Learning Express

Ages 5-6
K

Reading and Math

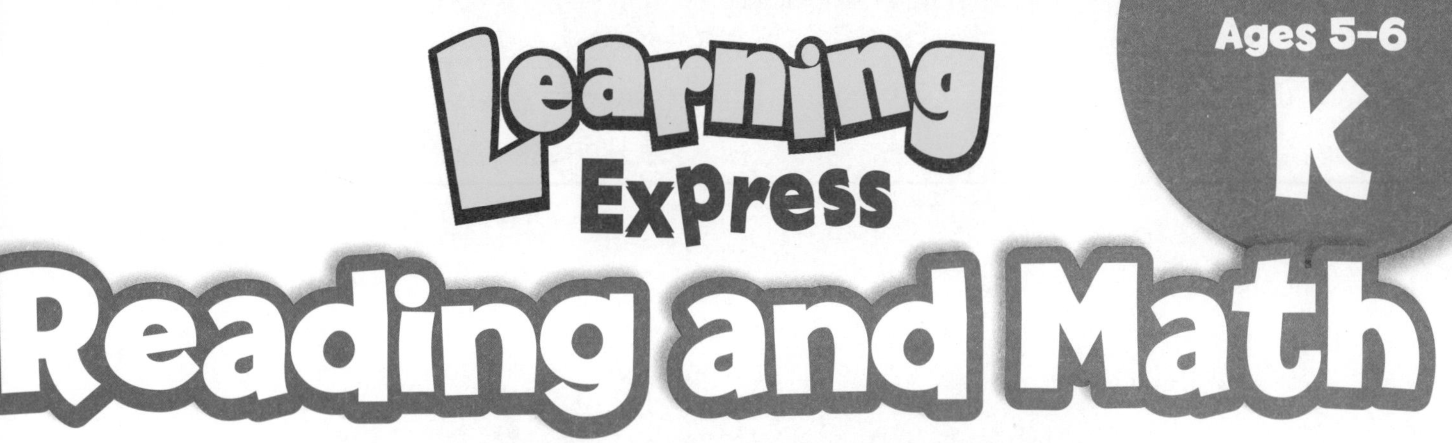

JUMBO WORKBOOK

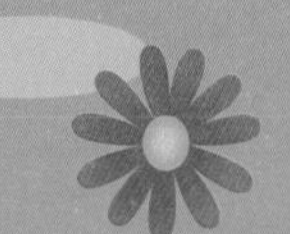

SCHOLASTIC

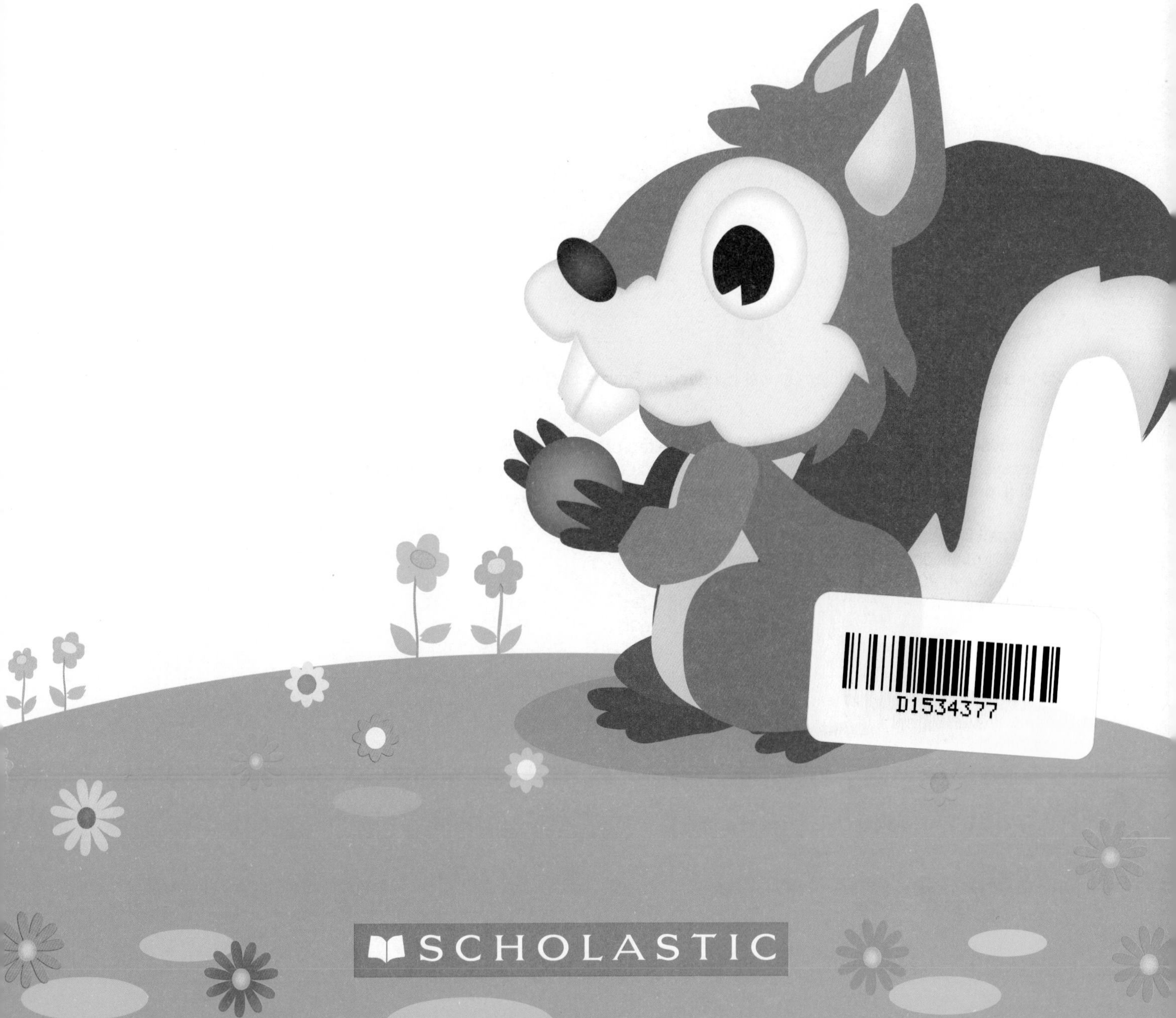

For information regarding permission, write to:
Scholastic Education International (Singapore) Pte Ltd
81 Ubi Avenue 4, #02-28 UB.ONE, Singapore 408830
Email: education@scholastic.com.sg

For sales enquiries write to:
Latin America, Caribbean, Europe (except UK), Middle East and Africa
Scholastic International
557 Broadway, New York, NY 10012, USA
Email: intlschool@scholastic.com
Rest of the World
Scholastic Education International (Singapore) Pte Ltd
81 Ubi Avenue 4 #02-28 UB.ONE Singapore 408830
Email: education@scholastic.com.sg

ISBN 978-981-07-7583-4
Printed in China

1 2 3 4 5 6 7 8 9 10 11 12 08 14 15 16 17 18 19/0

Dear Parents,

Independent practice is crucial to helping children develop essential learning skills. The Learning Express Reading and Math Jumbo Workbook is the perfect companion to providing the support your child needs to be successful in school.

This book includes teacher-approved activities that have been specially developed to make learning both accessible and enjoyable.

Topics covered include:
- Letter recognition
- Handwriting
- Phonics
- Reading Skills
- Number recognition
- Counting

You will also find assessments to help you keep track of your child's progress and evaluate your child's understanding.

A completion certificate and motivational stickers will mark and celebrate your child's learning milestones.

Let's get started!

Contents

Alphabet and Handwriting

"Look, mom, I can write the alphabet!" What a delightful thing to hear your child say. In this book, your child will practice writing upper and lowercase letters of the alphabet.

What to do

Have your child use a pencil to trace and then write each letter. Next, help your child identify and write words that start with that letter. He or she might choose words from the word and picture cards.

Invite your child to color the pictures. Review the flash cards frequently to help your child develop his or her vocabulary skills during the year.

Keep on going!

- As you drive or walk with your child, point out signs around the neighborhood. Have your child identify the letters on the signs. Then together, say the words.
- While reading a magazine or the newspaper, encourage your child to look for words on the page that begin with a particular letter, such as B. Then, circle the words.

I am learning about the letter A a.
This is how I write it:

A A

a a

Write two words that start with the letter A a:

This is my picture of an ____________________.

Date: ____________

Say the words. Color the pictures.

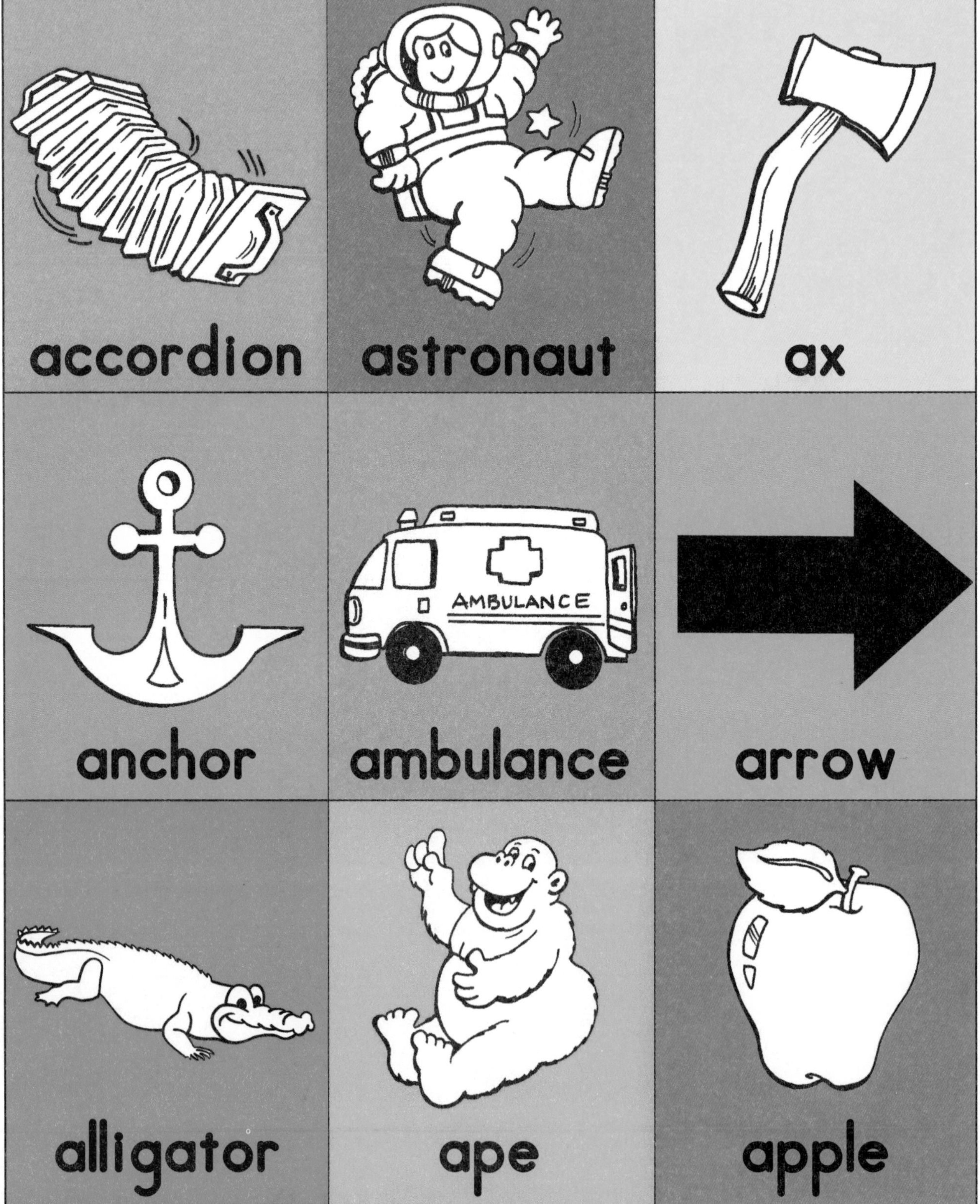

Date: ____________

I am learning about the letter B b.
This is how I write it:

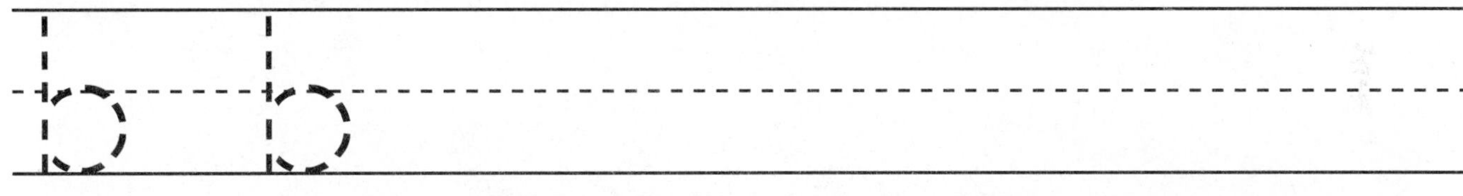

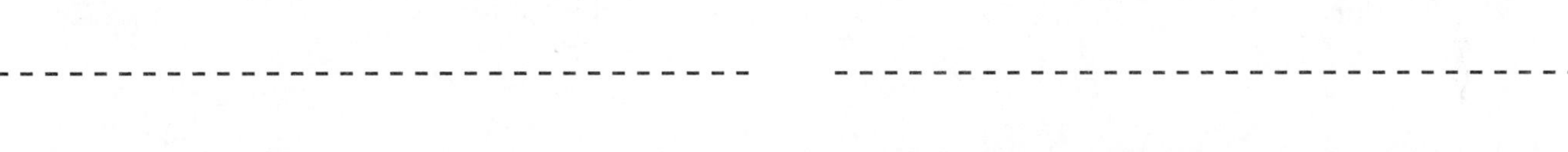

Write two words that start with the letter B b:

____________________ ____________________

This is my picture of a ______________________.

Date: ______________

Say the words. Color the pictures.

Date: ____________

I am learning about the letter C c.
This is how I write it:

C C

c c

Write two words that start with the letter C c:

____________ ____________

This is my picture of a ____________.

Date: ____________

Say the words. Color the pictures.

Date: __________

I am learning about the letter D d.
This is how I write it:

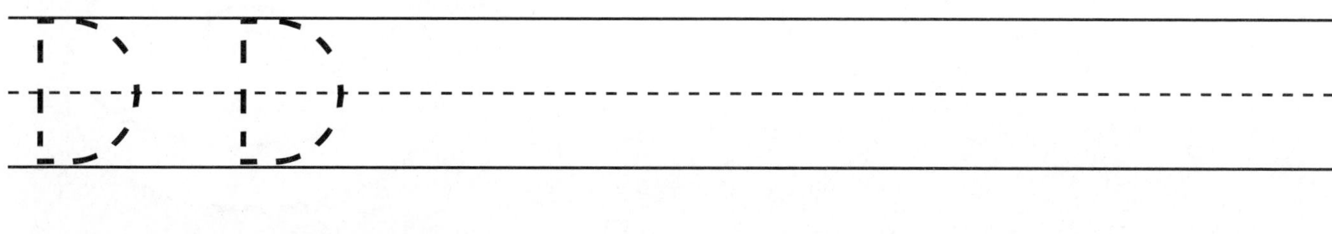

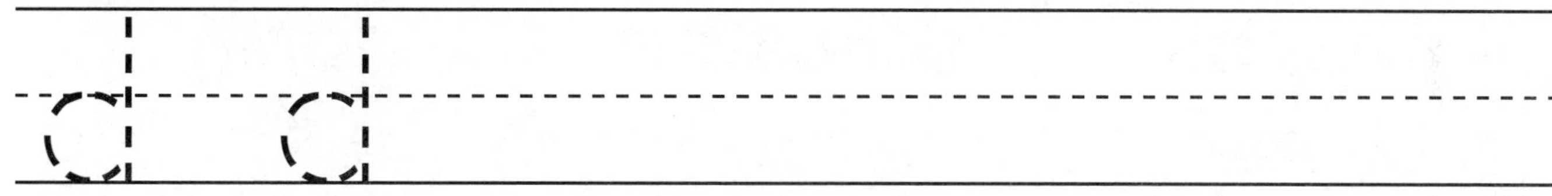

Write two words that start with the letter D d:

This is my picture of a ____________________.

Date: ____________

Say the words. Color the pictures.

Date: ____________

I am learning about the letter E e.
This is how I write it:

E E

e e

Write two words that start with the letter E e:

This is my picture of an ____________________.

Date: ____________

Say the words. Color the pictures.

Date: ____________

I am learning about the letter F f.
This is how I write it:

Write two words that start with the letter F f:

This is my picture of a ____________________.

Date: ____________

Say the words. Color the pictures.

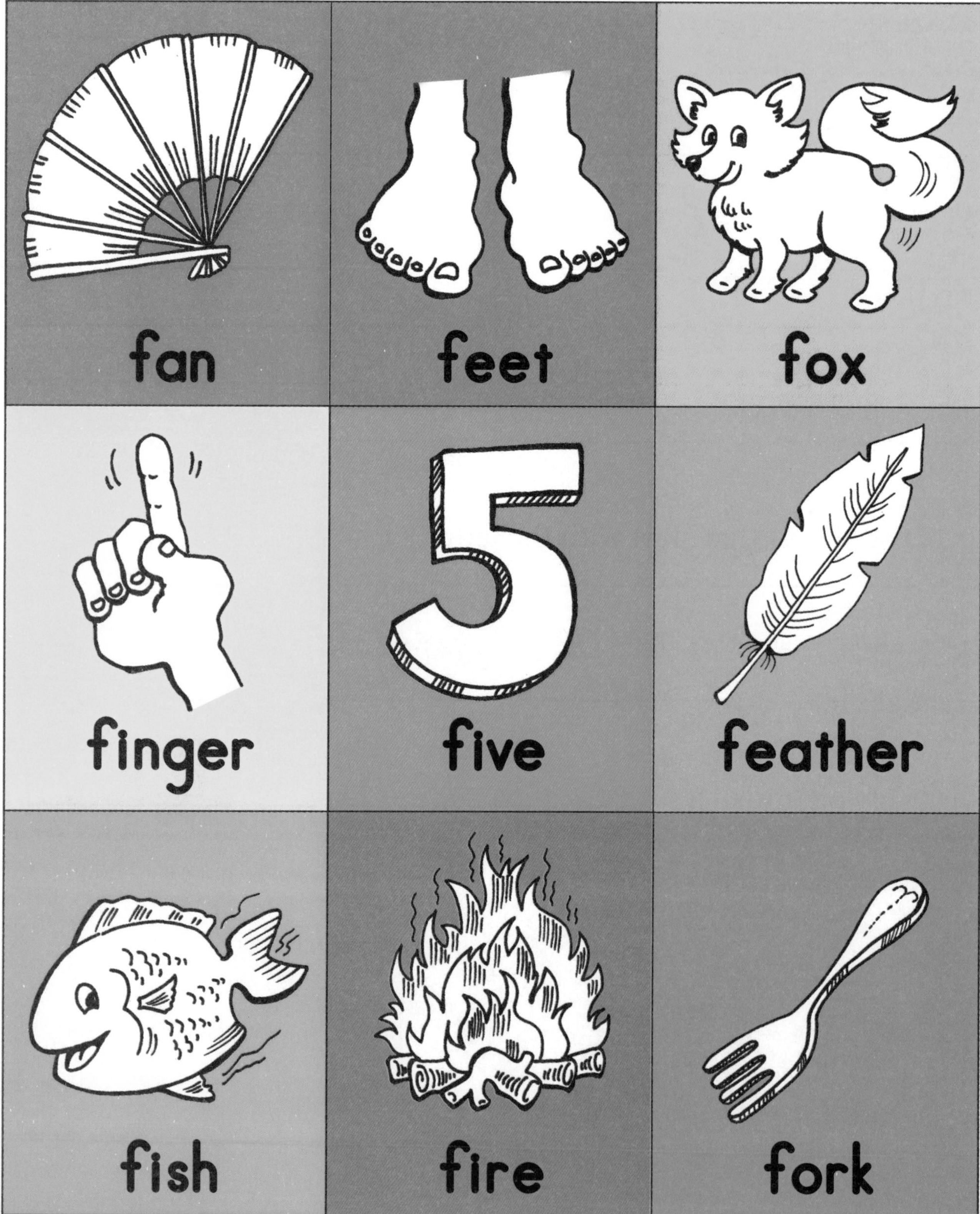

Date: ____________

I am learning about the letter G g.
This is how I write it:

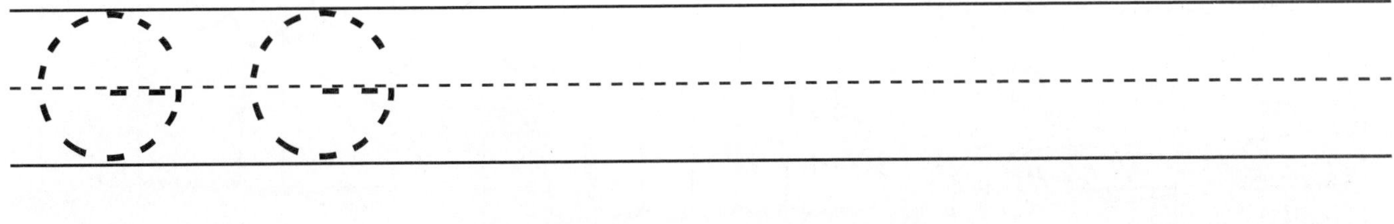

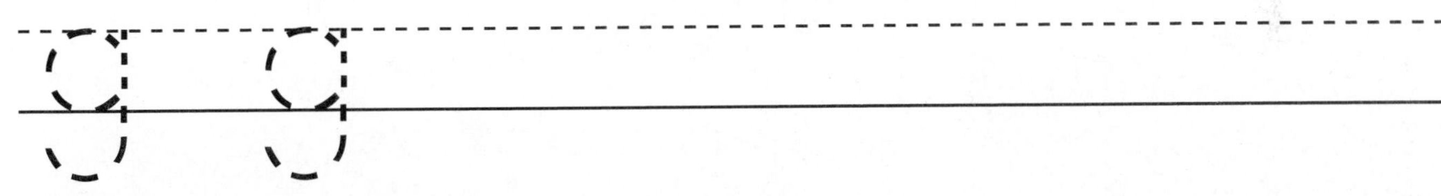

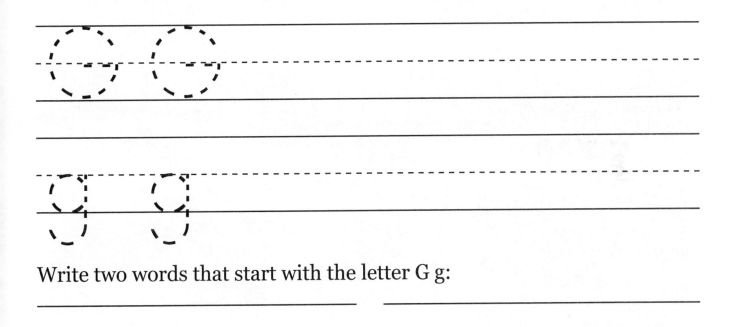

Write two words that start with the letter G g:

This is my picture of a ____________.

Date: ______________

Say the words. Color the pictures.

Date: ____________

I am learning about the letter H h.
This is how I write it:

H H

h h

Write two words that start with the letter H h:

This is my picture of a ____________.

Date: ______________

Say the words. Color the pictures.

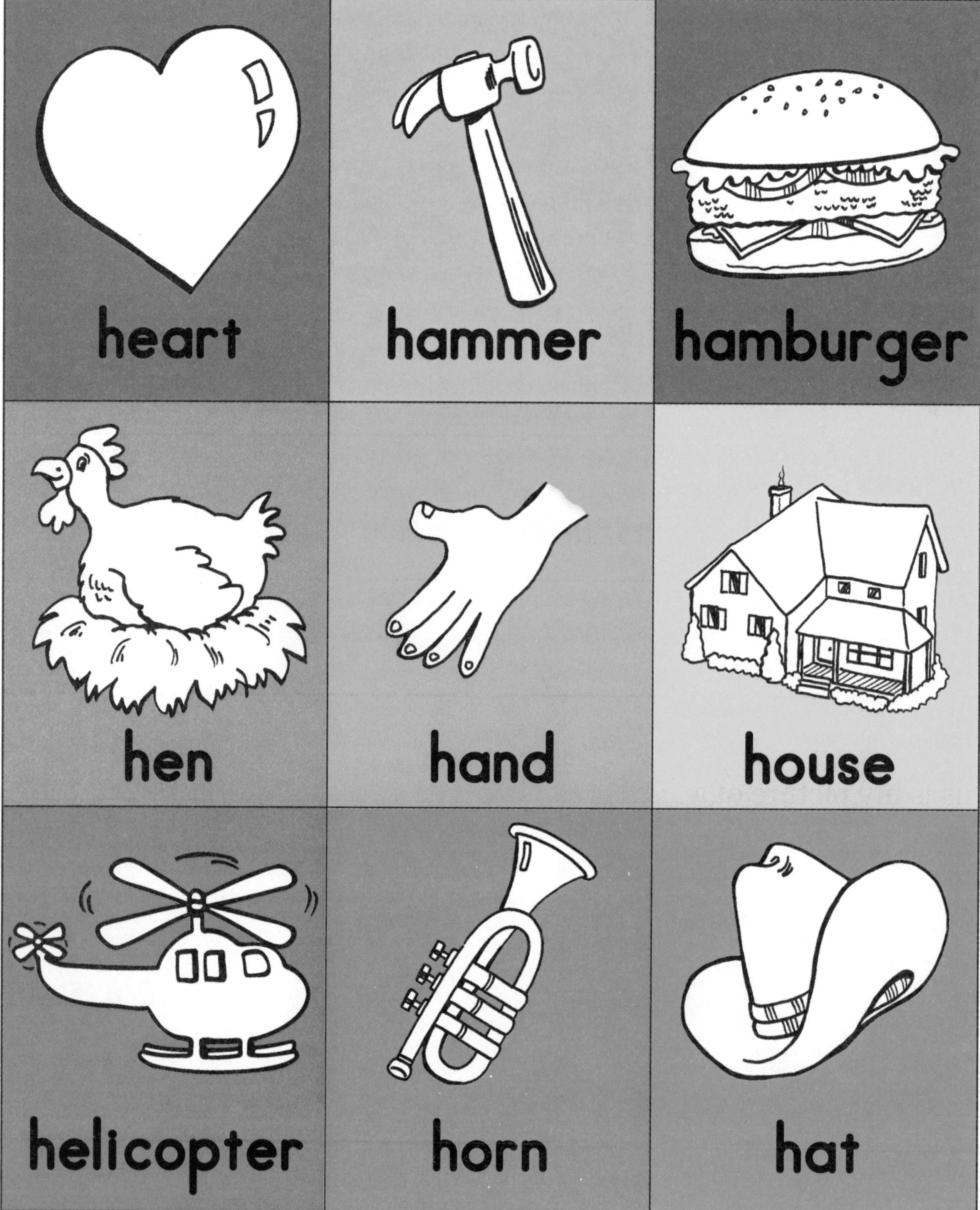

Date: ____________

Which letter comes next? Write it in the box.

Example

A B C D E

1. 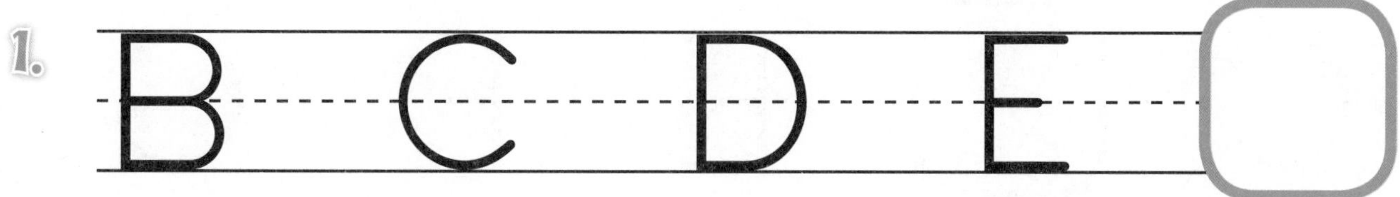

2. 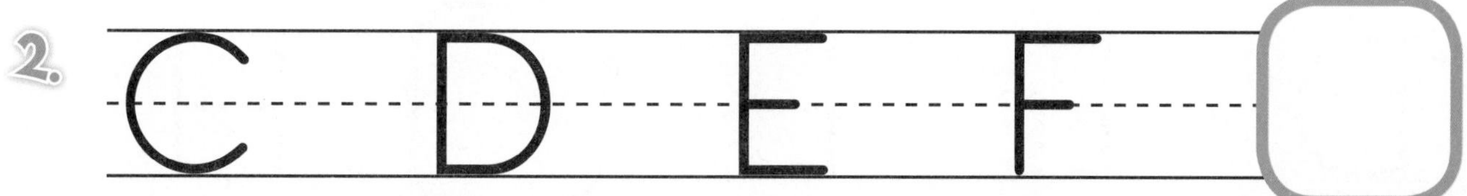

3. D E F G ☐

Date: ____________

Which letter is missing in the sequence?
Write it in the box.

Example

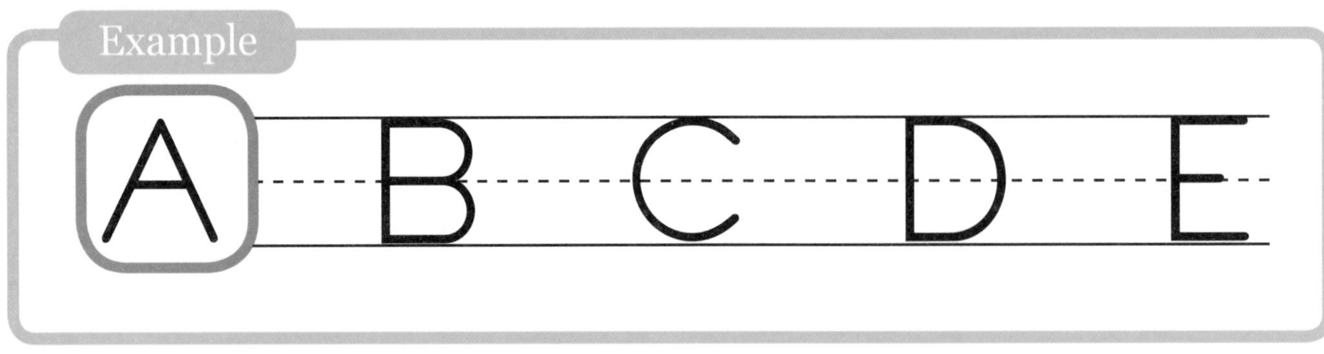

1.
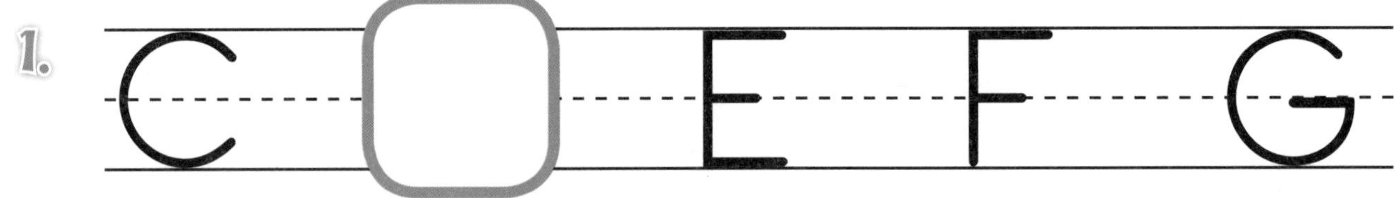

2.
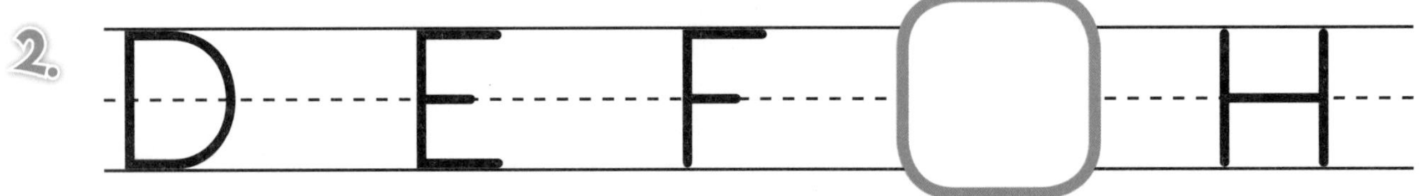

3. B C D F

Date: ____________

Which letter comes next? Write it in the box.

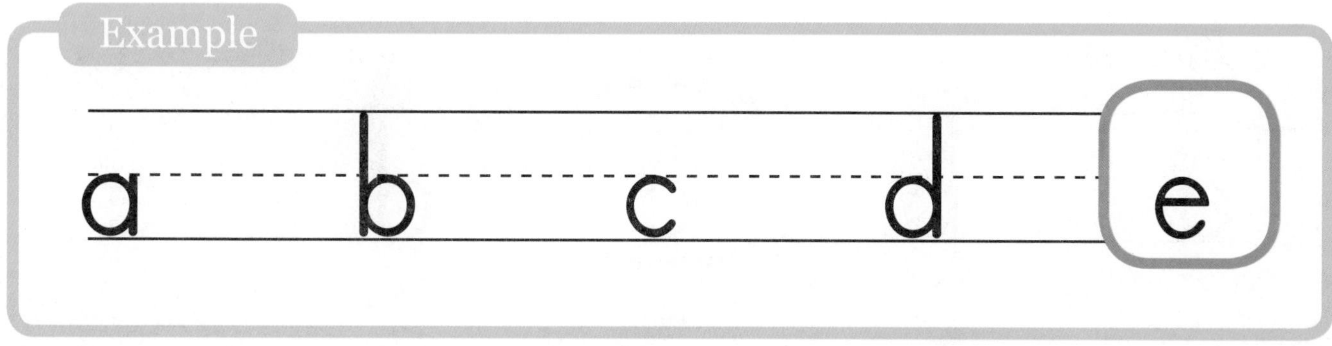

1. 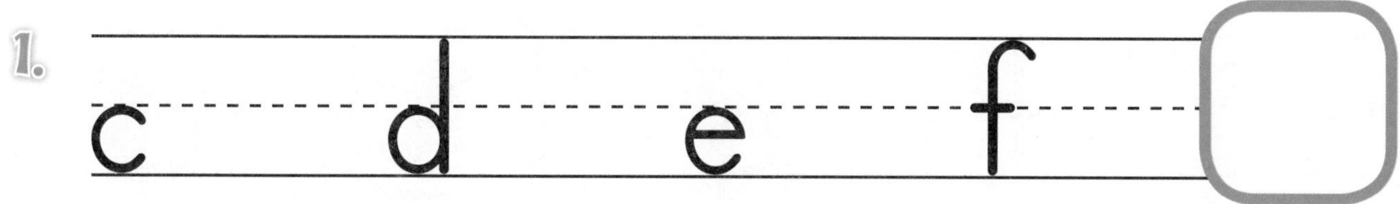

2. 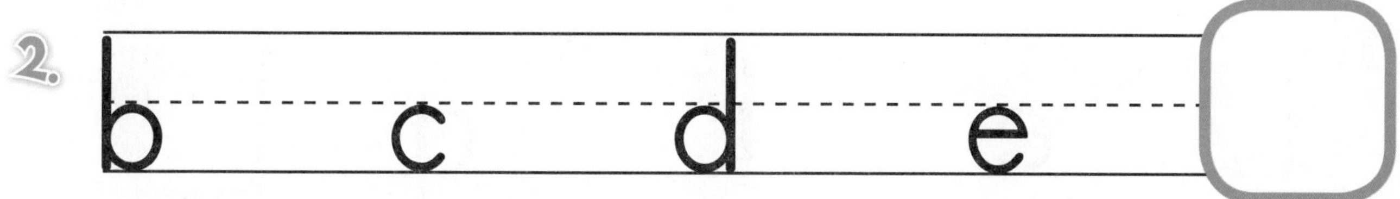

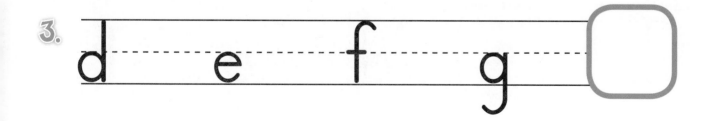

3. d e f g

Date: ______________

Which letter is missing in the sequence?
Write it in the box.

Example

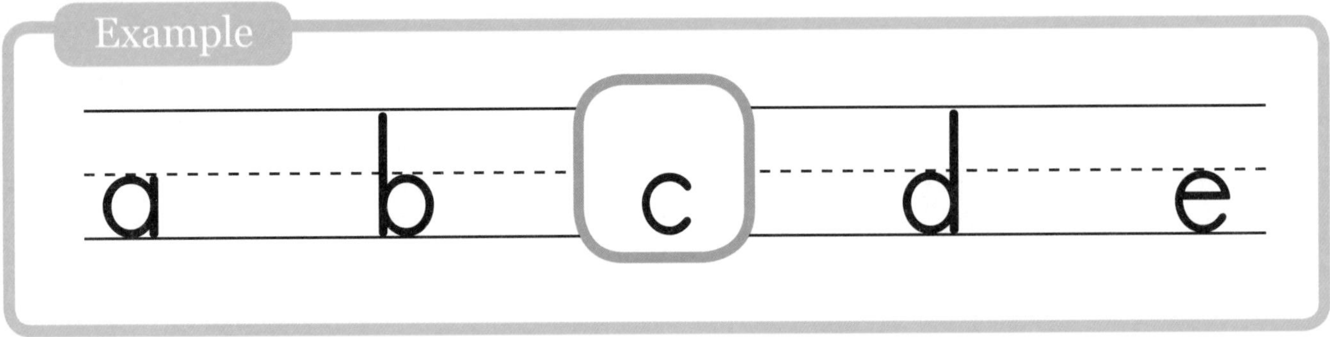

1.
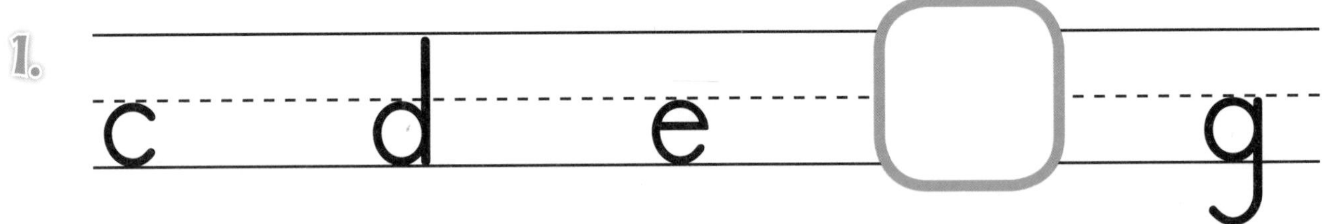

2.
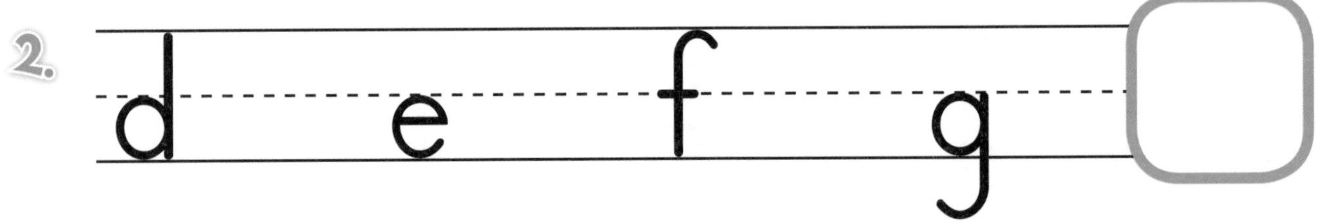

3.
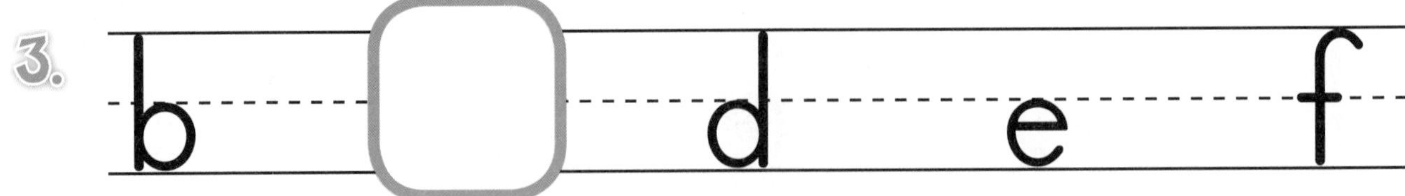

I am learning about the letter I i.
This is how I write it:

I I

i i

Write two words that start with the letter I i:

This is my picture of an ______________________________ .

Date: ____________

Say the words. Color the pictures.

Date: ____________

I am learning about the letter J j.
This is how I write it:

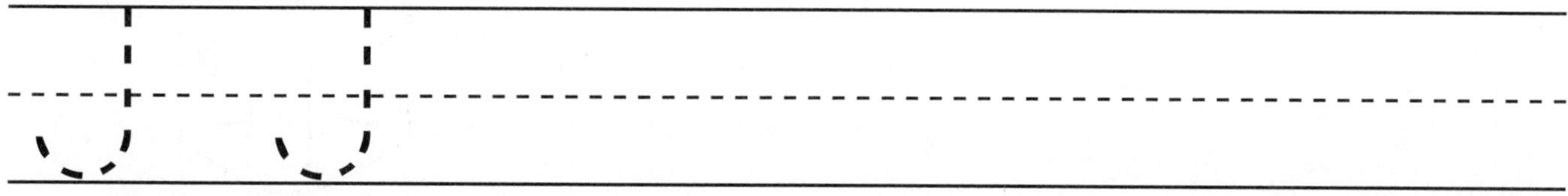

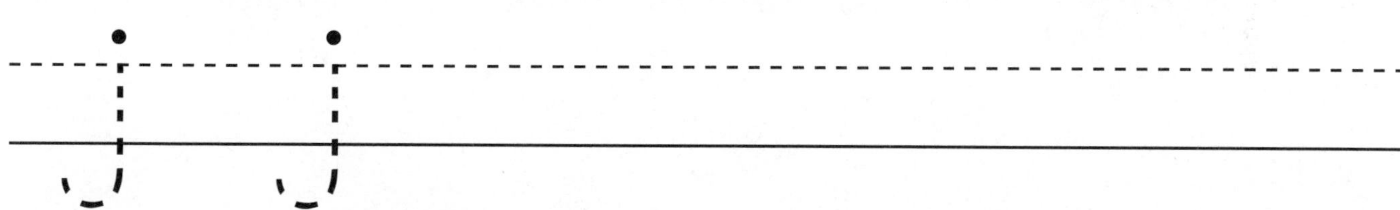

Write two words that start with the letter J j:

____________________ ____________________

This is my picture of a ____________________.

Date: ____________

Say the words. Color the pictures.

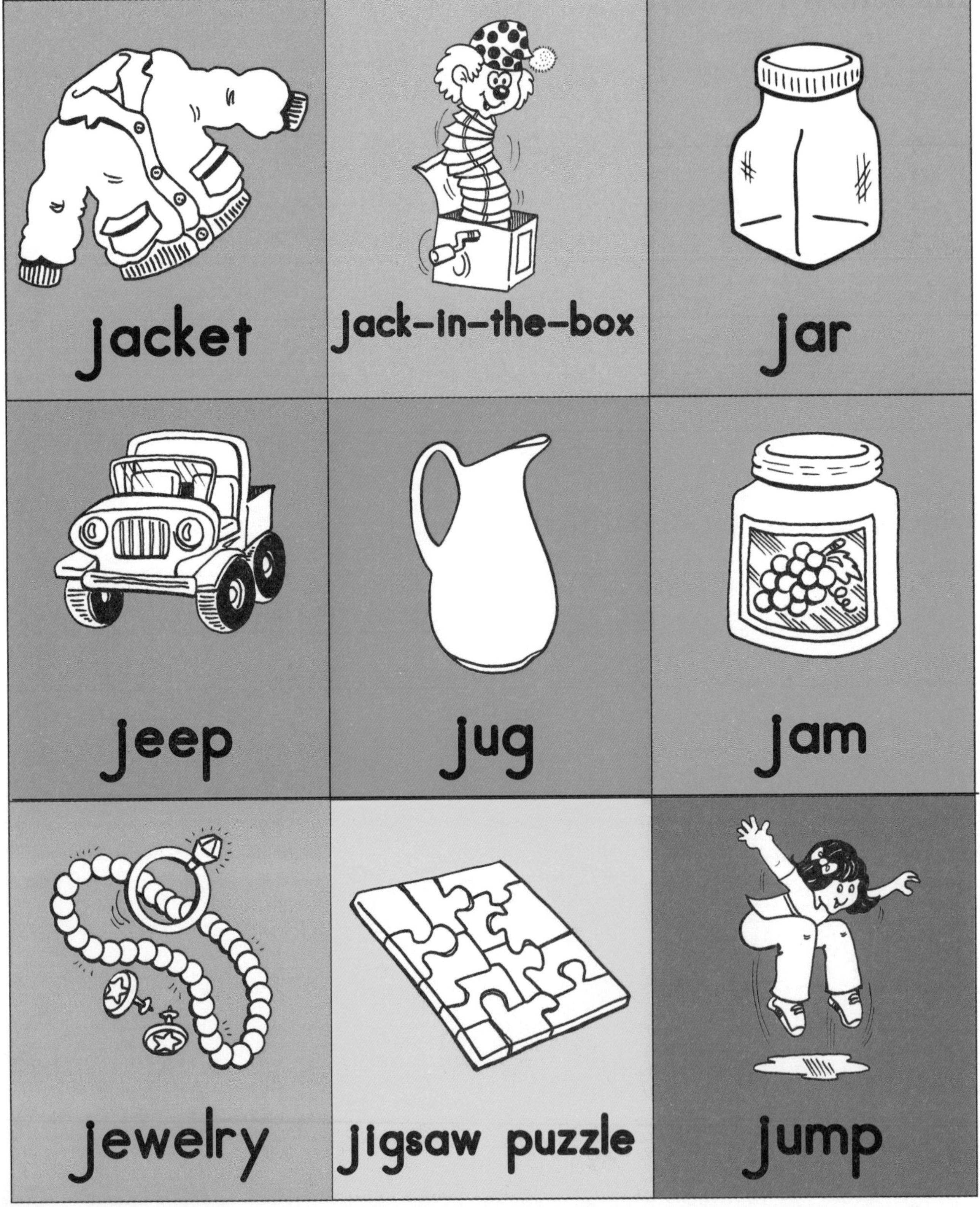

Date: ____________

I am learning about the letter K k.
This is how I write it:

K K

k k

Write two words that start with the letter K k:

______________________ ______________________

This is my picture of a ______________________ .

Date: ____________

Say the words. Color the pictures.

Date: ____________

I am learning about the letter L l.
This is how I write it:

Write two words that start with the letter L l:

This is my picture of a ____________________.

Date: ____________

Say the words. Color the pictures.

Date: __________

I am learning about the letter M m.
This is how I write it:

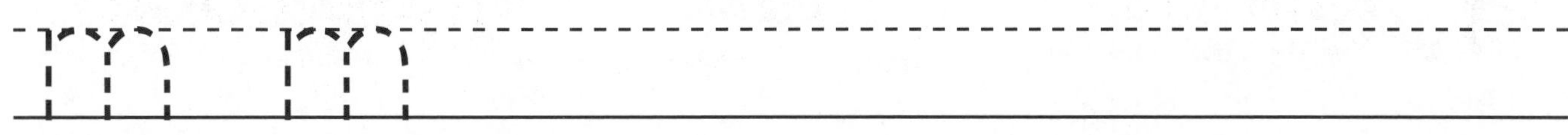

Write two words that start with the letter M m:

This is my picture of a ____________________ .

Date: ____________

Say the words. Color the pictures.

Date: ____________

I am learning about the letter N n.
This is how I write it:

N N

n n

Write two words that start with the letter N n:

This is my picture of a ____________.

Date: ____________

Say the words. Color the pictures.

Date: ______________

I am learning about the letter O o.
This is how I write it:

O O

o o

Write two words that start with the letter O o:

This is my picture of an ______________ .

Date: ____________

Say the words. Color the pictures.

Date: ____________

I am learning about the letter P p.
This is how I write it:

P P

p p

Write two words that start with the letter P p:

This is my picture of a ____________________.

Date: ____________

Say the words. Color the pictures.

Date: ____________

Which letter comes next? Write it in the box.

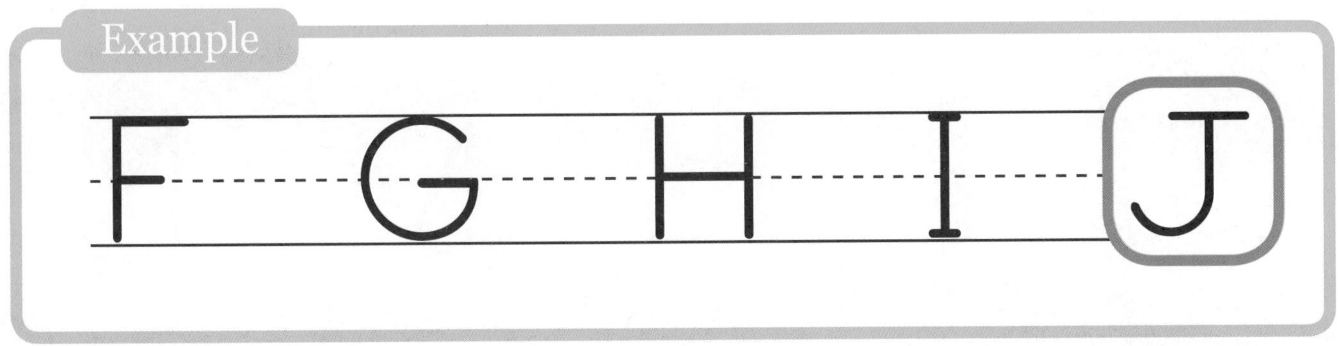

1. 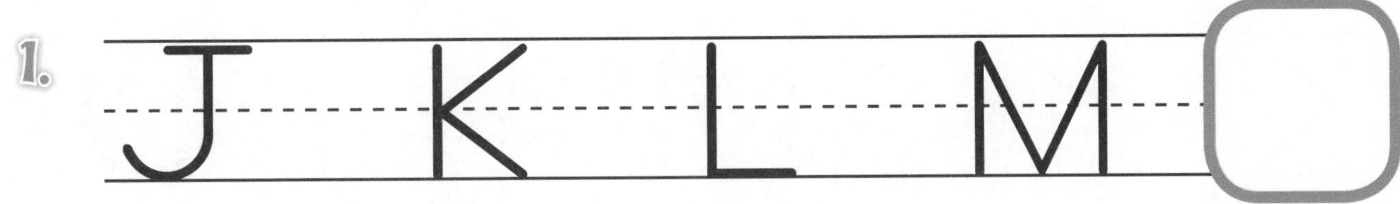

2. 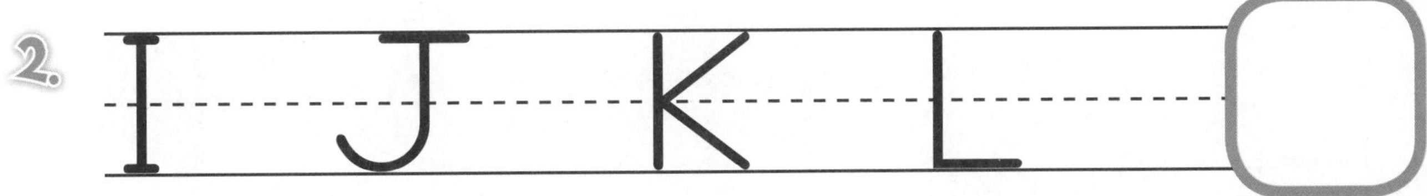

3. 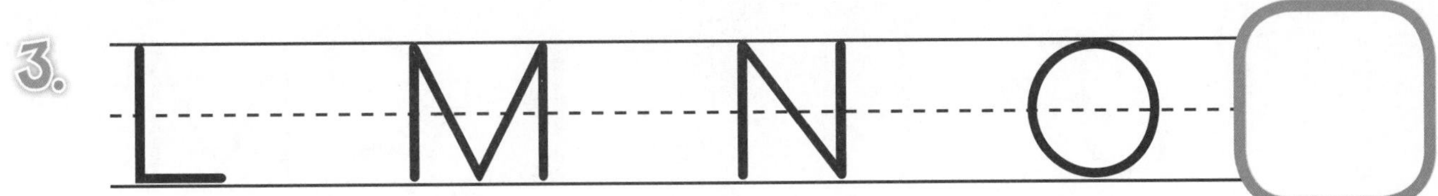

Date: ____________

**Which letter is missing in the sequence?
Write it in the box.**

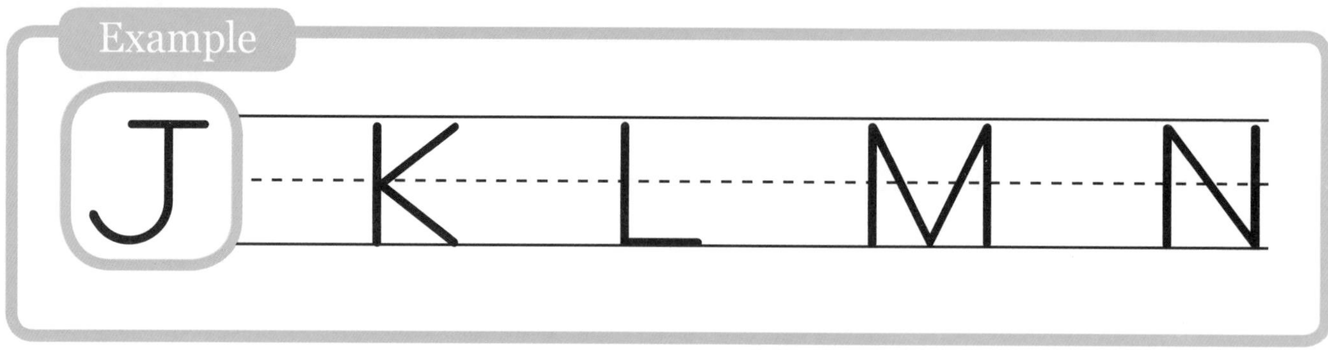

1. 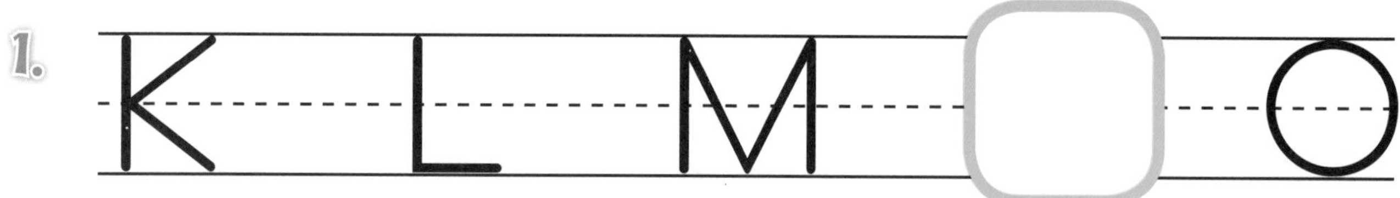

2. 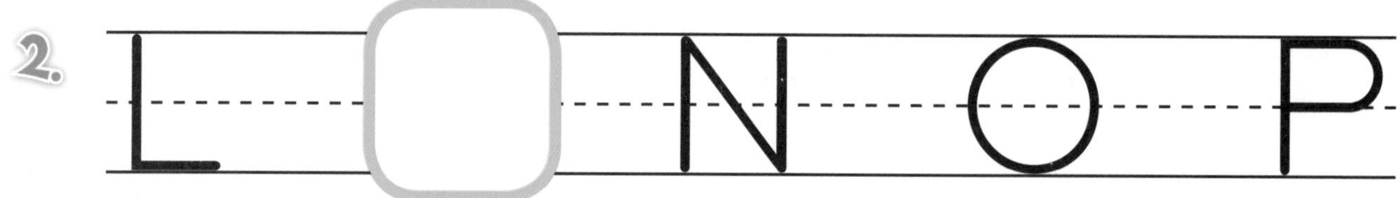

3. 

Date: ____________

Which letter comes next? Write it in the box.

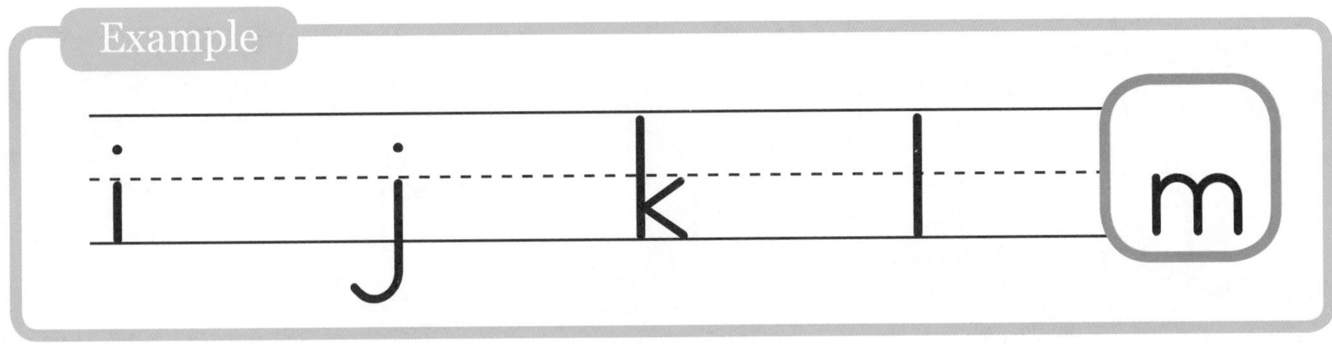

1. 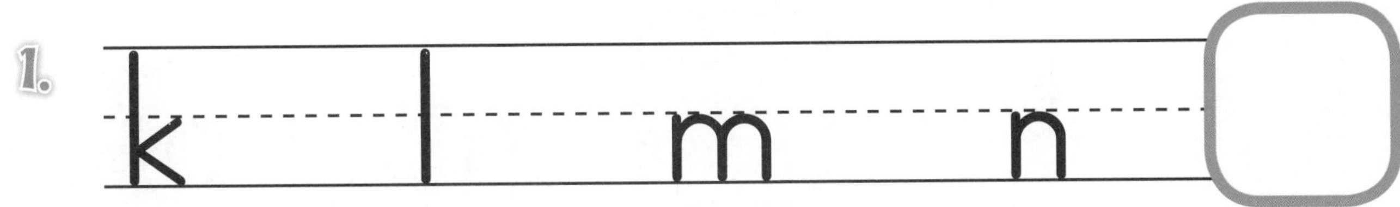

2. 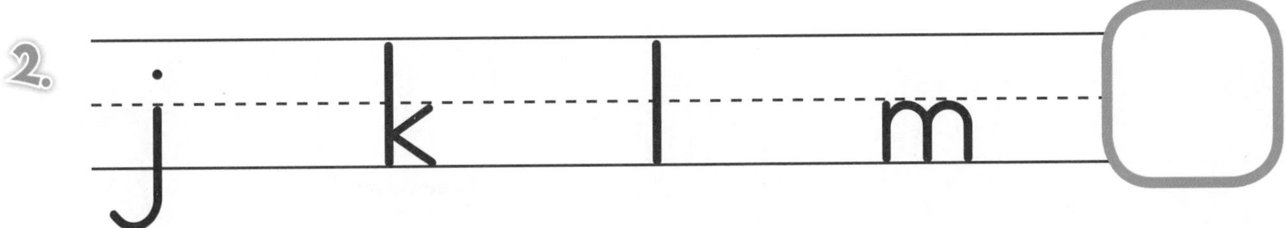

3. 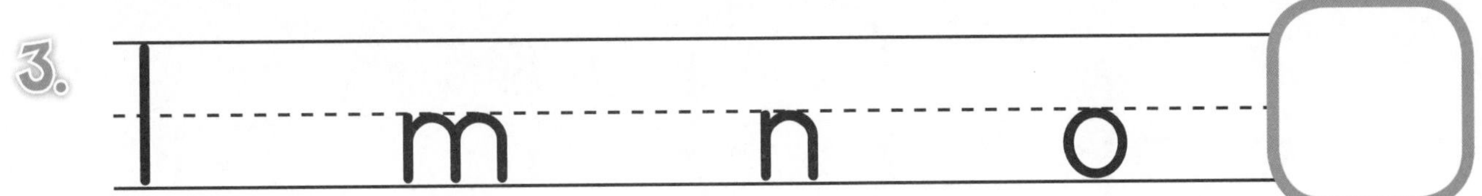

Date: ____________

Which letter is missing in the sequence? Write it in the box.

Example

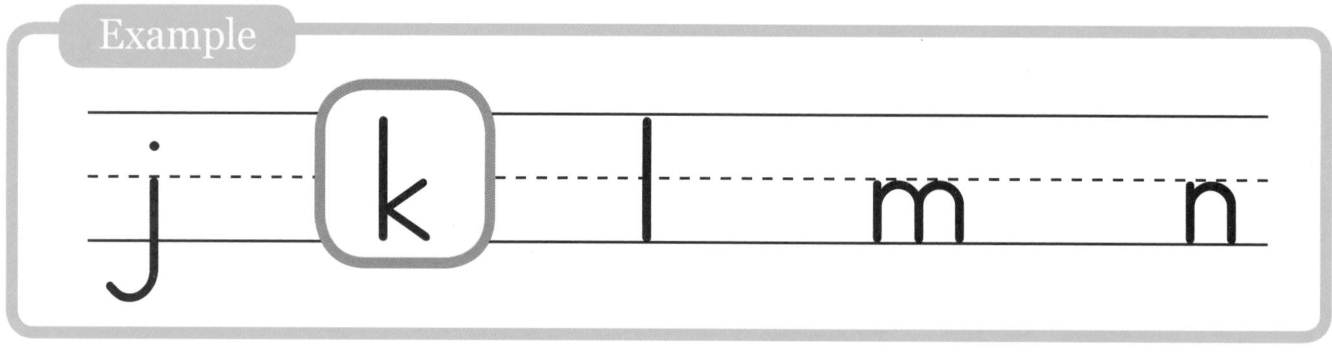

1. 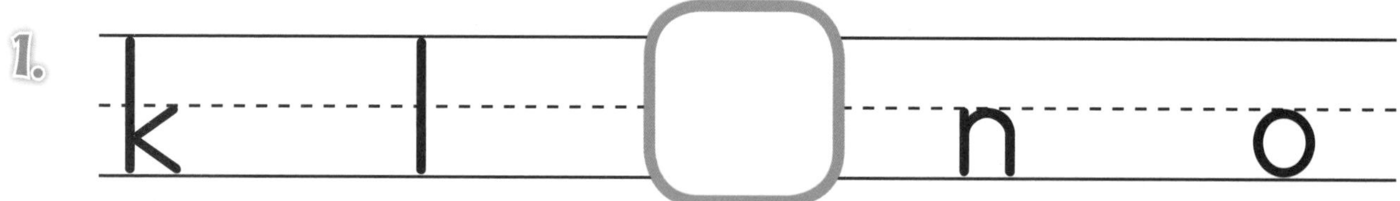

2. 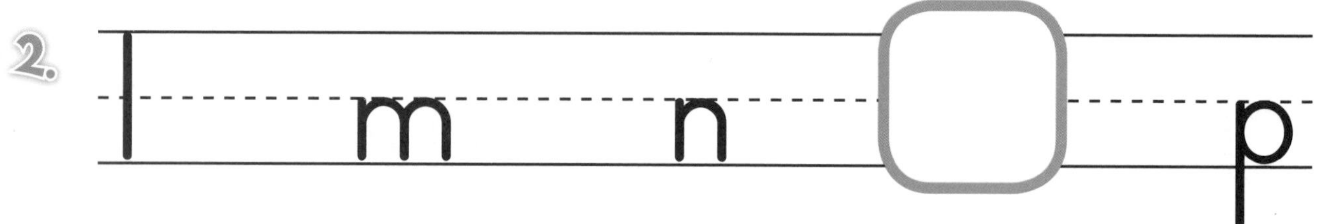

3. 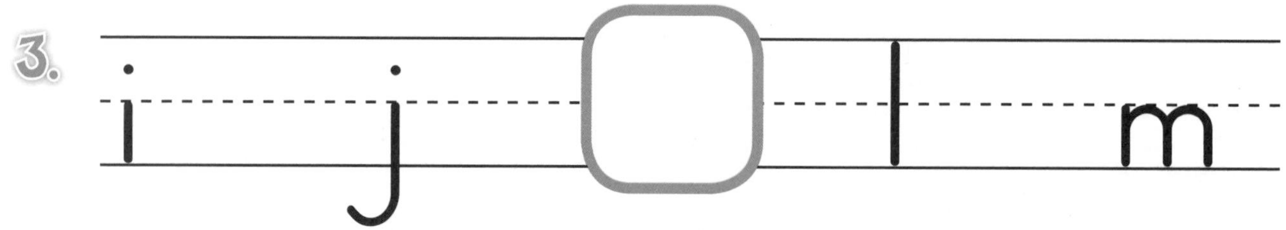

Date: ______________

I am learning about the letter Q q.
This is how I write it:

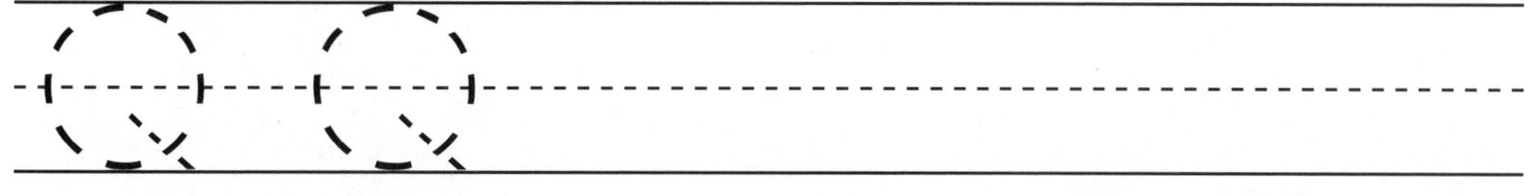

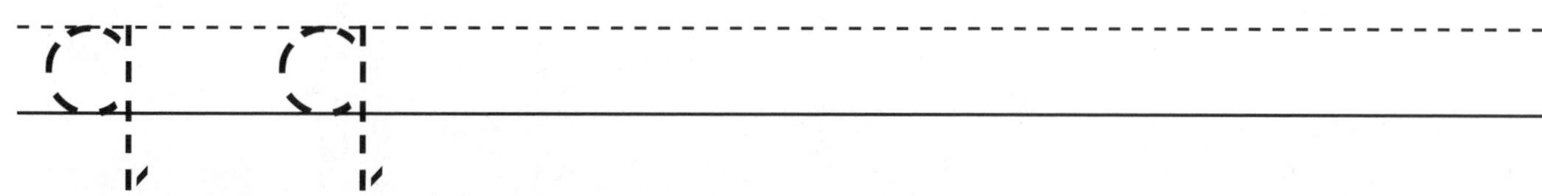

Write two words that start with the letter Q q:

This is my picture of a ______________________________ .

Date: ____________

Say the words. Color the pictures.

Date: __________

I am learning about the letter R r.
This is how I write it:

R R

r r

Write two words that start with the letter R r:

This is my picture of a ____________________ .

Date: ____________

Say the words. Color the pictures.

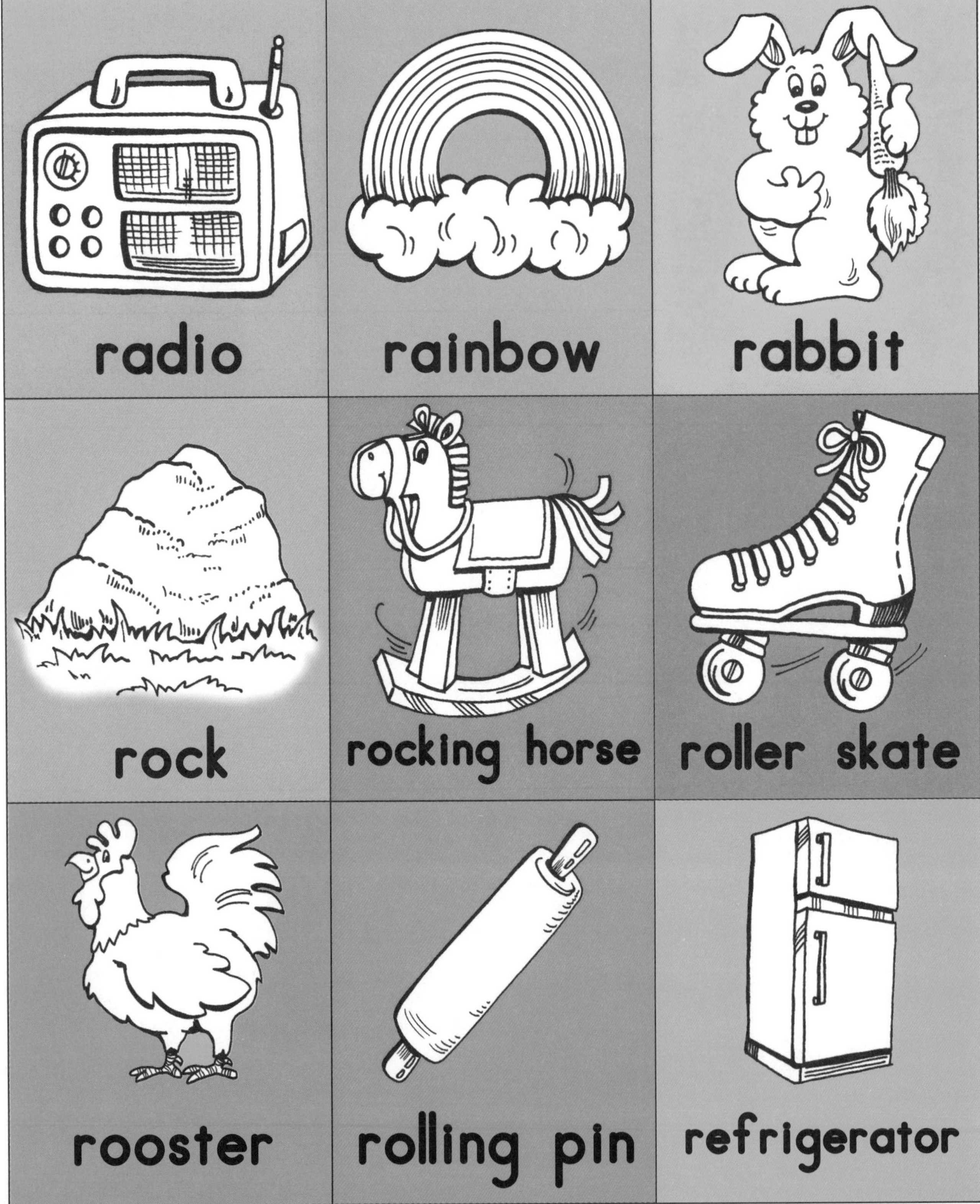

Date: ____________

I am learning about the letter S s.
This is how I write it:

S S

s s

Write two words that start with the letter S s:

____________ ____________

This is my picture of a ____________ .

Date: ______________

Say the words. Color the pictures.

Date: ____________

I am learning about the letter T t.
This is how I write it:

Write two words that start with the letter T t:

This is my picture of a ______________________________ .

Date: ____________

Say the words. Color the pictures.

Date: __________

I am learning about the letter U u.
This is how I write it:

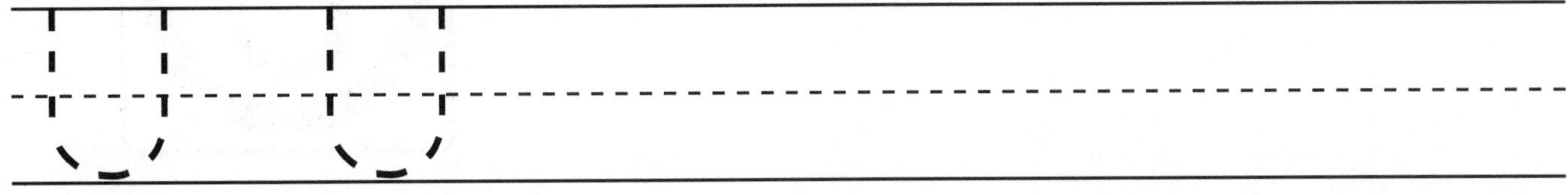

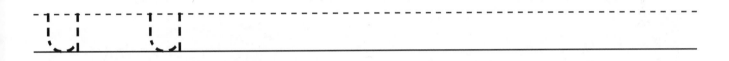

Write two words that start with the letter U u:

This is my picture of a/an __________.

Date: ____________

Say the words. Color the pictures.

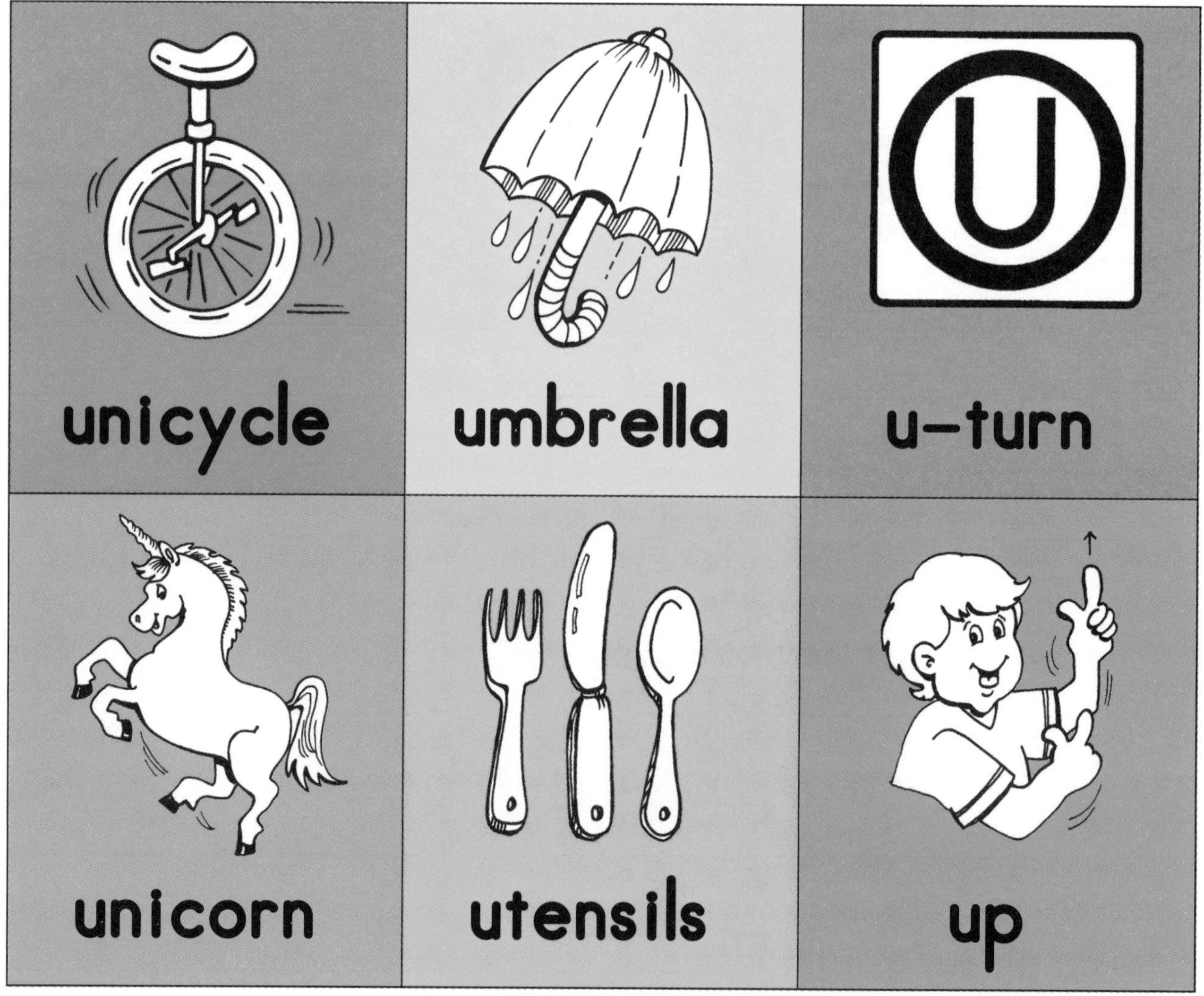

Date: ____________

I am learning about the letter V v.
This is how I write it:

V V

v v

Write two words that start with the letter V v:

This is my picture of a ____________________.

Date: ____________

Say the words. Color the pictures.

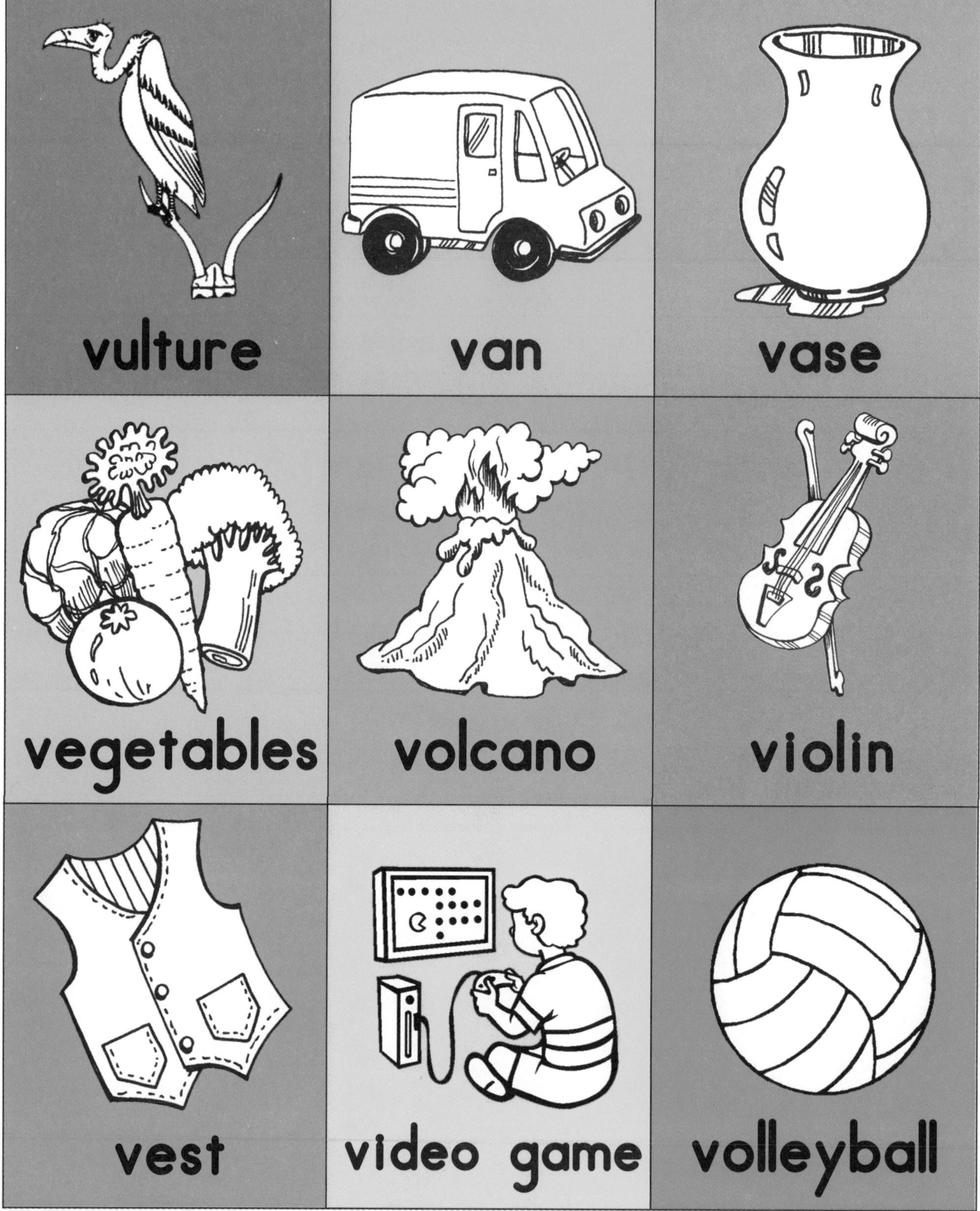

Date: ____________

I am learning about the letter W w.
This is how I write it:

W W

w w

Write two words that start with the letter W w:

This is my picture of a ____________.

Date: ____________

Say the words. Color the pictures.

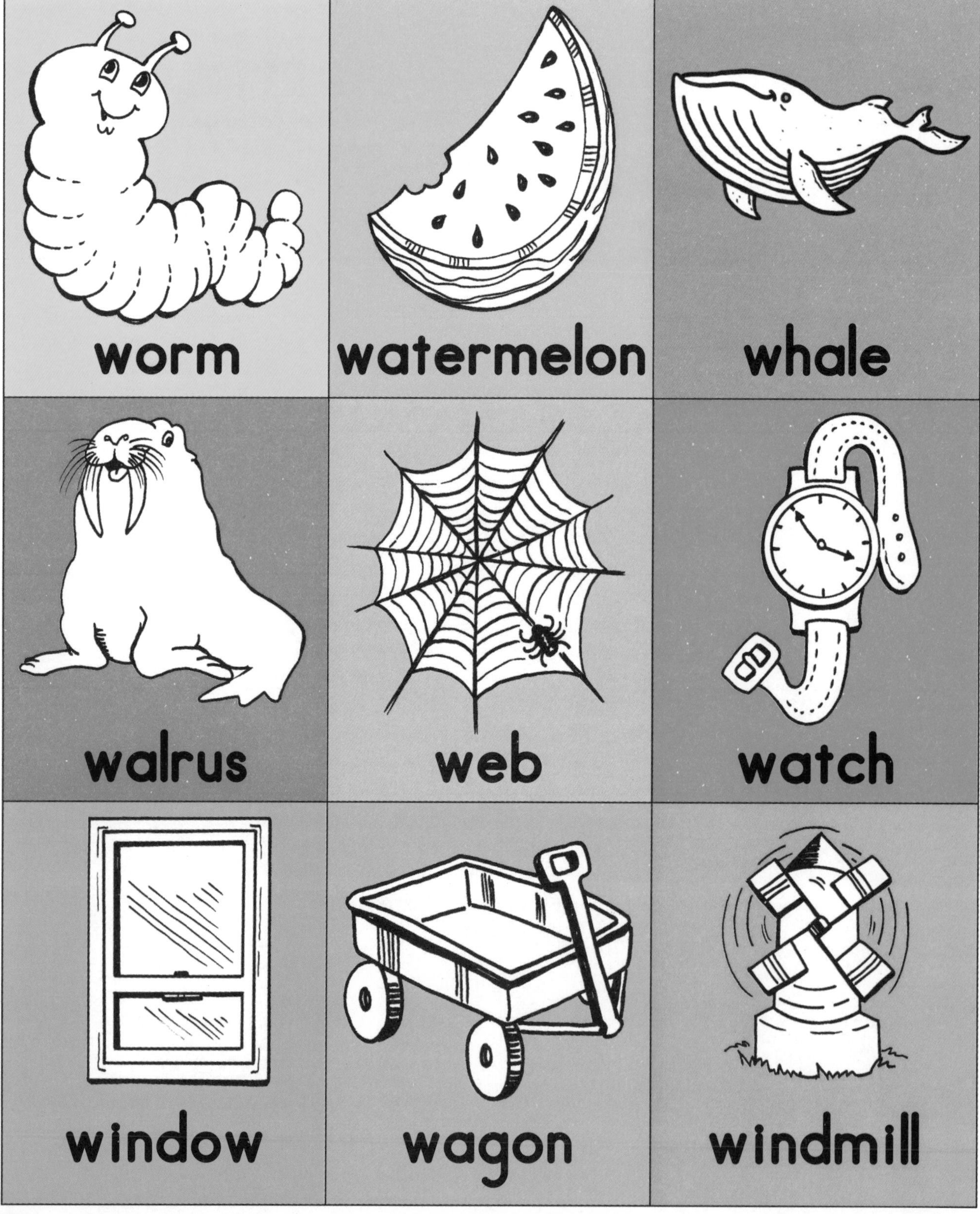

Date: ____________

I am learning about the letter X x.
This is how I write it:

X X

x x

Write two words that start with the letter X x:

______________ ______________

This is my picture of a ______________________.

Date: ______________

I am learning about the letter Y y.
This is how I write it:

Y Y

y y

Write two words that start with the letter Y y:

______________ ______________

This is my picture of a ______________ .

Date: ____________

I am learning about the letter Z z.
This is how I write it:

Z Z

z z

Write two words that start with the letter Z z:

This is my picture of a ______________________________.

Date: ____________

Say the words. Color the pictures.

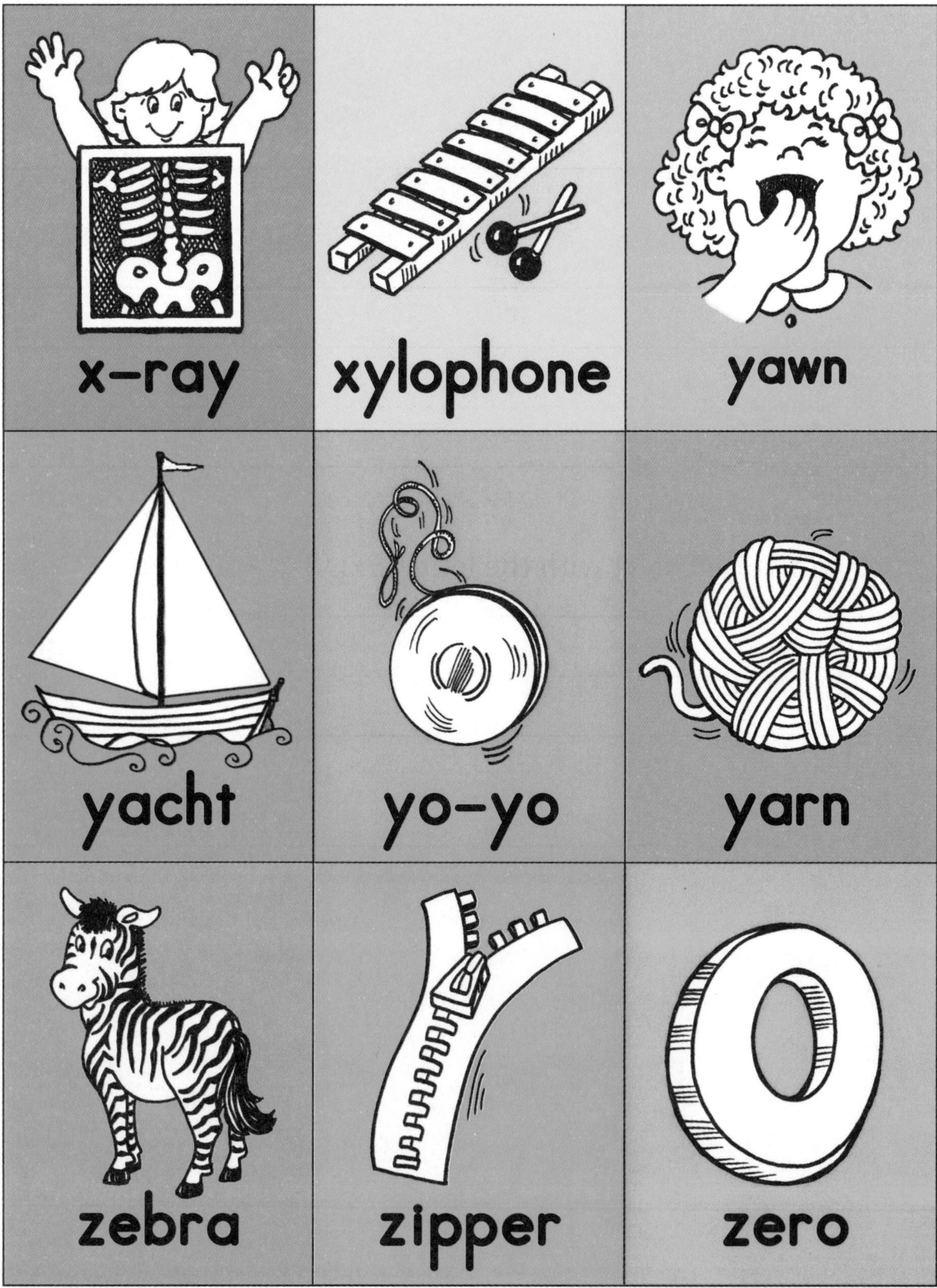

Date: ____________

Which letter comes next? Write it in the box.

Example

Q R S T U

1.

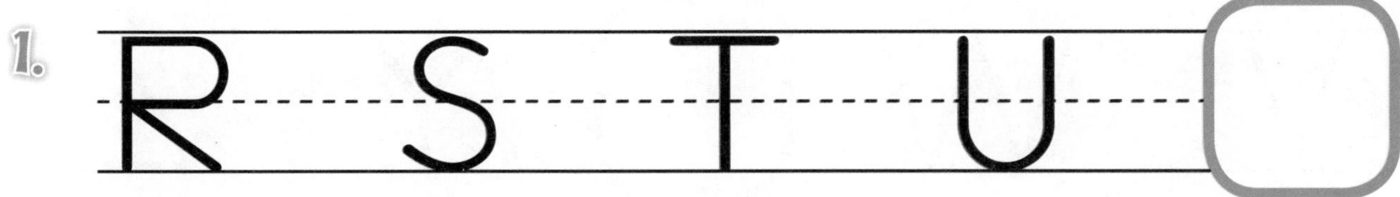

2.

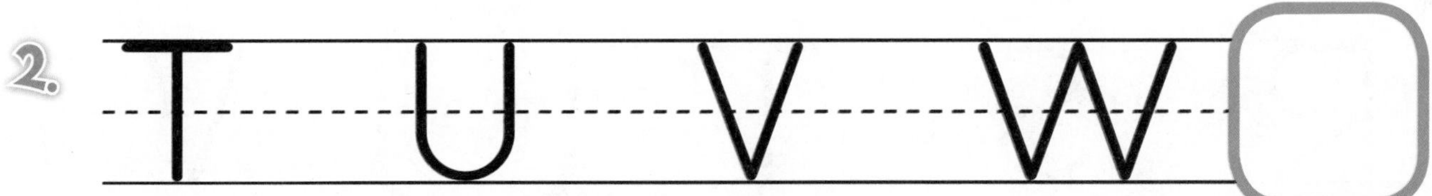

3.

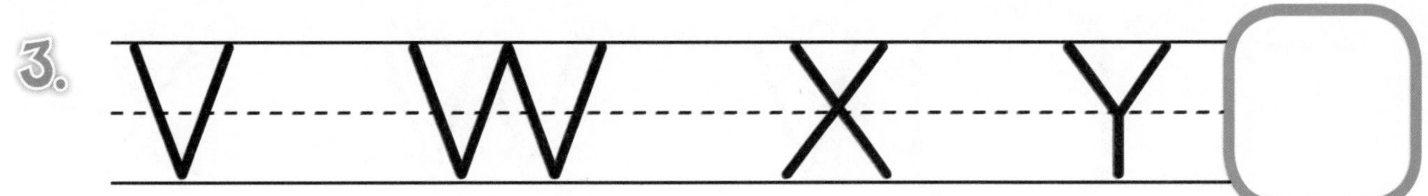

Date: ____________

Which letter is missing in the sequence? Write it in the box.

Example

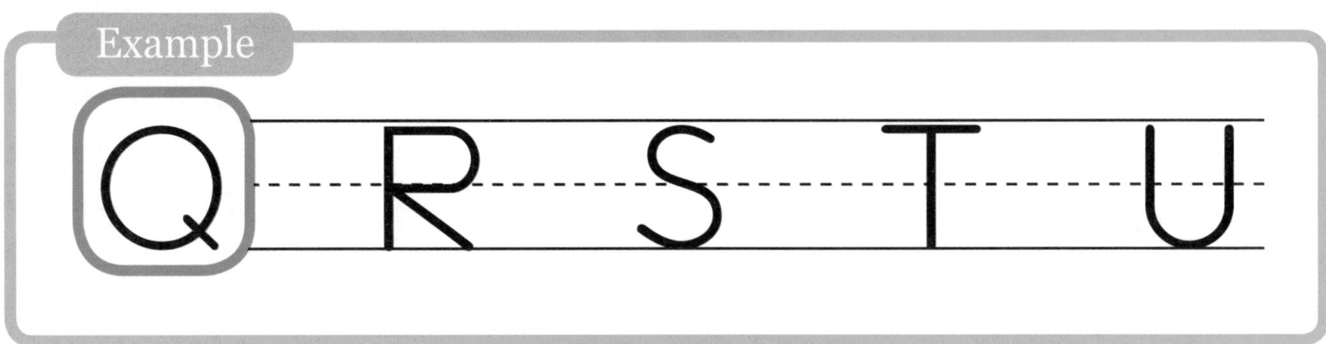

1.
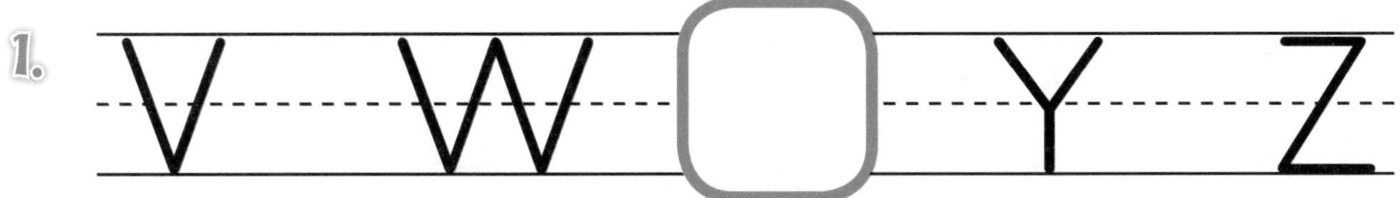

2.
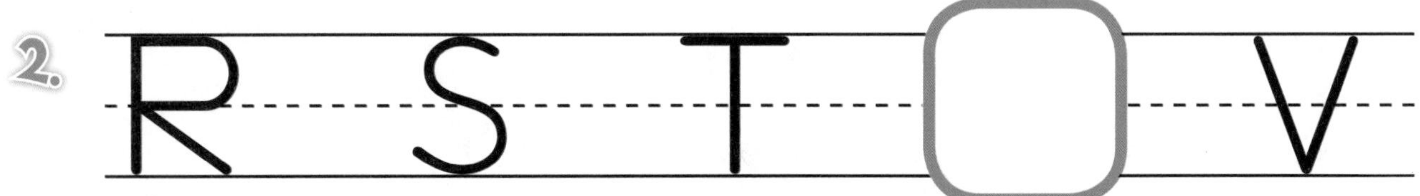

3.
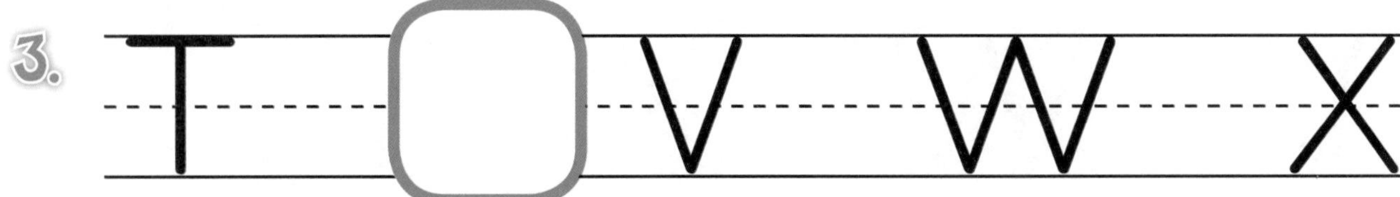

Which letter comes next? Write it in the box.

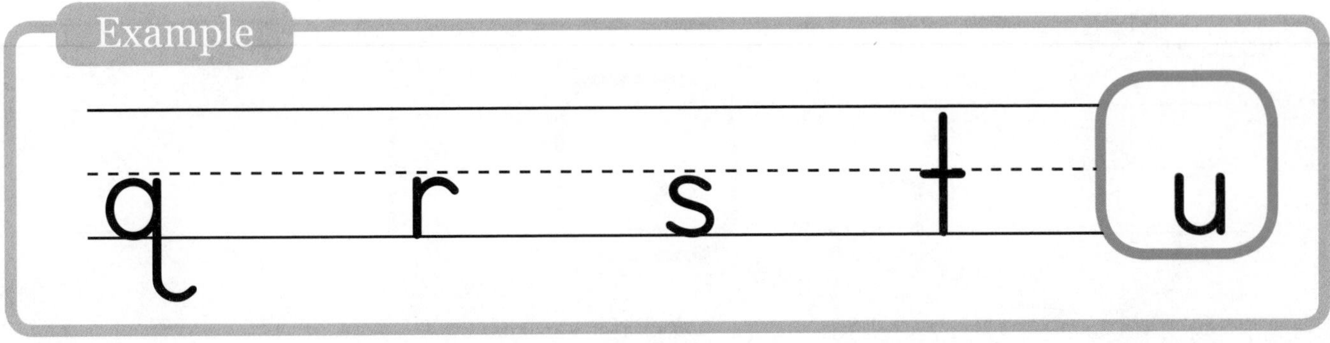

1.
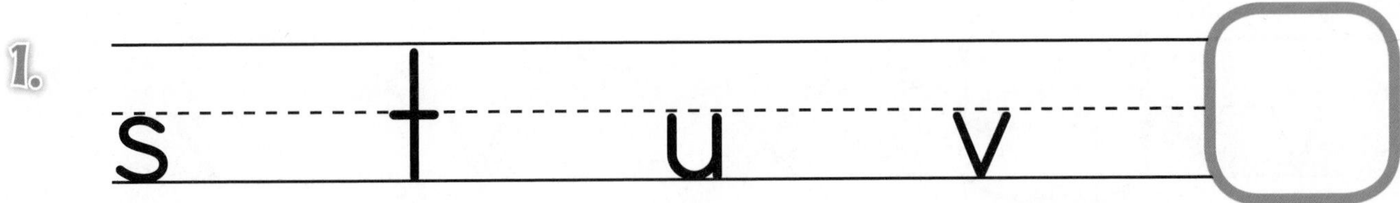

2.
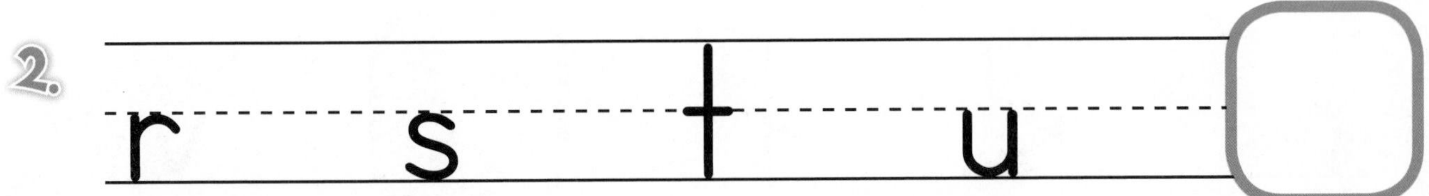

3.
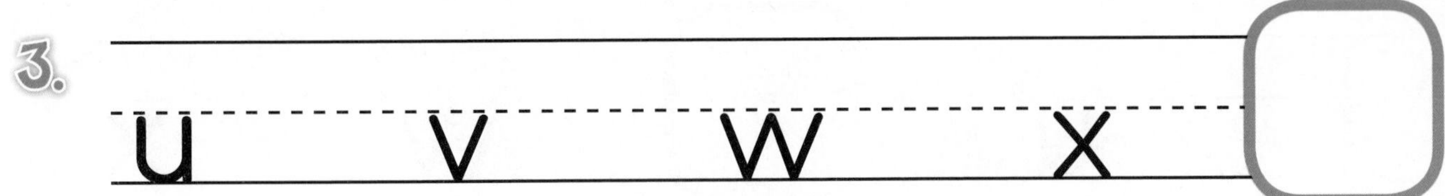

Date: ______

Which letter is missing in the sequence?
Write it in the box.

Example

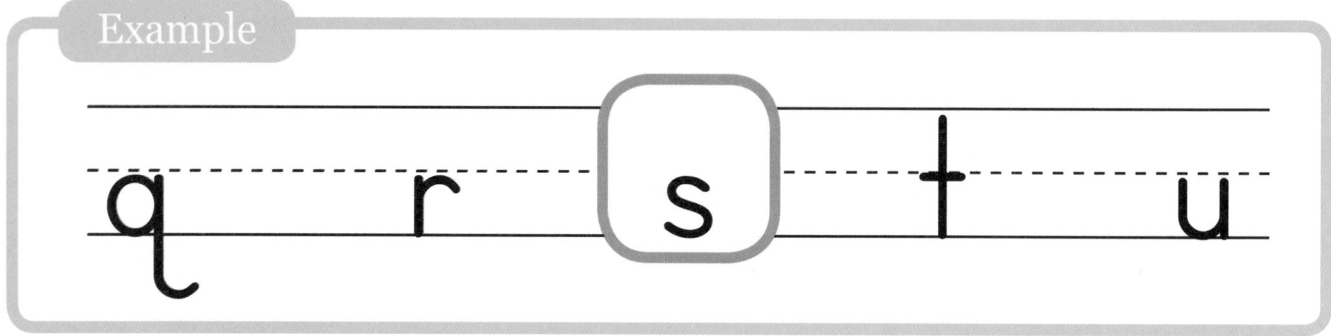

1.
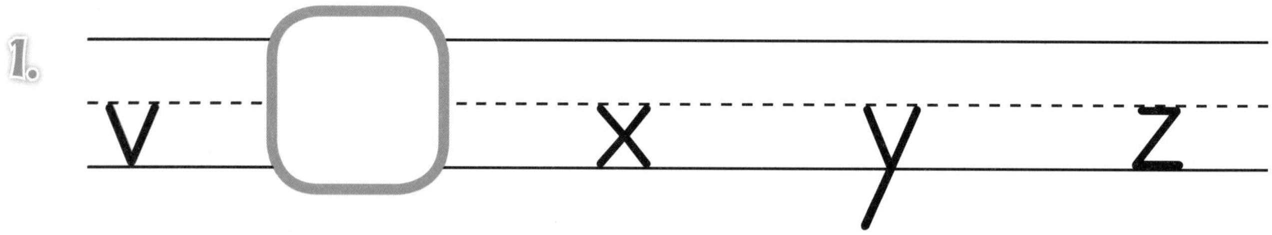

2.
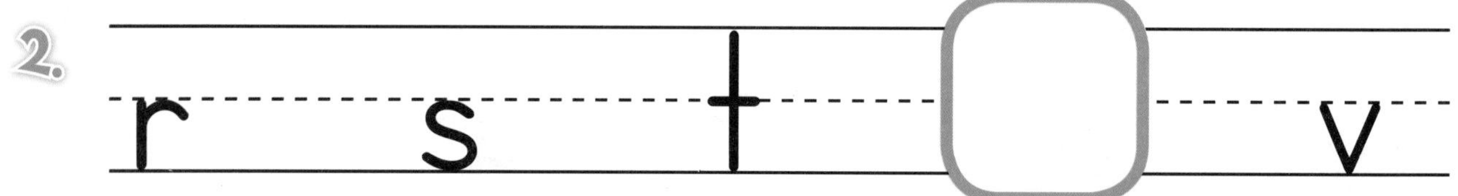

3.
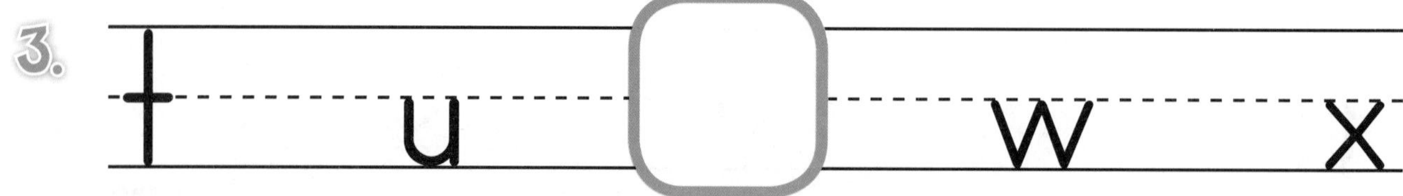

Date: ______________

Help the rabbit find its way home. Color the boxes with the letters A-Z in the right order.

	C	D	L	C	P	N
A	B	E	R	S	T	U
U	Y	F	Q	P	H	V
W	T	G	N	O	A	W
M	Q	H	M	G	C	X
P	V	I	L	E	D	Y
R	A	J	K	T	I	Z
K	L	A	F	S	J	

Date: ________________

Help the mouse find its food. Color the boxes with the letters a-z in the right order.

	a	b	c	d	f	r
t	v	g	f	e	a	c
u	s	h	o	q	t	x
m	g	i	j	k	l	m
b	s	r	q	p	o	n
c	t	u	d	e	t	e
e	l	v	w	x	y	z
t	v	t	s	u	v	

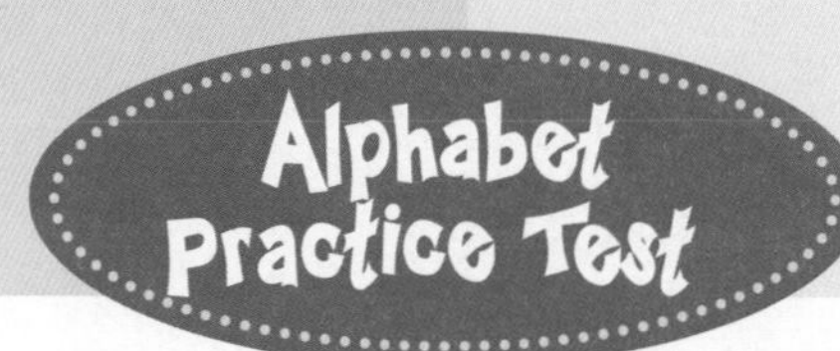

Choose the letters that come next? Color in the bubble next to those letters.

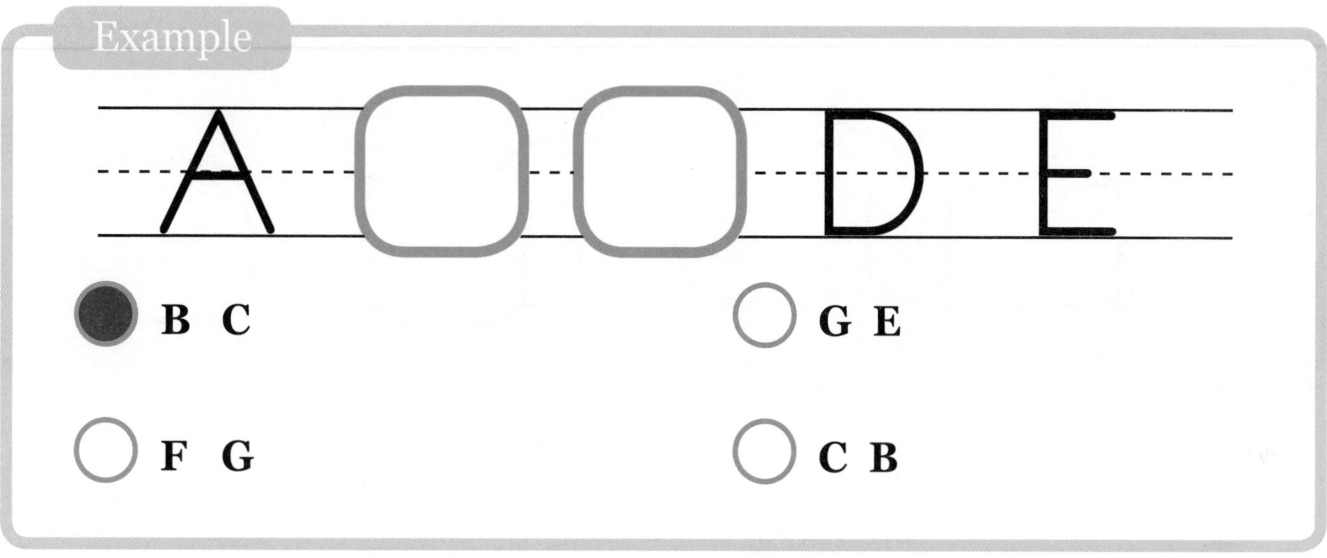

1. G H K

- B C
- I J
- F G
- X Y

2. E F G

- G L
- Q H
- C K
- H I

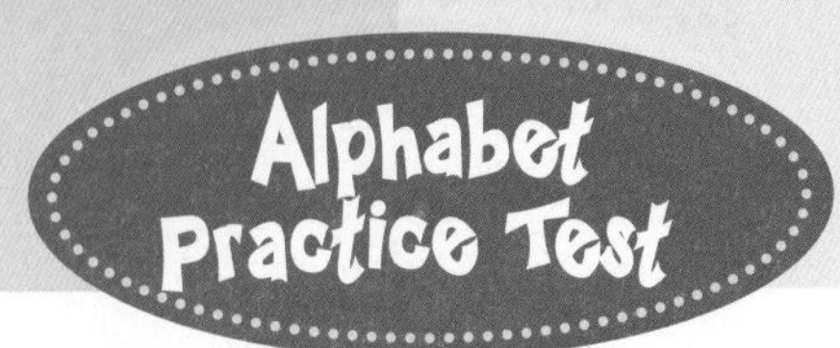

Choose the letters that come next? Color in the bubble next to those letters.

3. 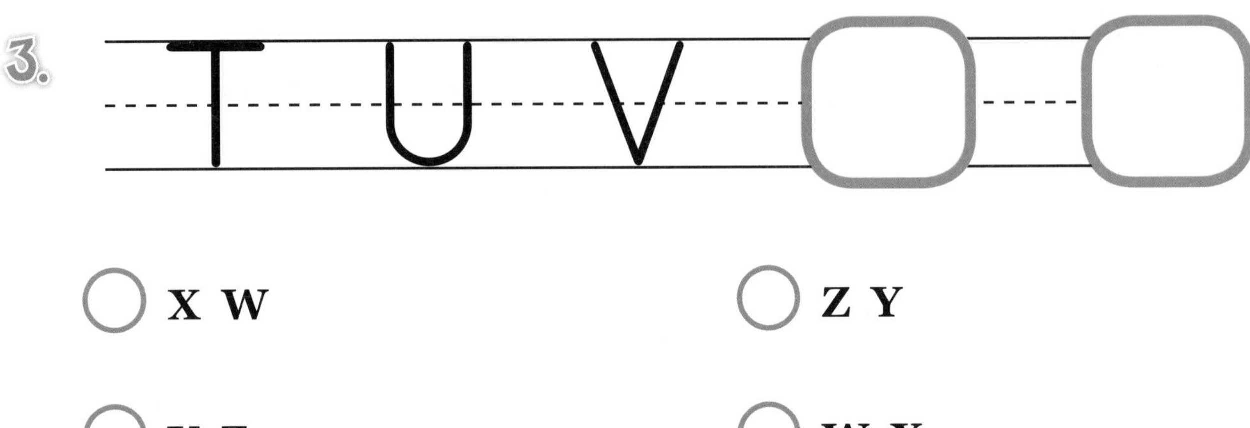

○ **X W** ○ **Z Y**

○ **Y Z** ○ **W X**

4. 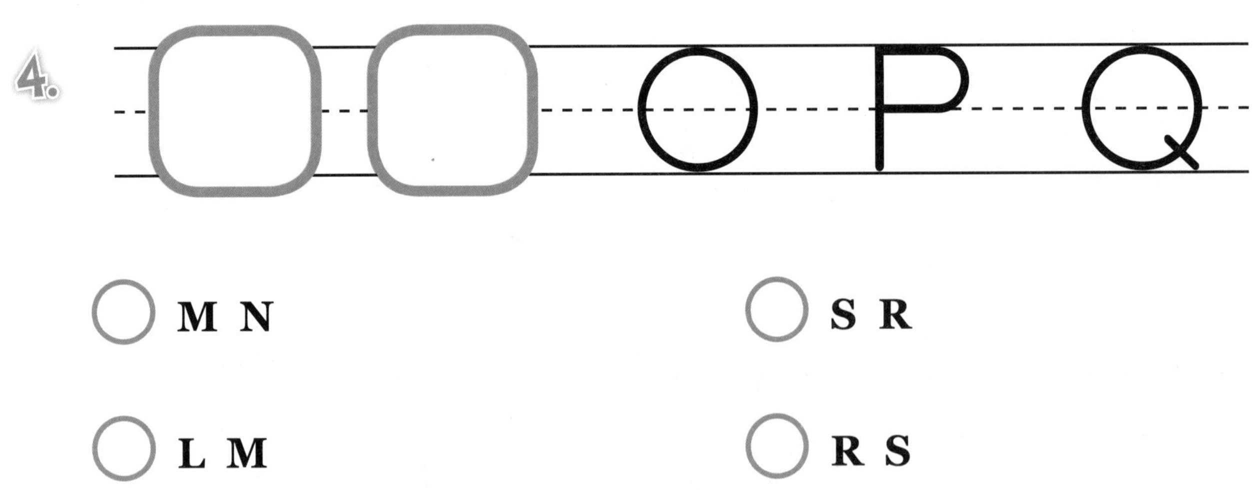

○ **M N** ○ **S R**

○ **L M** ○ **R S**

Choose the letters that come next? Color in the bubble next to those letters.

5. b ☐ ☐ e f

○ a c　　○ g h

○ c d　　○ c a

6. r s ☐ ☐ v

○ w x　　○ t u

○ p q　　○ w z

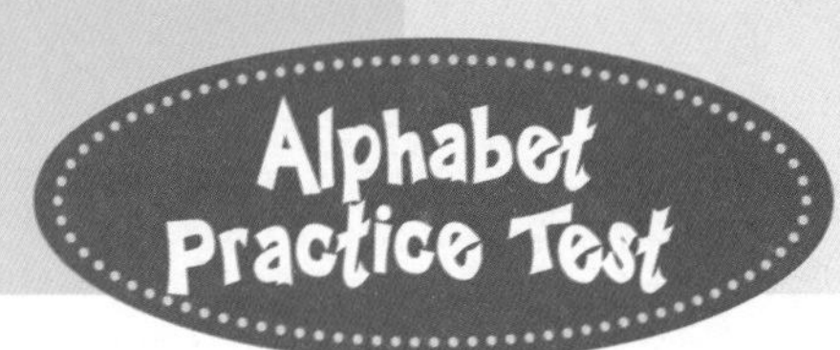

Choose the letters that come next? Color in the bubble next to those letters.

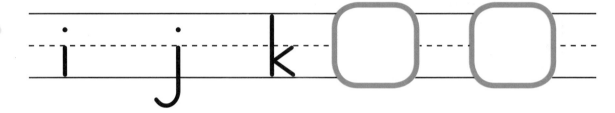

7. i j k ☐ ☐

○ m n ○ l m

○ n m ○ g h

8. p ☐ ☐ s t

○ o m ○ m n

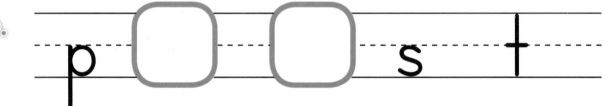

○ q r ○ r u

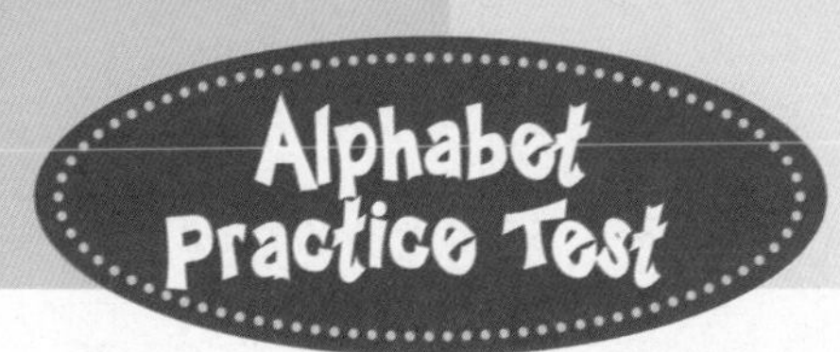

Choose the word that begins with the letter in the box. Color in the bubble next to that word.

9.

- ○ balloon
- ○ lizard
- ○ jacket
- ○ vest

10. q

- ○ penguin
- ○ guitar
- ○ banana
- ○ quilt

Choose the word that begins with the letter in the box. Color in the bubble next to that word.

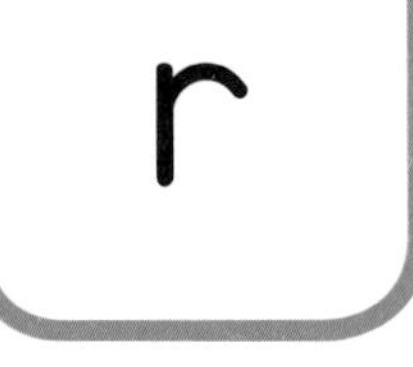

- ○ **moon**
- ○ **arrow**
- ○ **hair**
- ○ **rice**

12.

- ○ **insect**
- ○ **lemon**
- ○ **unicorn**
- ○ **water**

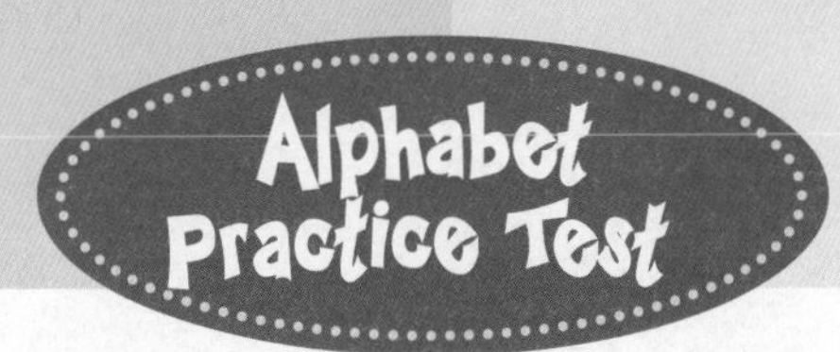

Choose the word that begins with the letter in the box. Color in the bubble next to that word.

○ **apple** ○ **queen**

○ **igloo** ○ **yacht**

○ **kite** ○ **dinner**

○ **bell** ○ **horse**

Phonics

"I know the sounds these letters make!" When you hear your child say that, you can rest assured he or she is building phonics skills. In this book, your child learns phonics, which is the relationship between letters and the sounds they make. Understanding this relationship is essential to learning to read.

What to do

The activity pages in this book will give your child practice in identifying vowels and consonants, beginning and ending sounds in words, short and long vowel sounds and spelling and consonant blends. Have your child complete each activity page and then review it together. On some pages you will see a light bulb. Spend time discussing the answers to these questions.

Keep on going!

- Point to objects around the house. Have your child identify the beginning or ending sounds and letters of the objects. Then have your child point to objects as you identify long and short vowel sounds. Take turns identifying the various letter-sound relationships.
- Create riddles with your child to practice beginning or ending consonant sounds. For example, "It's round and fun to play with. It ends with the *l* sound." (ball)

Date: ______________

There are 26 letters in the alphabet. Five of the letters are vowels: **A**, **E**, **I**, **O** and **U**. All the rest are consonants.

Look at the alphabet below. Put an X through the five vowels: A, E, I, O and U.

Now say the names of all the consonants.

A B C D E F G H I

J K L M N O P Q

R S T U V W X Y Z

How many consonants are there? ________

Color each balloon that has a consonant in it.

X

F M A B I J L

Date: ____________

B *makes the sound you hear at the beginning of the words* **Bobby** *and* **bear**.

Help Bobby the bear find ten things in this store that begin with b. Draw a circle around each one.

What insect buzzes around flowers and makes honey?

Date: ____________

D *makes the sound you hear at the beginning of the words* **doctor** *and* **Dave**.

Look in Doctor Dave's bag.
Color the pictures that begin with d.
Put an X on the pictures that do not begin with d.

She is another kind of doctor. She works on your teeth. Her job begins with *d*. Who is she?

Date: ____________

F *makes the sound you hear at the beginning of the words* **fancy** *and* **fish**.

Draw a circle around the pictures that begin with f. Put an X on the pictures that do not begin with f.

This word begins with *f*. It names a brave person who saves people if their houses are burning. Who is this person?

Date: ____________

L *makes the sound you hear at the beginning of the words* **lazy** *and* **lion**.

Help Lazy the lion find a word that begins with l to match each picture. Circle the correct word.

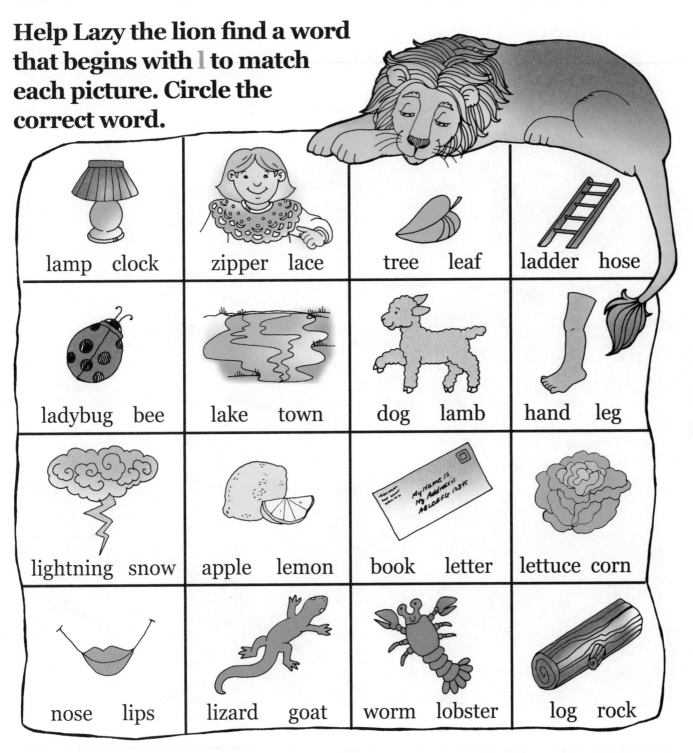

lamp clock	zipper lace	tree leaf	ladder hose
ladybug bee	lake town	dog lamb	hand leg
lightning snow	apple lemon	book letter	lettuce corn
nose lips	lizard goat	worm lobster	log rock

This word begins with *l*. It is a good feeling that you have about the people you like the most. It makes you want to hug someone! What is it?

Date: ______________

M *makes the sound you hear at the beginning of the words* **Mike** *and* **mailman**.

Look at the mail below. Circle the pictures that begin with m. Put an X on the pictures that do not begin with m.

I am a woman in your family. I take care of you. I love you. You call me a name that begins with *m*. Who am I?

Date: ____________

N makes the sound you hear at the beginning of the words **Nancy** *and* **nurse**.

Color the lollipops below that have pictures beginning with n.

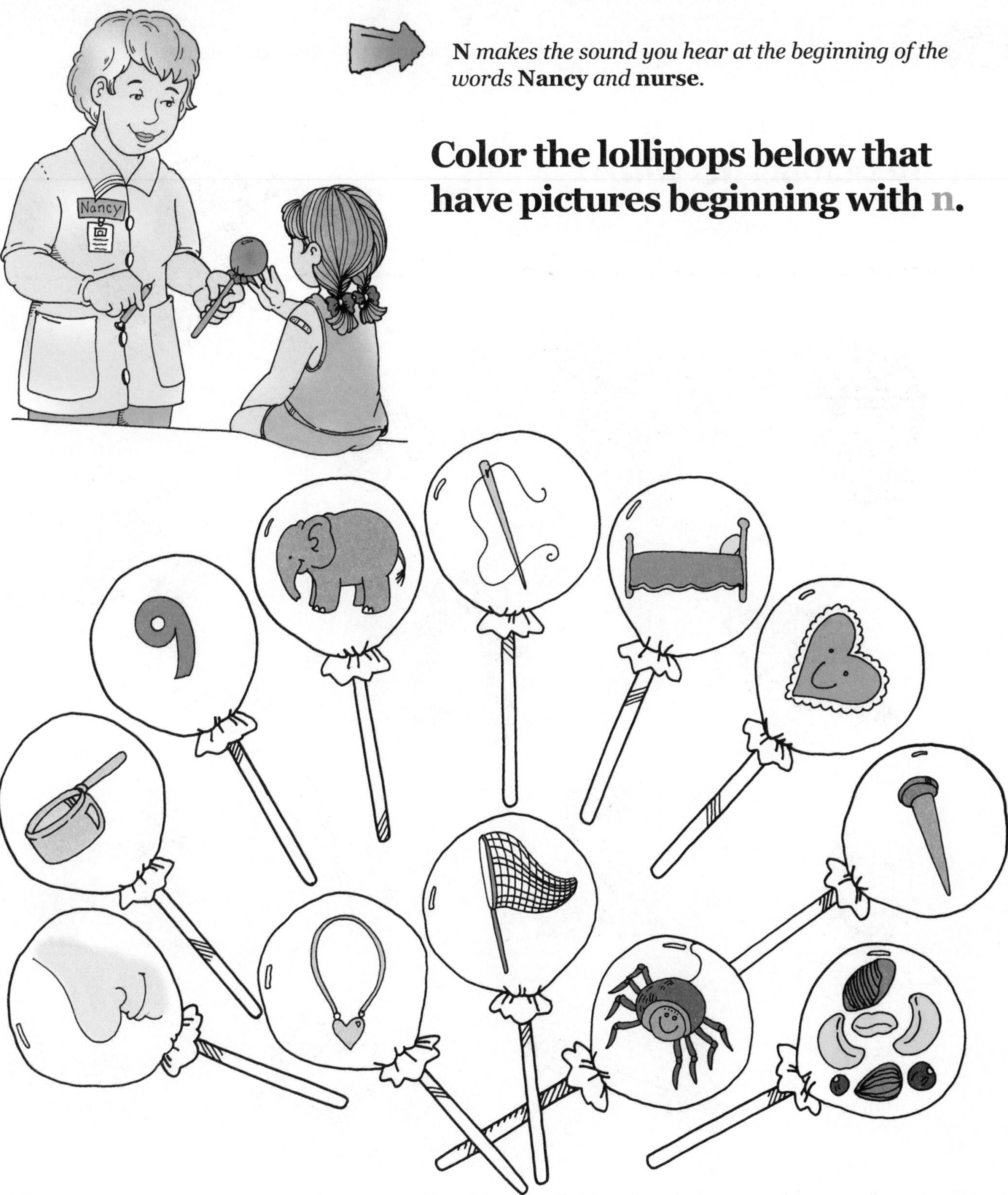

This thing begins with *n*. It is made of big sheets of paper. It has lots of pictures and words on it. It tells us what is happening in the world. Grownups like to read it. What is it? Find one of these and look at one page of it. Find words you know. Circle them with a marker. Show a grownup what you can read!

Date: ________

P *makes the sound you hear at the beginning of the words* **Patsy** *and* **parrot**.

Use a purple crayon to write the letter p on top of each picture that begins with p.

This food begins with *p*. It is round and has cheese on it. You can order it or make it at home. What is it?

Date: ______________

R *makes the sound you hear at the beginning of the words* **Ricky** *and* **rabbit**.

Circle the r word that tells what Ricky the rabbit is doing in each picture.

rest play	swim run	ride hug
rock look	climb rake	stand roll
read sing	rope feed	rip talk
row eat	race walk	sleep rush

This word begins with *r*. It blasts off into outer space. What is it?

Date: __________

S *makes the sound you hear at the beginning of the words* **Sally** *and* **silly**.

Draw a circle around the pictures that begin with s. Put an X on the pictures that do not begin with s.

If you take two pieces of bread and put peanut butter on one and jelly on the other, then stick them together, what have you made? It begins with *s*.

Date: ____________

T *makes the sound you hear at the beginning of the words* **Tammy** *and* **teacher**.

1. **Trace** the letter in each row.
2. **Color** the pictures in each row that begin with t.

t

t

t

t

This thing begins with *t*. Campers sleep in it. What is it?

Date: ____________

W *makes the sound you hear at the beginning of the words* **Willy** *and* **worm**.

In the story below, there are 11 words that begin with w. Draw a wiggly line under each one.

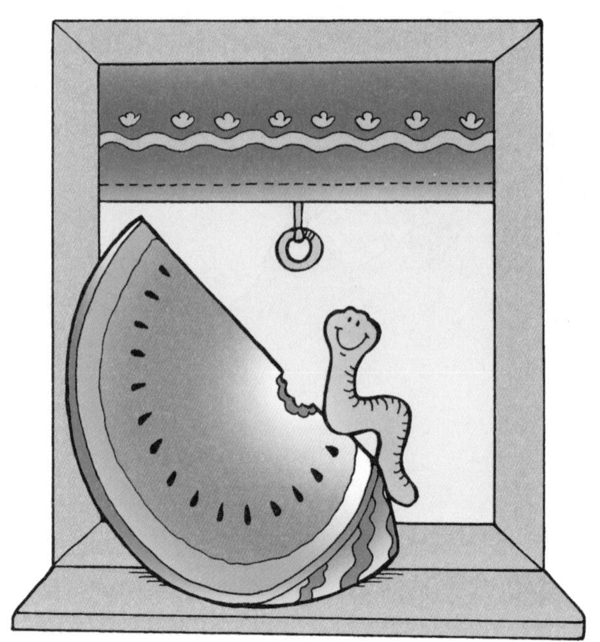

Willy the worm felt hungry. He wanted something to eat. He saw a watermelon in the window. He climbed up on the wagon. He wiggled up the wall. Then he took a bite. Wow! It was wonderful!

Now circle each word that you underlined in the puzzle. The words go across and down.

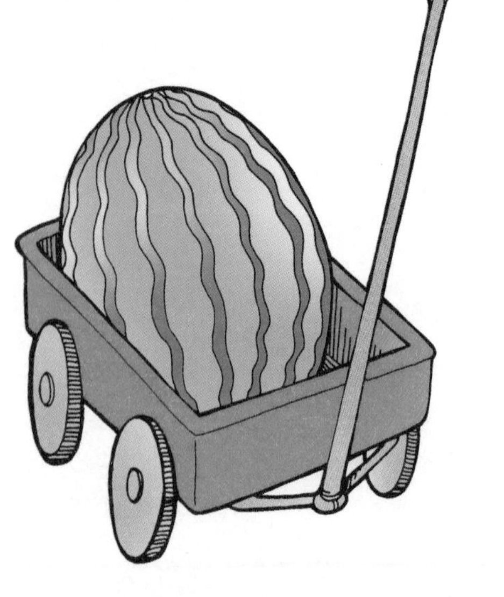

x	w	i	g	g	l	e	d	v	t
w	a	t	e	r	m	e	l	o	n
o	g	e	k	p	r	s	b	y	w
w	o	r	m	h	f	l	x	z	i
k	n	c	w	i	n	d	o	w	l
g	v	w	a	n	t	e	d	a	l
u	w	h	s	r	z	q	g	l	y
w	o	n	d	e	r	f	u	l	a

This begins with *w*. You cannot see it, but you can feel it. Sometimes you hear it blowing. It makes the trees sway. What is it?

Date: ____________

*C can make two sounds. If the vowels **e** or **i** come after the **c**, then **c** will have the **s** sound. If one of the other vowels (**a**, **o**, **u**) comes after the **c**, then **c** will have the **k** sound.*

Look at the pictures and words. If a word begins with an s sound, as in *city*, circle s. If it begins with a k sound, as in *country*, circle k.

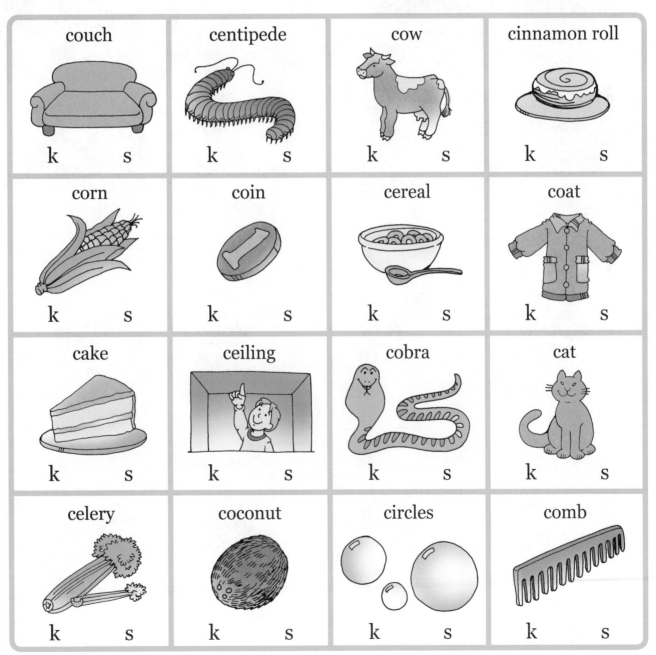

couch	centipede	cow	cinnamon roll
k s	k s	k s	k s
corn	coin	cereal	coat
k s	k s	k s	k s
cake	ceiling	cobra	cat
k s	k s	k s	k s
celery	coconut	circles	comb
k s	k s	k s	k s

Date: ____________

G can make two sounds. Usually, words that begin with **g** *make the same sound that you hear in* **Gary** *and* **goat**. *But sometimes* **g** *can sound like* **j**, *as in* **George** *and* **giraffe**. *This usually happens when the vowels* **e** *or* **i** *come after the* **g**, *but not always. The best way to figure out which* **g** *sound to use is to try both sounds and see which one makes sense. For example, try saying* goat *with both* **g** *sounds. See? One of them does not make sense!*

Look at the pictures and words. If the word begins like *goat*, circle g. If the word begins like *giraffe*, circle j.

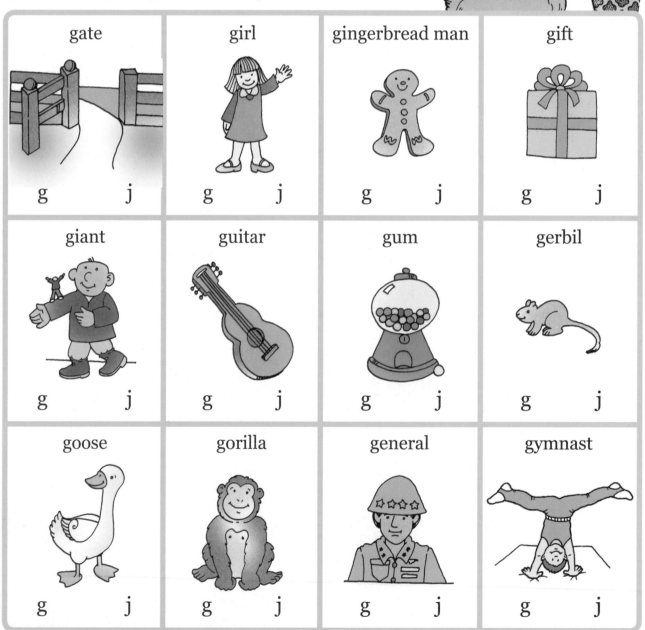

gate	girl	gingerbread man	gift
g j	g j	g j	g j
giant	**guitar**	**gum**	**gerbil**
g j	g j	g j	g j
goose	**gorilla**	**general**	**gymnast**
g j	g j	g j	g j

Date: ____________

H *makes the sound you hear at the beginning of the words* **happy** *and* **hippo**.

Help Happy the hippo find h words. Name the picture in each box. Color the pictures that begin with h.

This game begins with *h*. One child counts to ten and then tries to find the other children who are hiding. Do you know what it is?

Date: ____________

V *makes the sound you hear at the beginning of the words* **Vicki** *and* **vacation**.

Vicki is going on a vacation. Help Vicki load her van with things that begin with v. Draw a line from the v words to the van.

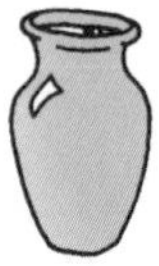

Date: ______________

K *makes the sound you hear at the beginning of the words* **Katie** *and* **kangaroo**.

Draw a circle around the pictures that begin with k. Put an X on the pictures that do not begin with k.

Date: ____________

Say the name of each picture and listen to the beginning sound. Choose the correct beginning sound from the box below. Write it next to each picture.

q	r	y	h	v	w

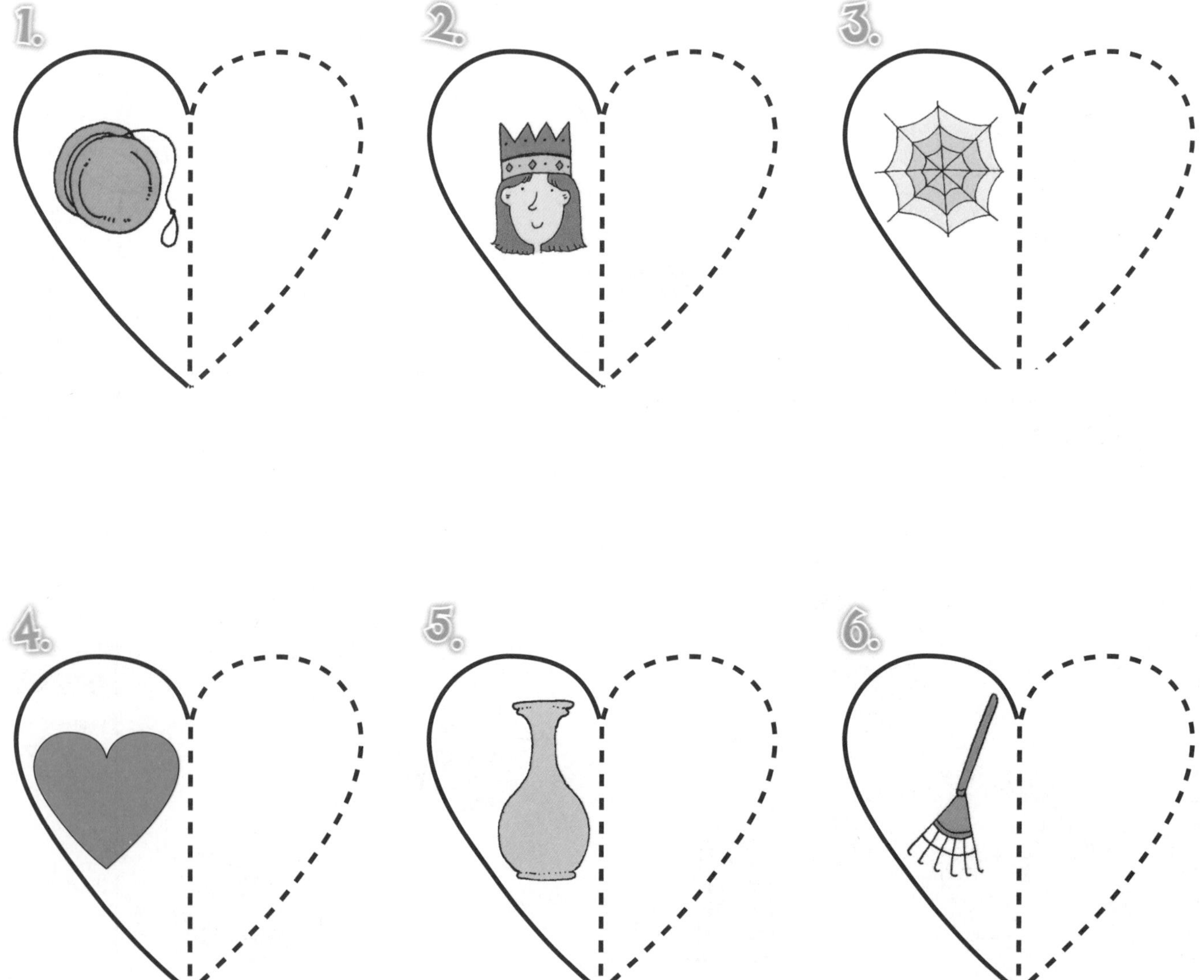

Date: ____________

Say the name of each animal and listen to the beginning sound. Draw lines to match the animals with the same beginning sound. Write the correct letter beside each box .

1. 
lion

2. 
cat

3. 
dog

4. 
fox

5. 
bear

Date: ____________

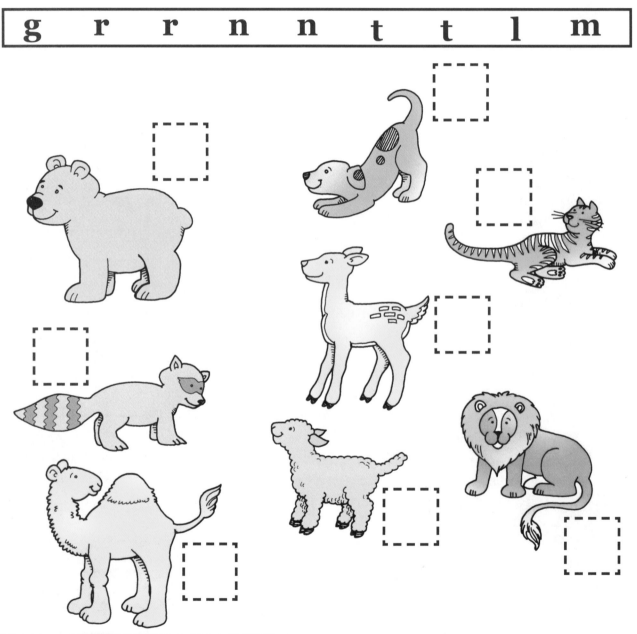

To help you hear the ending sound, say the word and stretch out the last sound. For example, when you see the picture of the bear, say **"bear-r-r-r-r-r"**.

Say the name of each animal. Choose an ending sound from the box below. Write the correct ending sound next to each animal.

g	r	r	n	n	t	t	l	m

This creature lives in the sea. It does not have a tail. It has eight arms. Its head looks like a balloon. It ends with *s*. What is it?

Date: ________________

Help Larry Last find the last sound that each word makes. Circle the correct letter under each lunchbox.

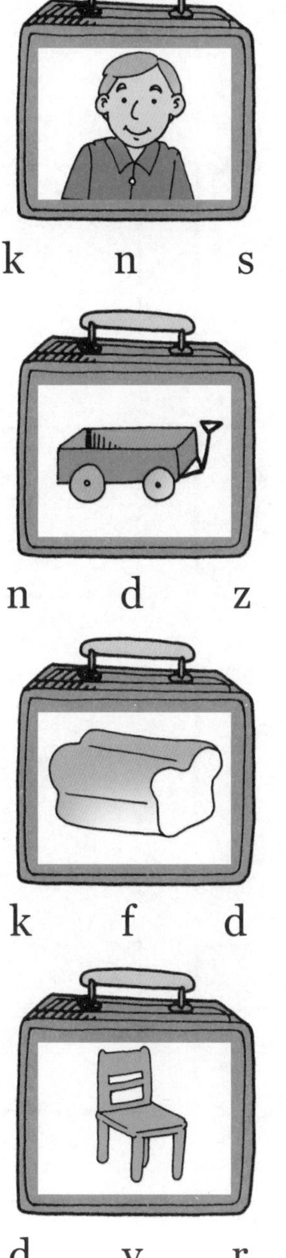

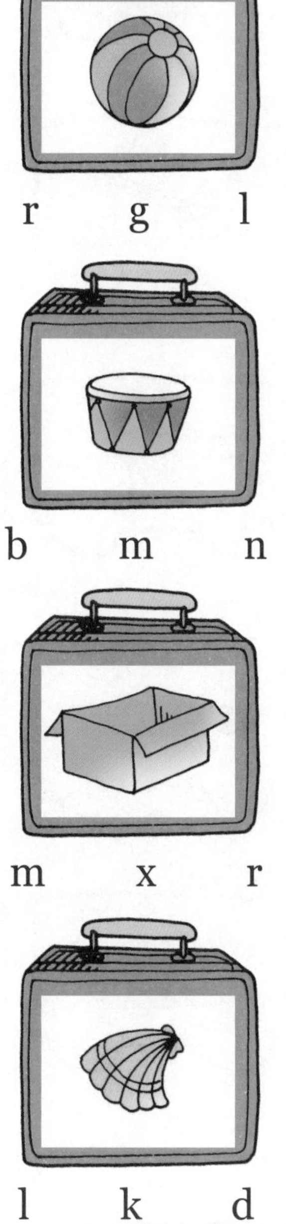

k n s   r g l   s f r

n d z   b m n   t k p

k f d   m x r   g z l

d v r   l k d   g t f

You do this while you are asleep. It is like watching a movie in your head. It ends with *m*. What is it?

Date: ____________

Find two pictures on each train that end with the same sound in the box. Circle them.

1. g

2. n

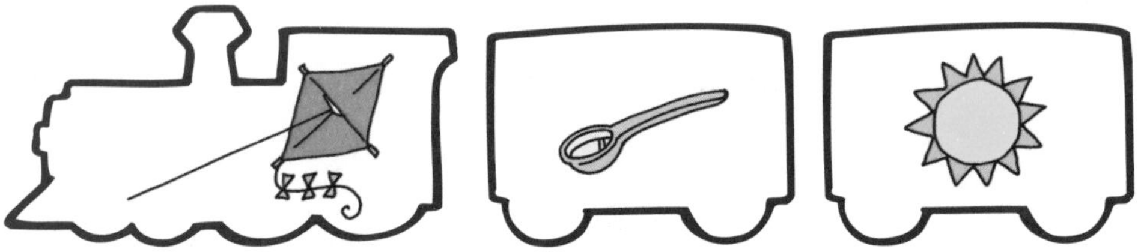

3. r

4. m

5. t

6. l

Date: ____________

It's time to raise the flags! Listen to the ending sound of each picture.

1. **Color** the s picture flags orange.

2. **Color** the l picture flags purple.

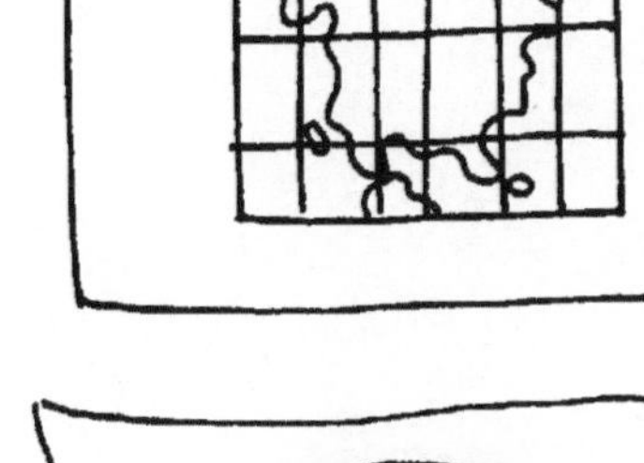

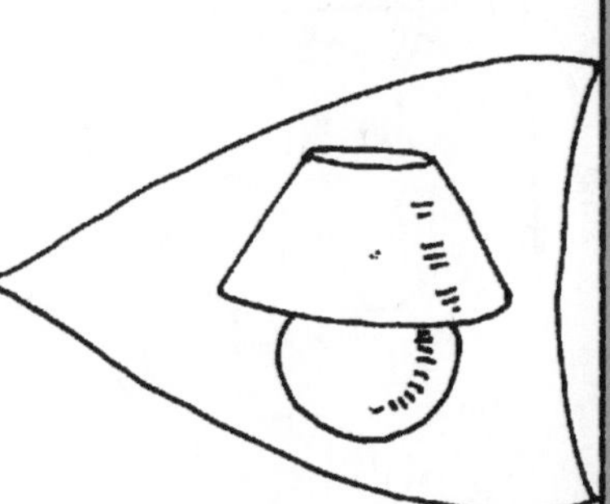

3. **Color** the p picture flags green.

Date: ____________

Draw lines to match each object to each clue.

1. It ends like

2. It ends like

3. It ends like

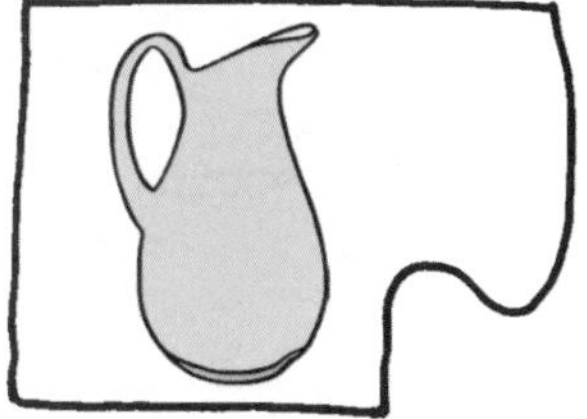

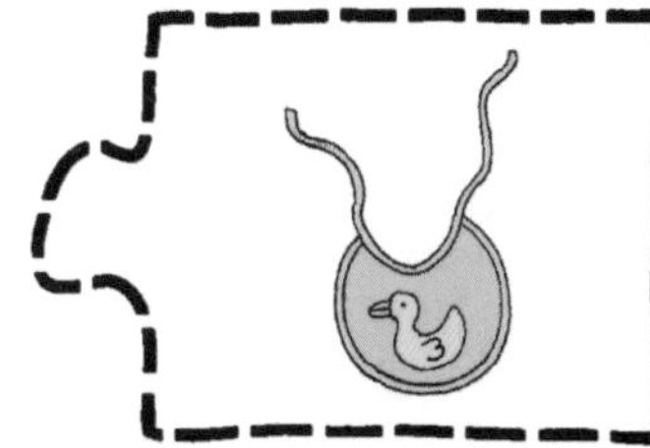

4. It ends like

5. It ends like

Date: ____________

Read the letter in each row. Fill in the bubble next to each picture that begins with that sound.

 1. p 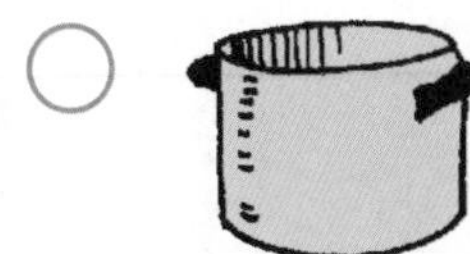    

2. n     

 3. d    

 4. f      

Read the letter in each row. Fill in the bubble next to each picture whose name ends with that sound.

 5. k      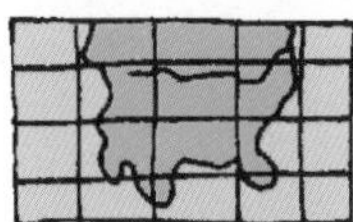

6. s    

7. t 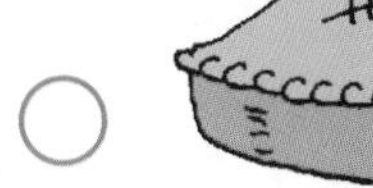   

8. l      

Date: ____________

Draw lines to match each object to each clue.

1. It begins with  and ends like 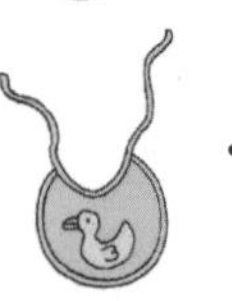.

2. It begins with  and ends like .

3. It begins with  and ends like .

4. It begins with  and ends like 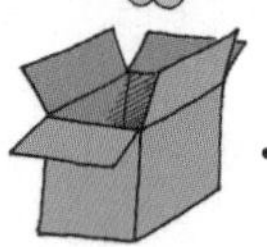.

5. It begins with  and ends like .

Date: ____________

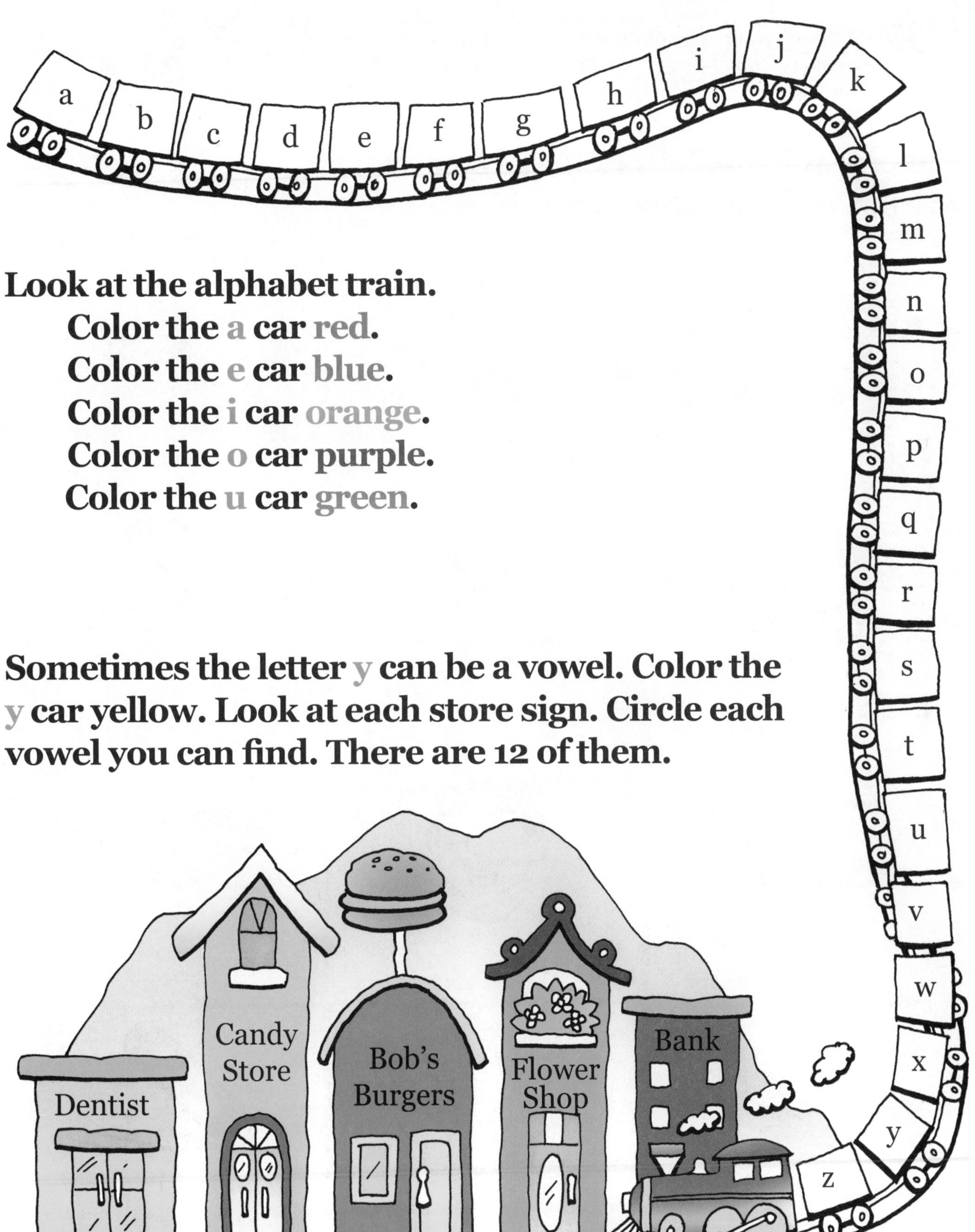

Look at the alphabet train.

Color the a car red.
Color the e car blue.
Color the i car orange.
Color the o car purple.
Color the u car green.

Sometimes the letter y can be a vowel. Color the y car yellow. Look at each store sign. Circle each vowel you can find. There are 12 of them.

Date: ____________

The **consonant-vowel-consonant rule**: *When only one vowel comes between consonants, that vowel is usually short.*

Unscramble the letters to spell each word. Circle the short vowels.

1. atr ____________

2. aht ____________

3. ktac ____________

4. mkas ____________

5. naf ____________

6. plam ____________

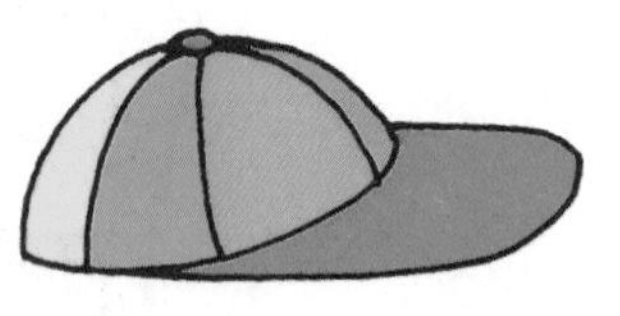

7. pca ____________

8. dDa ____________

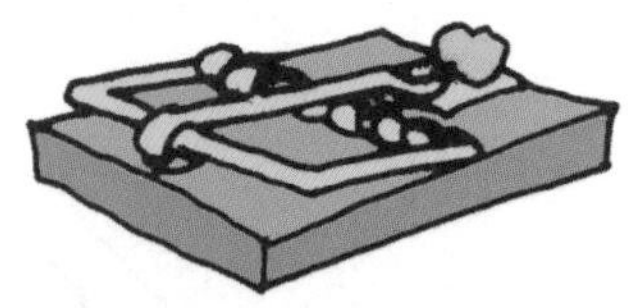

9. tarp ____________

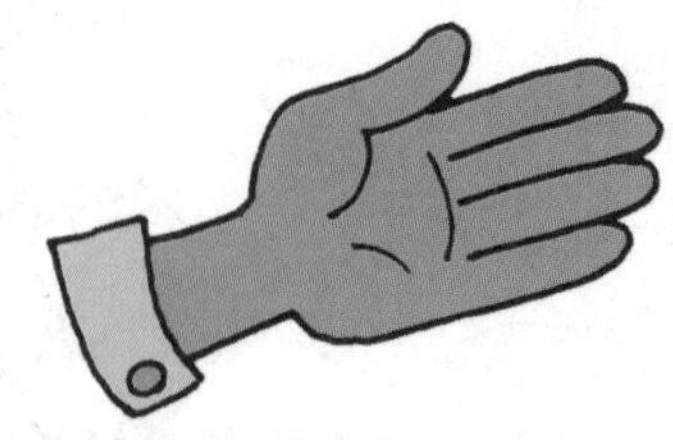

10. dahn ____________

11. palc ____________

12. cklab ____________

Date: __________

Use a list word to complete each sentence.

List Words: at had an can as and

1. We went to __________ apple farm.
2. We picked green __________ red apples.
3. One apple was as big __________ a ball.
4. We __________ lots of fun!
5. We went home __________ dinnertime.
6. Now Mom __________ make apple pie.

Write the challenge word that matches each clue.

lamp fast

7. I can be turned off and on.
   I am a __________.
8. I am not slow.
   I am __________.

 Date: ____________

Short e *makes the sound you hear at the beginning of* **egg**. *To help you remember the* ***short -e*** *sound, stretch out the beginning of the word like this: e-e-e-egg.*

Help Ed find the eggs that have pictures with the short -e sound. Color these eggs brown.

When you say this word you nod your head up and down. It means the opposite of no. It has the *short -e* sound. What word is it?

Date: ____________

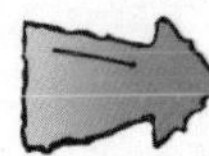

The **short -e** *sound is the beginning sound of the word* **elephant**.

Read each list word. Circle the letter that makes the short -e sound.

Read.

Copy.

Organize.

1. end ____________
2. get ____________
3. let ____________
4. red ____________
5. ten ____________
6. yes ____________

list words with **en**

____

____

list words with **et**

____

____

Write the list word that begins with the same sound as each picture.

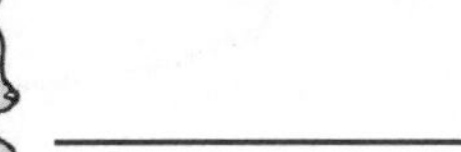

7. ____________

8. ____________

9. ____________

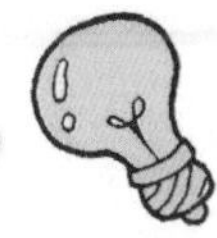

10. ____________

11. ____________

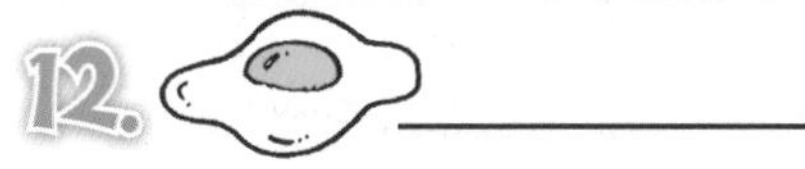

12. ____________

Date: ____________

Short i *makes the sound you hear at the beginning of* **igloo**. *To help you remember the* **short -i** *sound, stretch out the beginning of the word like this: i-i-i-igloo.*

Color the pictures with the short -i sound blue. Put an X on the pictures that do not have a short -i sound.

IGLOO INN

Date: ____________

*The **short -i** sound is the beginning sound for the word **inchworm**.*

Read each list word. Circle the letter that makes the short -i sound.

 **Read.**  **Copy.**  **Organize.**

Read.	Copy.	Organize.
		list words that begin with **i**
1. if	____________	____________
2. is	____________	____________
3. big	____________	list words that begin with **h**
4. him	____________	____________
5. his	____________	____________
6. sit	____________	

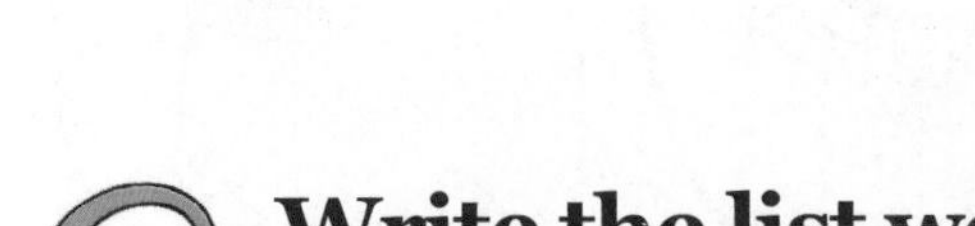

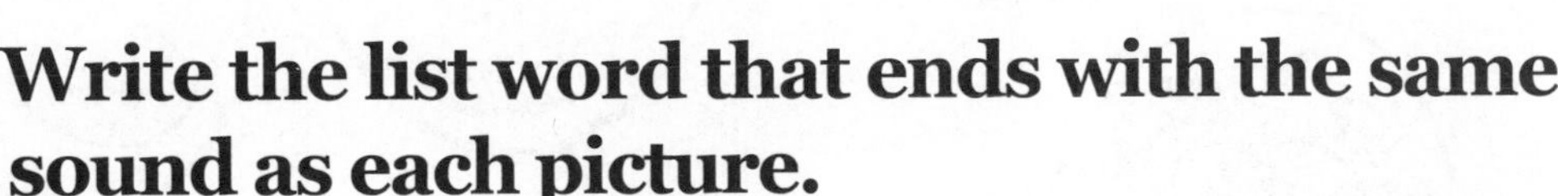

Write the list word that ends with the same sound as each picture.

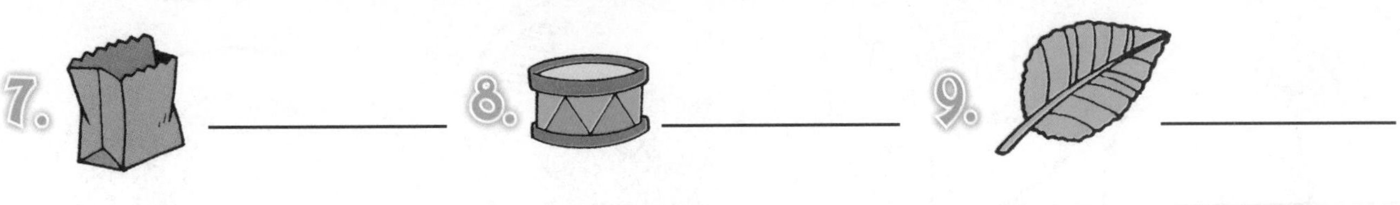

7. ____________ 8. ____________ 9. ____________

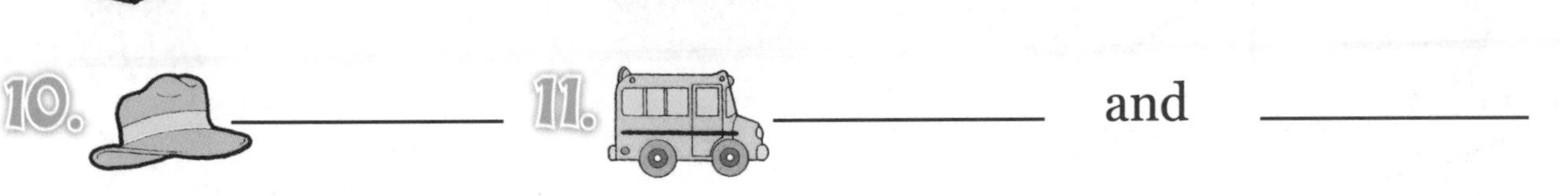

10. ____________ 11. ____________ and ____________

Date: ______________

Short o *makes the sound you hear at the beginning of* **olive**. *To help you remember the* **short -o** *sound, stretch out the beginning of the word like this: o-o-o-olive.*

Help Oliver find the olives that have pictures with the short -o sound. Color these olives green. If the picture does not have the short -o sound, color the olive black.

Date: __________

*The **short -o** sound is the beginning sound of the word **octopus**.*

Read each list word. Circle the letter that makes the short -o sound.

Read.

Copy.

Organize.

1. on __________

2. got __________

3. hop __________

4. fox __________

5. top __________

6. not __________

list words with **op**

____

____

list words with **ot**

____

____

Write the list word that matches each picture.

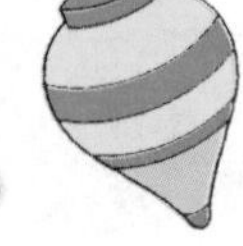

7. __________

8. __________

9. __________

10. __________

Date: ____________

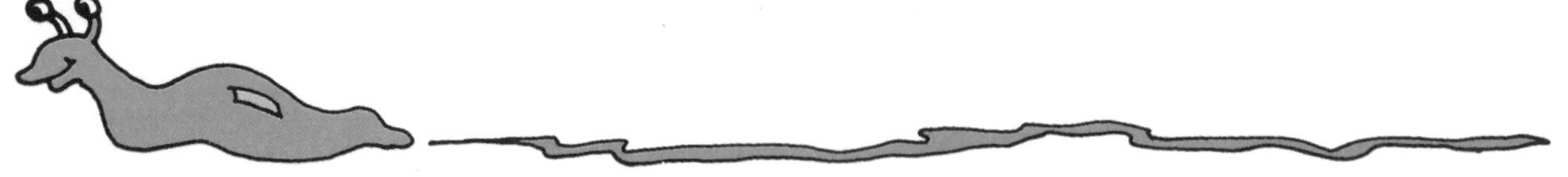

The **consonant-vowel-consonant rule**: *When only one vowel comes between consonants, that vowel is usually short.*

Circle each word with the short -u sound. Then join the words with the short -u sound to help Slug Bug find its way home.

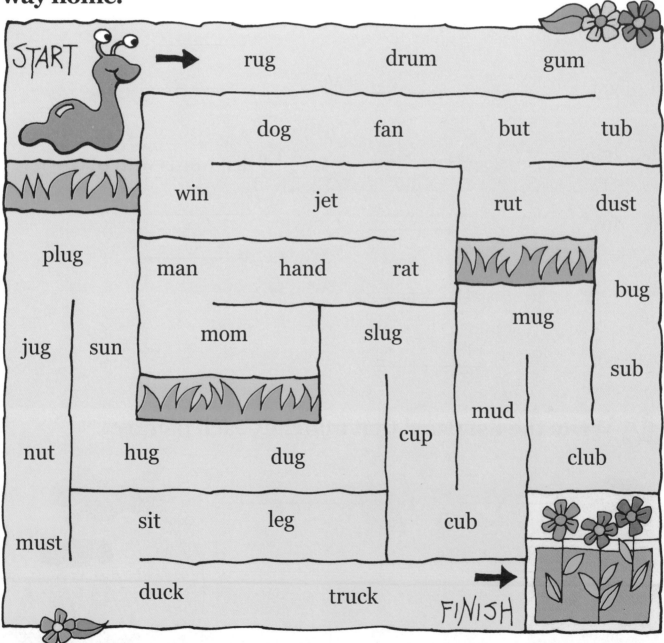

START

rug drum gum

dog fan but tub

win jet rut dust

plug man hand rat bug

mug

jug sun mom slug

sub

mud

cup

nut hug dug club

sit leg cub

must

duck truck

FINISH

Date: ____________

The **short -u** *sound is the beginning sound for the word* **umbrella**.

Read each list word. Circle the letter that makes the short -u sound.

Read.

Copy.

Organize.

1. up ____________
2. but ____________
3. run ____________
4. bug ____________
5. mud ____________
6. jump ____________

two-letter list word

____

three-letter list words

____

____

____

____

Write the list word that rhymes with each word.

7. bud ____________
8. lump ____________
9. hut ____________
10. sun ____________
11. tug ____________
12. cup ____________

Date: ______________

Circle the things in the picture that rhyme with rat .

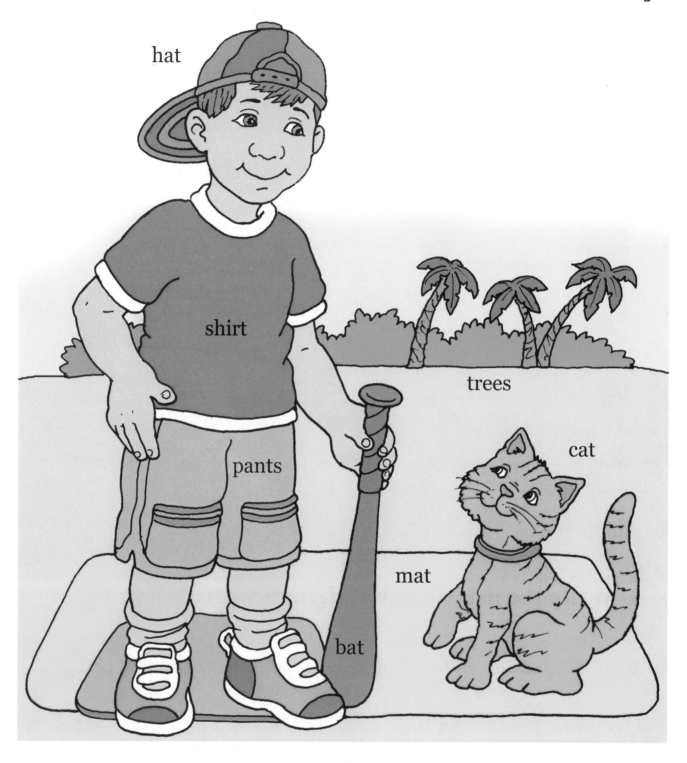

hat

shirt

trees

cat

pants

mat

bat

Name two things that rhyme with *rat* that are not in the picture.

Date: ________________

Help Tad Frog find his way across the pond. Color the pictures that rhyme with pad green.

Date: ____________

Circle each word that rhymes with van. Then join the words to help the van make the delivery.

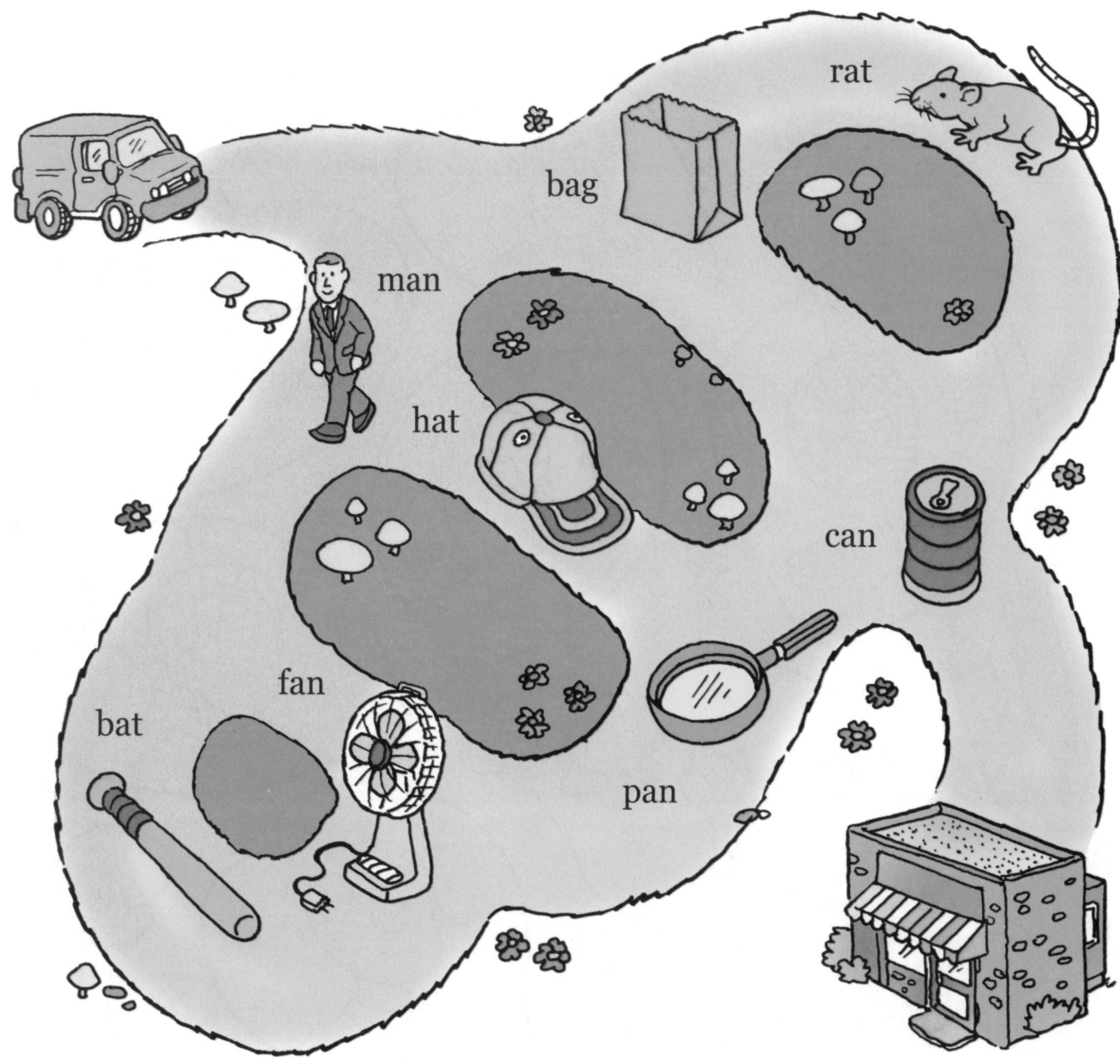

Date: ____________

Color the picture in each row that rhymes with the first picture.

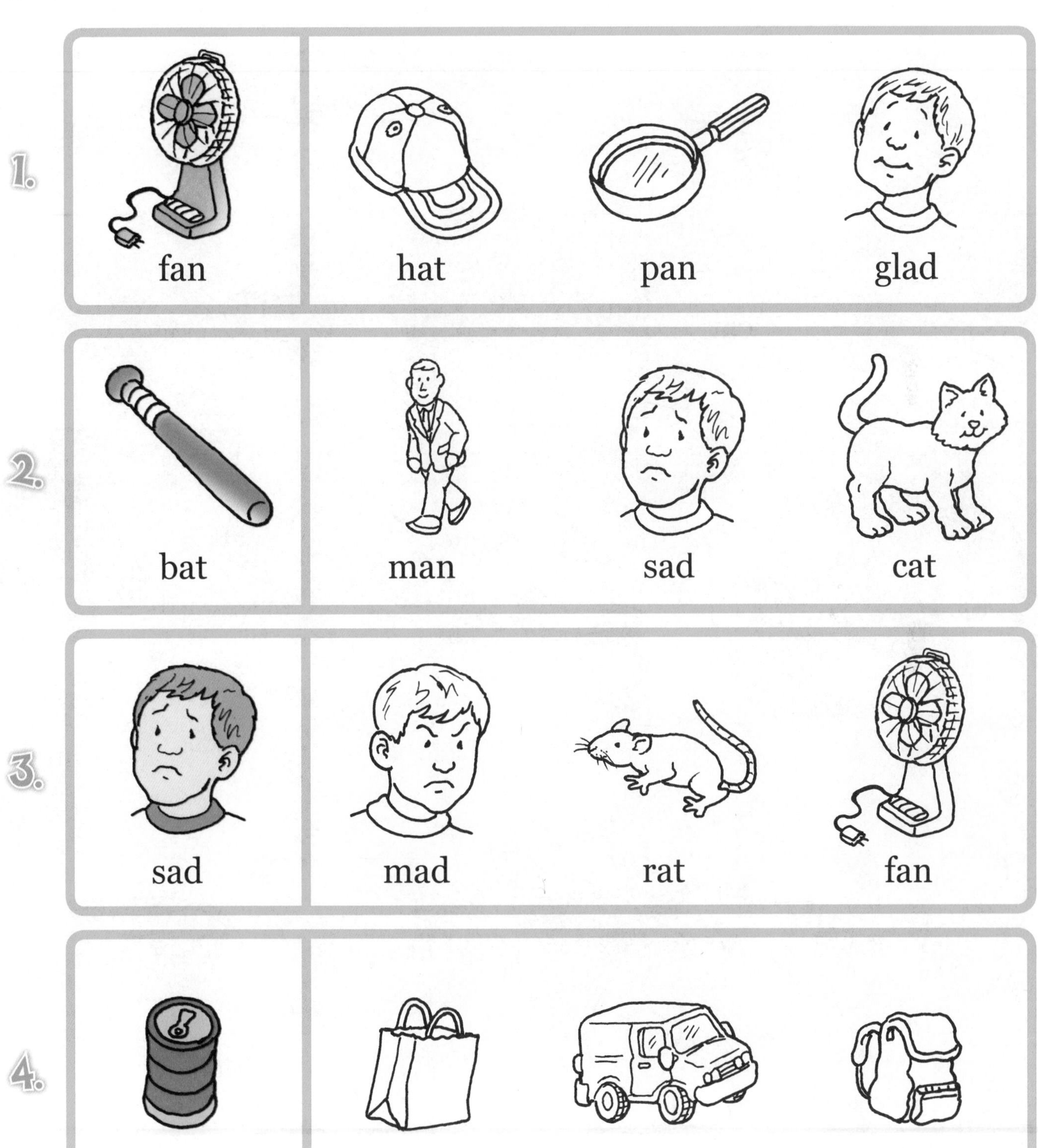

Date: ____________

Circle the things in the picture that rhyme with den **.**

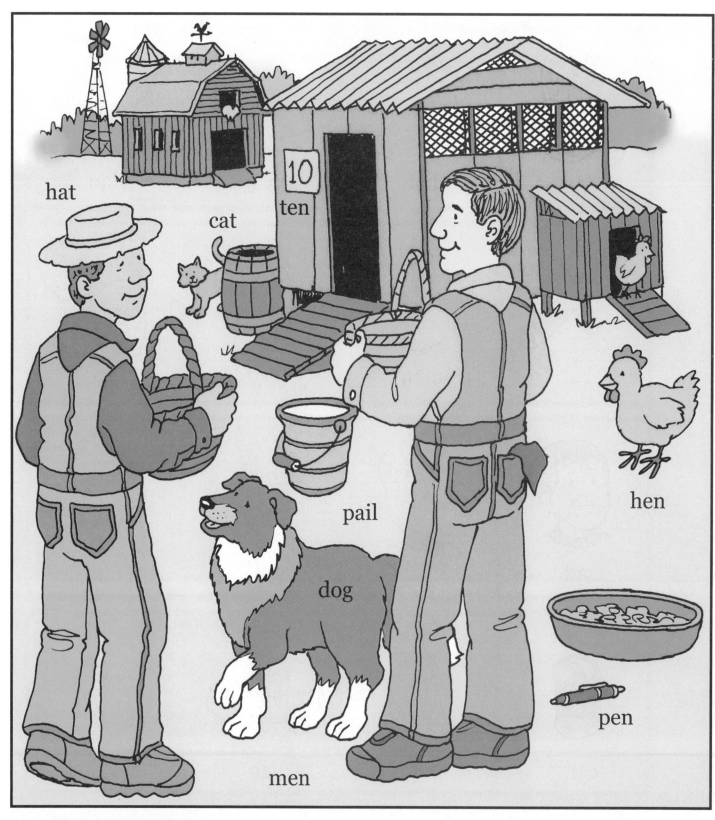

hat

cat

10

ten

hen

pail

dog

pen

men

Date: ____________

Circle each word that rhymes with shed. Then join the words to help Ted find his way down the hill.

red

bed

hen

bell

nest

pen

sled

shell

well

Finish

Date: ______________

Color the pictures that rhyme with met  **.**

jet	pet	hen
sled	net	wet
bed	pen	vet

Date: ____________

Color the pictures on the crown that rhyme with king  **.**

wing

wig

ring

string

sing

pin

fin

Date: ____________

Read the story. From the objects below, select one that rhymes with big in the story and write the alphabet in the box.

Once there was a cow who wanted to go to a party. She put on her pretty

pink [ ] . On the way to the party, the [ ] got stuck on a

[ ] that was on a [ ] tree. The cow lost her [ ] .

A. B.

C. D. E.

Date: ____________

Read the story. From the objects below, select one that rhymes with jog in the story and write the alphabet in the box.

Freddy is a very large bull [ ]. He is as big as a [ ]. His best friend is a bull [ ]. Together they play leap [ ]. See them jump over the [ ].

A. B.

C. D. E.

Date: ____________

Color the pictures that rhyme with pop .

mop

hop

dog

pot

STOP

stop

top

lock

Date: ____________

Read the story. From the objects below, select one that rhymes with dug in the story and write the alphabet in the box.

Once there was a lady [ ]. She liked to dance on a [ ]. Her favourite dance was the jitter [ ]. She won a first-place [ ]. Everyone gave her a [ ] for being the best dancing lady [ ].

A. B. C.

D. E. F.

Date: ______________

Randy hit a home run. Start at home plate and color the bases that rhyme with fun .

Date: ____________

Rhyming words *sound alike. They are made by changing only the beginning sound of a word. The rest of the word stays the same.*

The word puzzle below shows how to make a rhyming word.

Example

man – m + f = fan

1. 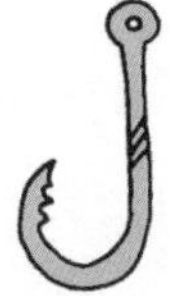 hook – h + b = ____________ 

2.  cake – c + r = ____________ 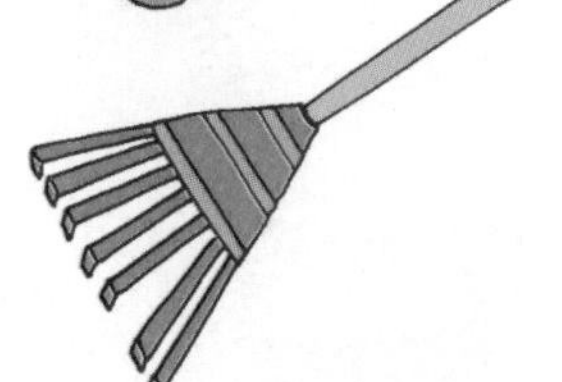

3.  dog – d + l = ____________ 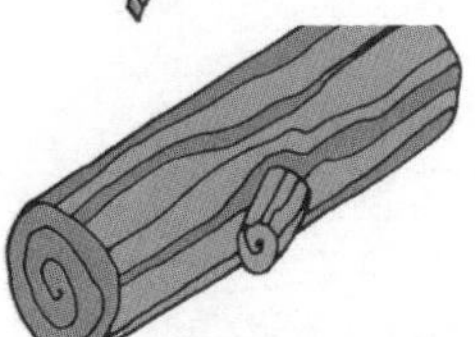

4. 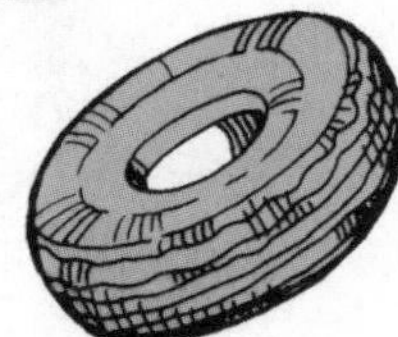 tire – t + f = ____________ 

5. 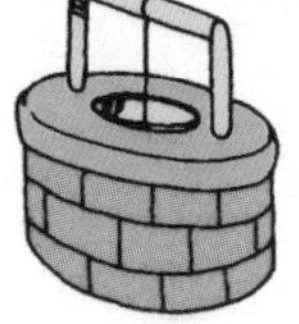 well – w + b = ____________ 

6.  king – k + r = ____________ 

Date: ____________

Look at the word on each basket. Change the first letter to make new words. Use the letters on each snake to help you. Write the words on the blanks below each snake.

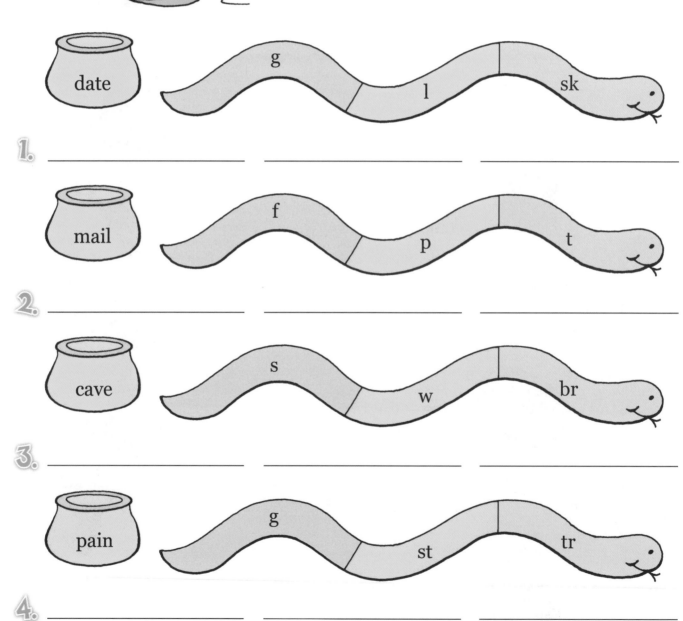

date — g, l, sk

1. ____________ ____________ ____________

mail — f, p, t

2. ____________ ____________ ____________

cave — s, w, br

3. ____________ ____________ ____________

pain — g, st, tr

4. ____________ ____________ ____________

Date: ____________

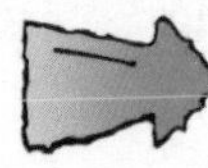

*The **long -a** sound can be spelled with the letters **ay** like in the word **may** and the letters **ai** like in the word **mail**.*

Read each list word. Circle the letters that makes the long -a sound.

 **Read.**  

Read.	Copy.	Organize.
1. day	____________	list words with long -a sound spelled **ay**
2. rain	____________	____________
3. tail	____________	____________
4. play	____________	____________
5. wait	____________	list words with long -a sound spelled **ai**
6. stay	____________	____________
		____________
		____________

Write the list word that begins with the same sound as each picture.

  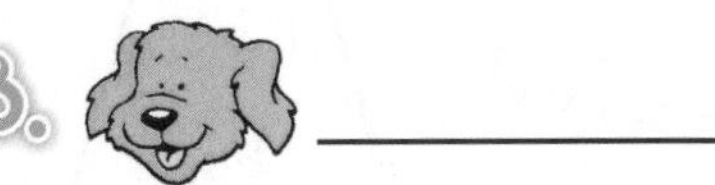 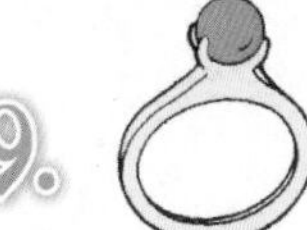

7. ____________ 8. ____________ 9. ____________

10. ____________ 11. ____________ 12. ____________

Date: ____________

Long e *makes the sound you hear at the beginning of* **eagle**. *To help you remember the* **long -e** *sound, stretch out the beginning of the word like this: e-e-e-eagle.*

Help Ethan find the eagles that have pictures with long -e sound. Color these eagles brown. Put an X on the eagle that does not have a long -e sound.

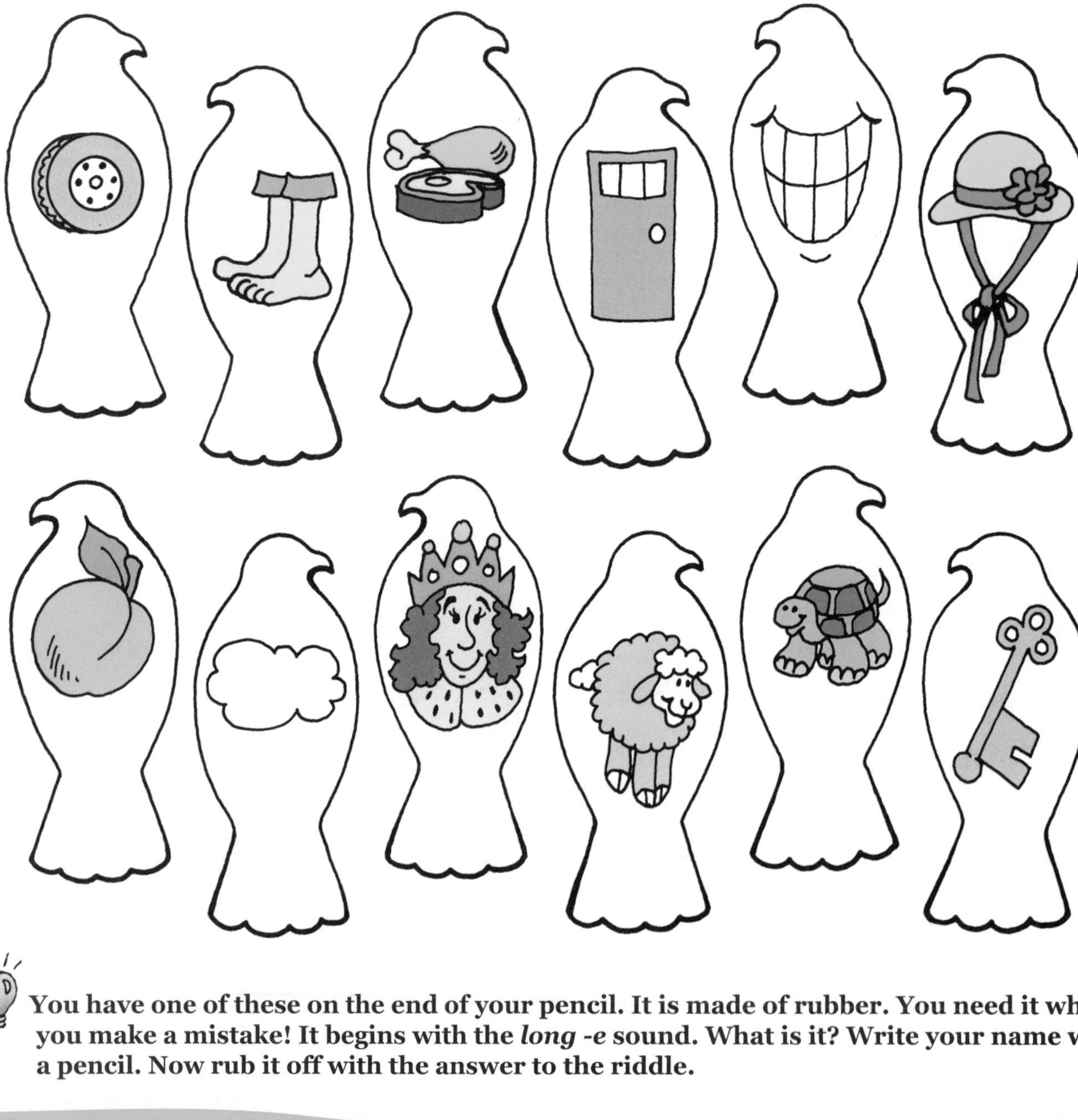

You have one of these on the end of your pencil. It is made of rubber. You need it when you make a mistake! It begins with the *long -e* sound. What is it? Write your name with a pencil. Now rub it off with the answer to the riddle.

Date: ____________

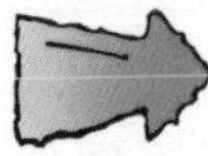

*The **long -e** sound can also be spelled with the letter **e** like in the word **he** and the letters **ee** like in the word **need**.*

Read each list word. Circle the letters that makes the long -e sound.

 **Read.**  **Copy.** 

Organize.

1. me ____________
2. tree ____________
3. we ____________
4. need ____________
5. see ____________
6. feet ____________

list words with long - e sound spelled **ee**

____

____

____

____

Write the list word that begins with the same sound as each picture.

7. 6 ____________
8. ____________
9. ____________
10. ____________
11. ____________
12. ____________

Date: ____________

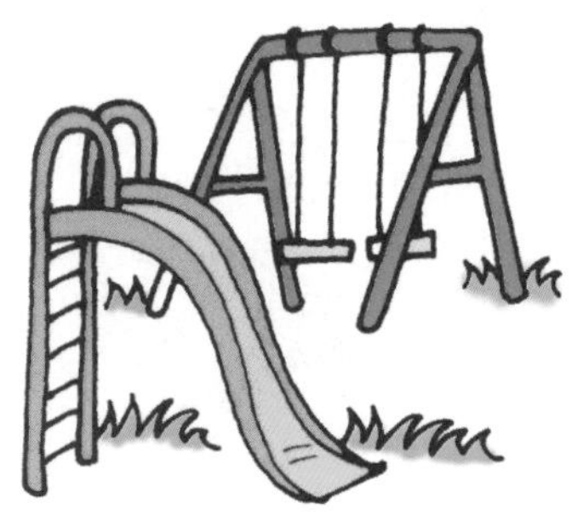

Look at the word on each slide. Change the first letter to make new words. Write the words on the slide.

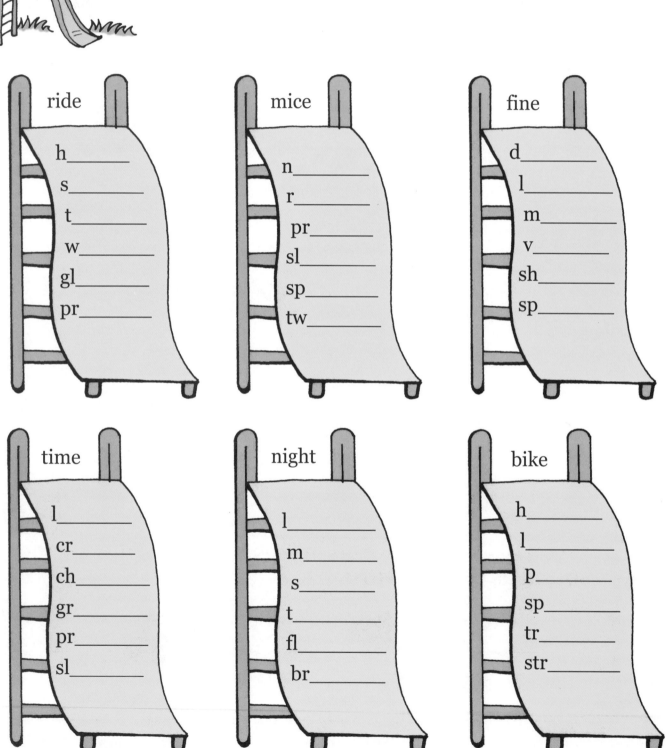

ride

h______
s______
t______
w______
gl______
pr______

mice

n______
r______
pr______
sl______
sp______
tw______

fine

d______
l______
m______
v______
sh______
sp______

time

l______
cr______
ch______
gr______
pr______
sl______

night

l______
m______
s______
t______
fl______
br______

bike

h______
l______
p______
sp______
tr______
str______

Date: ____________

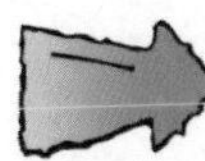

*The **long -i** sound can be spelled with the letters **i_e** like in the word **ice** and the letter **y** like in the word **try**.*

Read each list word. Circle the letters that makes the long -i sound.

 **Read.**  **Copy.**  **Organize.**

1. by ____________
2. like ____________
3. I ____________
4. my ____________
5. kite ____________
6. fly ____________

list words with **i_e**

____

____

list words with **y**

____

____

Write the list word that rhymes with each picture.

  ____________

 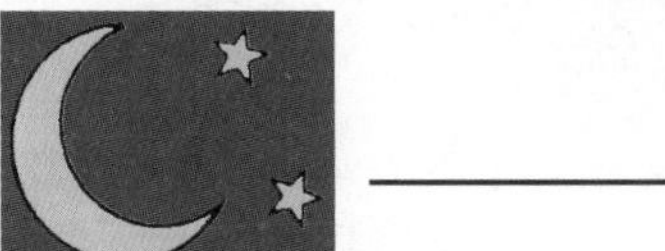 ____________

Write four list words that rhyme with each other.

9. ____________ 10. ____________ 11. ____________ 12. ____________

Date: ____________

The **consonant-vowel-vowel-consonant rule**: *When two vowels come together, the first vowel is usually long and the second vowel is silent. You can think of it this way, "When two vowels go walking, the first one does the talking!"*

Look at all the boats. Find the word that matches the picture on the boat and write it on the blank line.

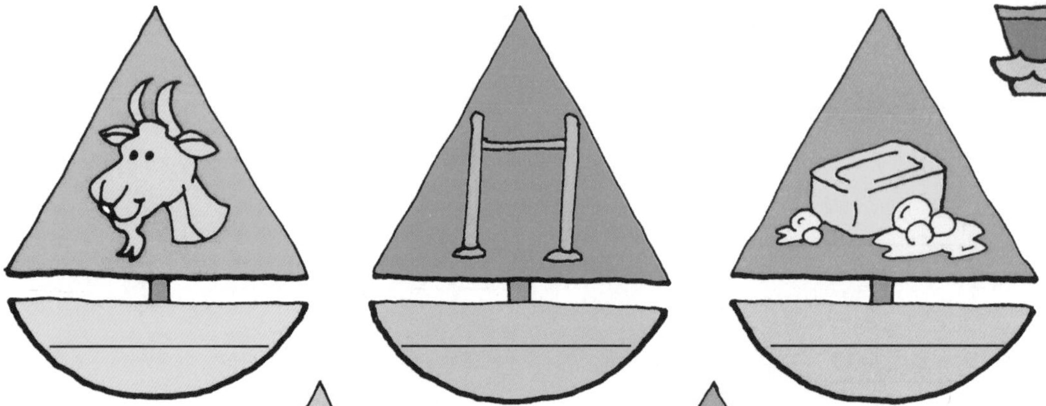

toast
road
soap
goat
toad
goal
foam
roast
coat

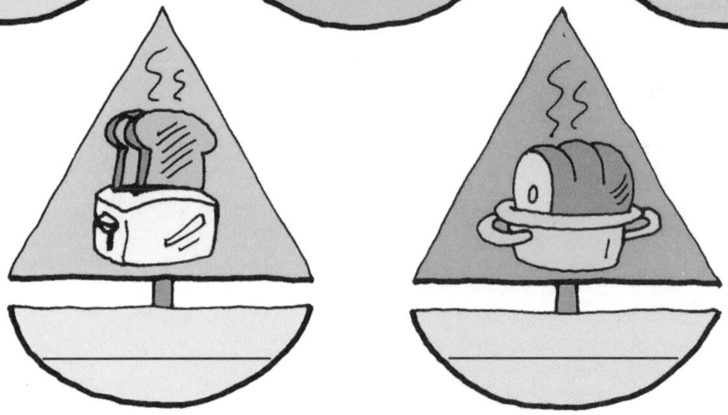

The word croak has a *long o* and silent *a*. What is another word with a *long o* and silent *a* that names an animal that makes a croak sound?

*The **long -o** sound is sometimes spelled with the letter **o** like in the word **no** and the letters **o_e** like in the word **cone**.*

Read each list word. Circle the letters that makes the long -o sound.

 **Read.**  **Copy.**  **Organize.**

1. so ____________

2. home ____________

3. go ____________

4. bone ____________
5. note ____________

6. rope ____________

list words with long -o sound spelled **o_e**

____

____

____

____

Write the list word that ends with the same sound as each picture.

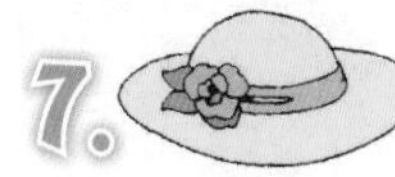 ____________ 

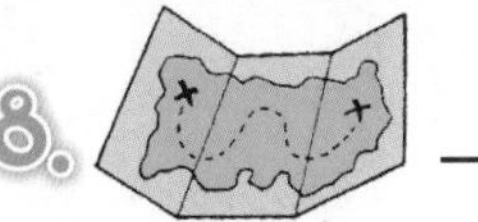 ____________

  ____________

  ____________

  ____________ and ____________

 Date: ____________

Look at the word on each fruit. Change the first letter to make a rhyming word. Write the word on the fruit.

1. suit fr______ crude r______ Luke d______

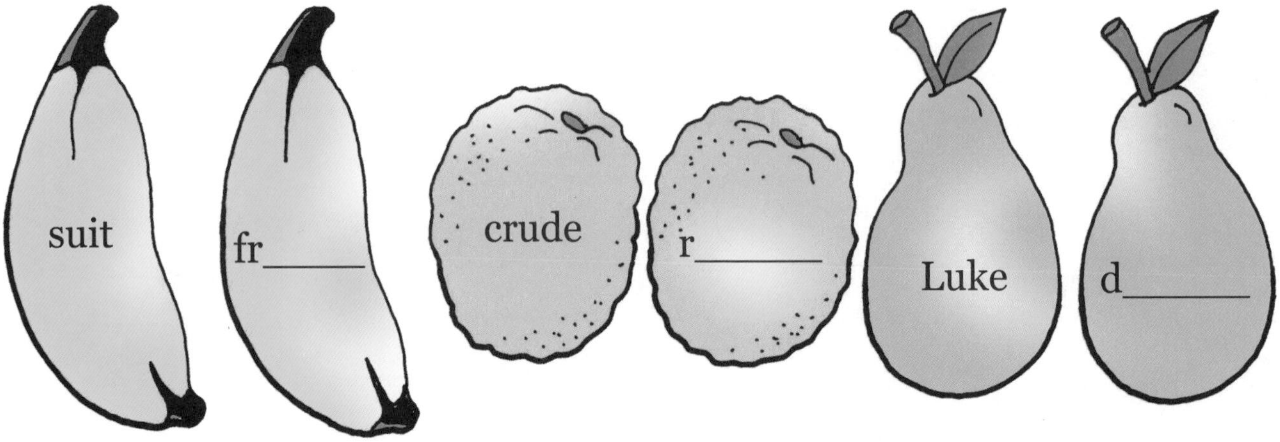

2. tube c______ cute fl______ blue cl______

3. mule r______ tune J______ glue tr______

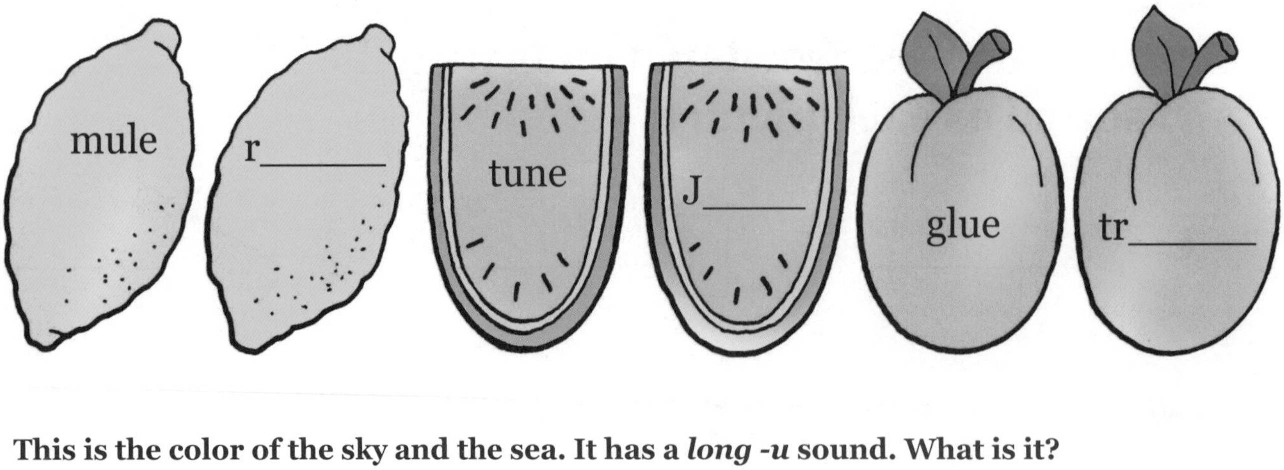

This is the color of the sky and the sea. It has a *long -u* sound. What is it?

Date: ____________

The **consonant-vowel-consonant-silent e rule**: *When a word ends in a silent* **e**, *the vowel that comes before the* **e** *will be long and will say its name.*

Mr Mule has all the answers! He wants you to choose one of his words to complete each sentence. Write the word on the blank.

chute huge rude
dune flute June
cute

1. It is _________ to talk back to you mother.
2. She plays the _________ in the band.
3. Throw your dirty socks down the clothes _________.
4. It is fun to roll down a big sand _________.
5. The giant had _________ feet!
6. My birthday is in _________.
7. This baby is so _________!

Date: ____________

There are 26 letters in the alphabet.
The vowels are **A**, **E**, **I**, **O** and **U**.
All the rest are consonants.

Color each consonant yellow.

A **consonant blend** *is when two consonants are side by side in a word, and you hear both sounds together. For example, in the word* **tree** *you hear both* **t** *and* **r** *blend together.*

Draw a circle around the two consonants that are side by side.

tree

snow

fly

drum

Date: ____________

Bl *makes the sound you hear at the beginning of the words* **Blake** *and* **bluebird**.

Draw a line to match each bl word with a picture. Then draw a circle around the letters bl in each word.

blanket •

blimp •

blindfold •

blocks •

blizzard •

blouse •

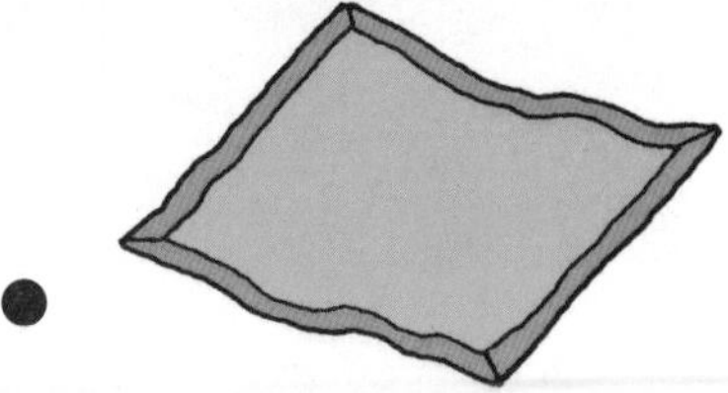

You have this inside you. It is red. Your heart pumps it through your body. It begins with *bl*. What is it?

Date: ____________

Br *makes the sound you hear at the beginning of the words* **Brady** *and* **brontosaurus**.

Brady the brontosaurus has made a puzzle for you. Use the picture clues and the Word Box to help you. Write the answers in the puzzle next to the correct number.

Word Box

brain	bride	broom	bridge
bread	brush	bricks	bracelet

Across

2.

4.

6.

8.

Down

1.

3.

5.

7.

1.

2.

3.

4.

5.

6.

7.

8.

This makes a blue or purple spot on your skin when you get hurt. It is sore when you push on it. It begins with *br*. What is it?

Date: ____________

Cl *makes the sound you hear at the beginning of the words* **Clara** *and* **clown**.

See Clara juggle the balls. Color the balls orange that have pictures beginning with cl. Color all the other balls blue.

Now write "Clara" on her costume.

This is part of your room. You keep your clothes and shoes in it. It begins with *cl*. What is it?

Date: ____________

Cr *makes the sound you hear at the beginning of the words* **crazy** *and* **Crystal**.

Find out about the crazy things Crystal does in the sentences below. Fill in the blanks with cr to complete the words. Then write the number of the sentence in the box by the picture that matches it.

1. ____ystal wears a ____ash helmet to bed.
2. She makes ____ ispy, ____unchy ice ____eam.
3. She buys ____owns with her ____edit card.
4. She keeps her pet ____ab in a ____ib.
5. She feeds ____ackers to ____ocodiles.
6. Her glasses are ____ooked.

Date: ____________

Dr *makes the sound you hear at the beginning of the words* **dragon** *and* **dream**.

This drowsy dragon wants to dream only about things that begin with dr. Color the pictures that it should dream about. Put an X on the pictures that do not begin with dr.

Fill in the bubble next to the correct answer.

1. Which of the letters is a consonant?

○ E ○ C

○ U ○ O

2. Which of the letters is a vowel?

○ A ○ C

○ B ○ D

3. Which of the letters is a consonant?

○ A ○ Y

○ I ○ E

4. Which of the letters is a vowel?

○ X ○ W

○ U ○ R

Color the bubble next to the correct answer.

Example

Which picture begins with **b**?

A

C

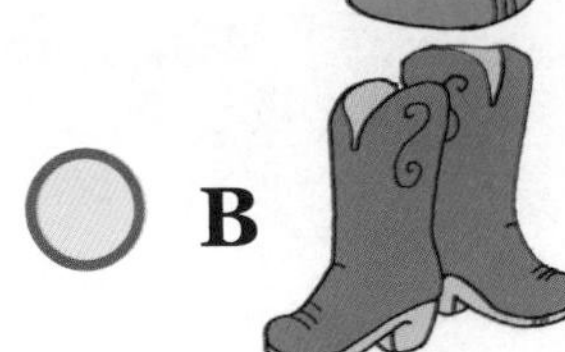

B

D

5. Which picture begins with **d**?

A

C

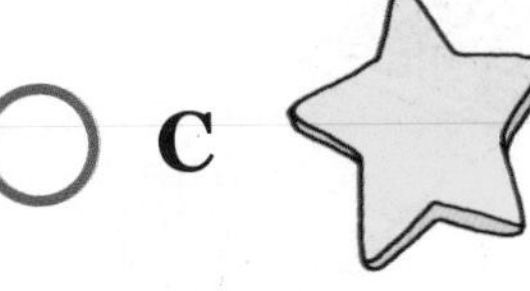

B

D

6. Which picture ends with the **m** sound?

A

C

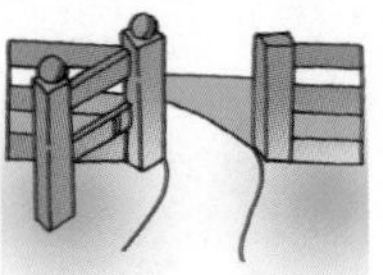

B

D

Fill in the bubble next to the correct answer.

7. Which picture has the **short -e** sound?

○ A 

○ B 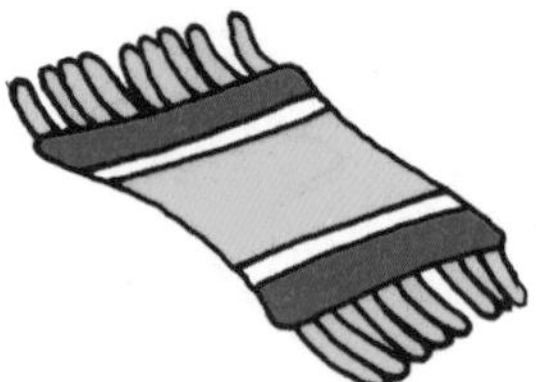

○ C 

○ D 

8. Which picture rhymes with hop?

○ A 

○ B 

○ C 

○ D 

Fill in the bubble next to the correct answer.

9. Which picture begins with the **br** consonant blend?

○ A

○ B

○ C

○ D

10. Which picture begins with the **dr** consonant blend?

○ A

○ B

○ C

○ D

In this section, your child is introduced to important reading skills. These skills will show your child how to make meaning out of what he or she reads.

What to do

Have your child complete the activities on each page. Review his or her answers. Let your child know that he or she is doing an excellent job.

Keep on going!

Ask your child questions about his or her day at school. *What did you do first? Next? Last? How did you make that art project?* Have your child look at objects and tell how they are alike and different. Or read a book with your child. Have your child look at the cover of the book and predict what the story will be about. Have your child identify where the story takes place. Have him or her describe the characters in the story. When you have finished reading, ask your child to retell the story in his or her own words.

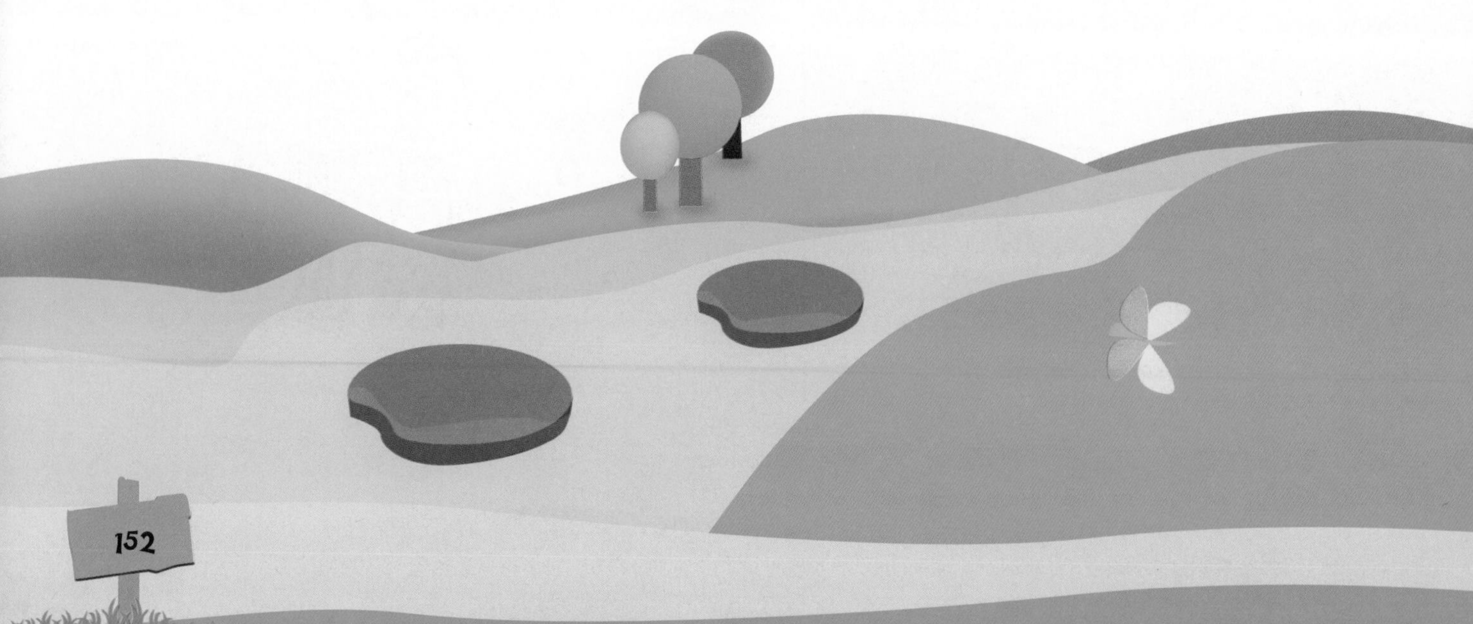

Date: ____________

The sequence is the order in which things happen.

Example

What happens first?
Write 1.

1

What happens next?
Write 2.

2

What happens last?
Write 3.

3

1.

2.

Date: ____________

Devin makes a birthday card for his grandmother.

1. **Look** at the pictures below.
2. What happens first? **Write** 1.
3. What happens next? **Write** 2.
4. What happens last? **Write** 3.
5. **Match** each number to the correct word.

First	Next	Last

Tim builds a house.

1. **Look** at the pictures below.
2. What happens first? **Write** 1.
3. What happens next? **Write** 2.
4. What happens last? **Write** 3.
5. **Match** each number to the correct word.
6. **Color** the pictures.

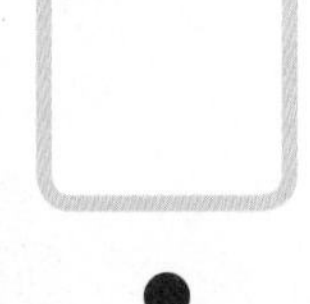

First	Next	Last

Date: ____________

1. **Look** at the big picture.
   Which small picture comes ***next***?

2. **Place** a ✔ for that picture.

☐ ☐

Date: ____________

1. **Look** at the big picture.
   Which small picture comes ***before***?

2. **Place** a ✔ for that picture.

Date: ______________

1. **Look** at the big picture.
   Which small picture comes ***before***?

2. **Place** a ✔ for that picture.

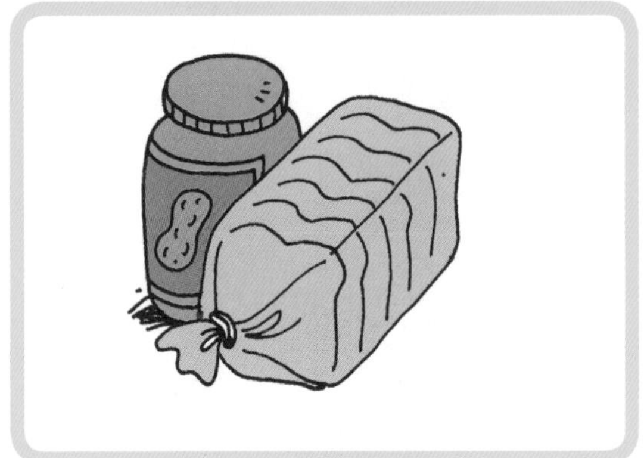

☐ ☐

Date: ____________

Read each sentence. Think and draw.

1. Draw a * to the **left** of the tree.

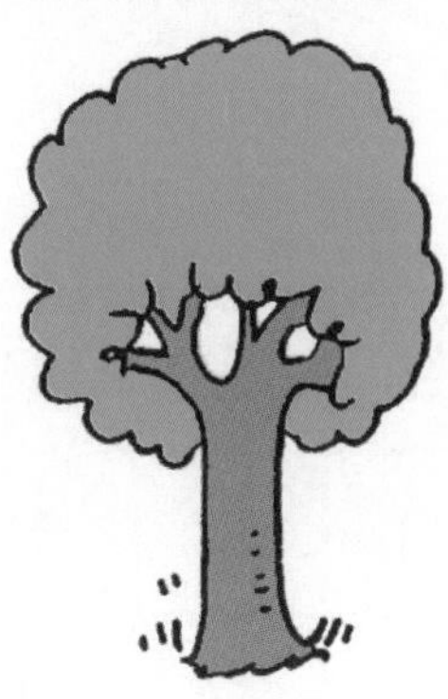

2. Draw a * to the **right** of the apple.

3. Draw a * to the **right** of the pencil.

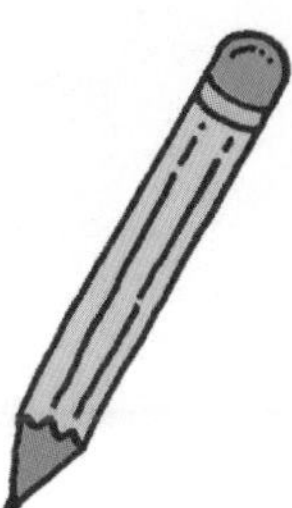

4. Draw a * to the **left** of the box.

5. Draw a * to the **left** of the circle.

6. Draw a * to the **right** of the ladder.

Date: ____________

1. **Read** the words below.
2. **Find** each word in the puzzle. You will have to look up, down and across.
3. **Circle** the word.

q	u	e	e	n	f	t	h	s	m
c	u	y	y	c	z	u	n	u	j
u	b	e	k	a	u	r	m	n	n
d	u	c	k	t	i	g	e	r	e
n	k	p	l	p	i	v	f	n	s
q	z	b	a	l	l	h	f	w	t

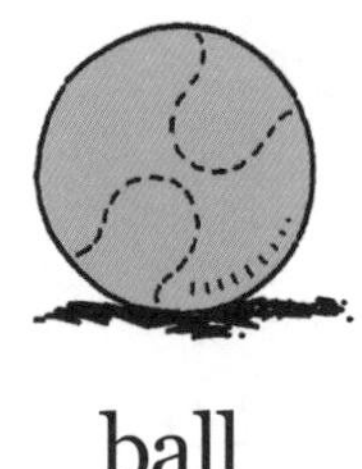

ball

tiger

sun

nest

queen

duck

Date: ____________

Read each sentence. Write the word on the line.

1. Write a word that begins with **p**. ____________
2. Write a word that begins with **m**. ____________
3. Write a word that begins with **b**. ____________
4. Write a word that begins with **s**. ____________
5. Write a word that ends with **g**. ____________
6. Write a word that ends with **t**. ____________
7. Write a word that ends with **y**. ____________
8. Write a word that ends with **e**. ____________

Date: ____________

Read each sentence. Think and draw.

1. Draw a △ **above** the car.

2. Draw a △ **below** the bat.

3. Draw a △ **under** the snail.

4. Draw a △ **on** the dinosaur.

5. Draw a △ **behind** the group.

6. Draw a △ **ahead** of the cowboy.

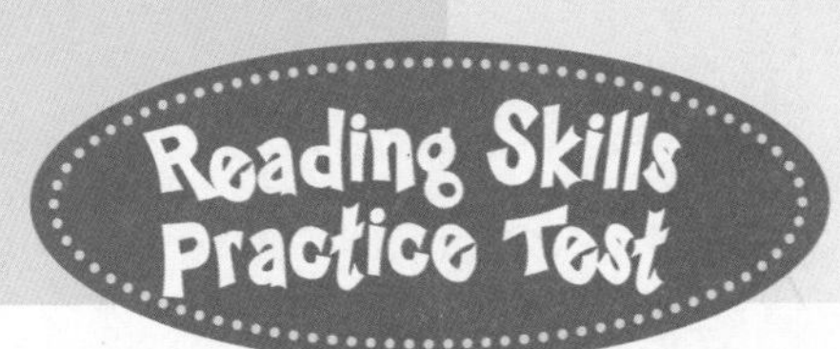

Color the bubble next to the correct answer.

1. Which picture shows a * to the **left** of the tree?

○ A 

○ B 

○ C 

○ D 

2. Which would you do **first** to make a cake?

○ A Add an egg to the cake mix.

○ B Put the cake mix into a bowl.

○ C Eat the cake.

○ D Add milk to the cake mix.

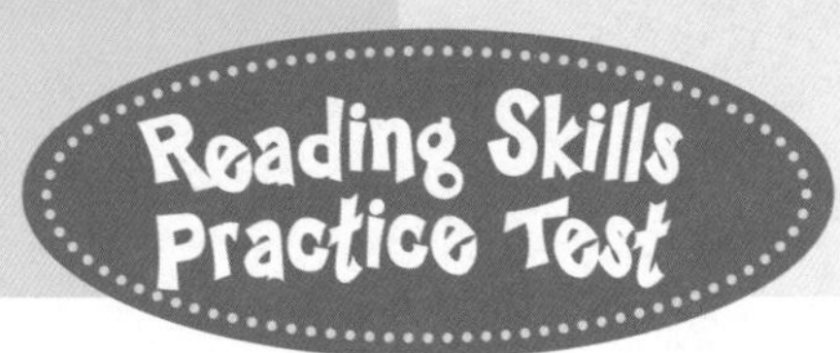

Color the bubble next to the correct answer.

3. Which comes **last** when you cook scrambled eggs?

◯ **A** Crack the eggs into a bowl.

◯ **B** Scramble the eggs.

◯ **C** Put eggs on a plate and eat them.

◯ **D** Turn on the stove.

4. Which picture shows a * to the **right** of the pencil?

◯ **A** 

◯ **B** 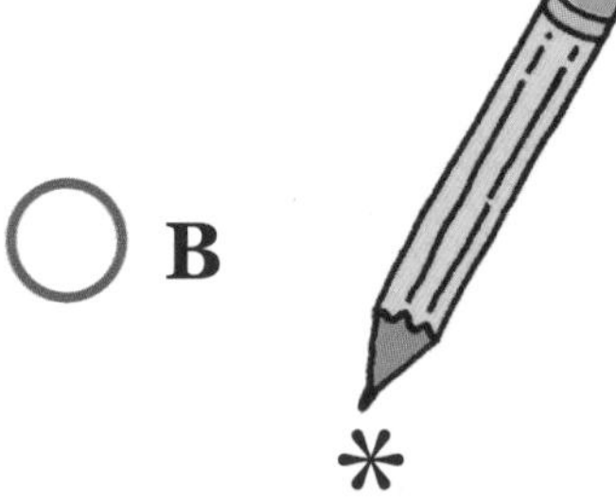

◯ **C** 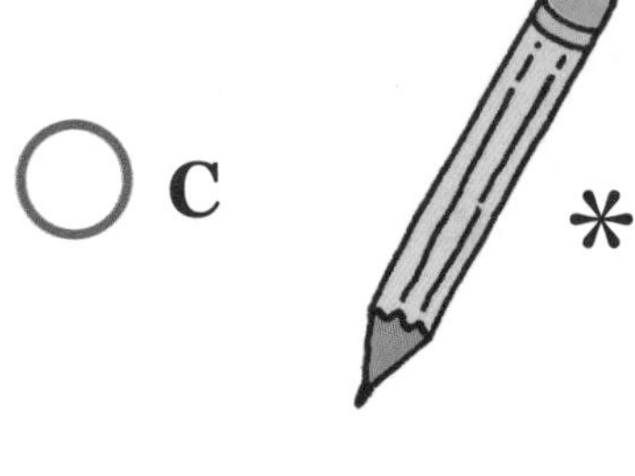

◯ **D** 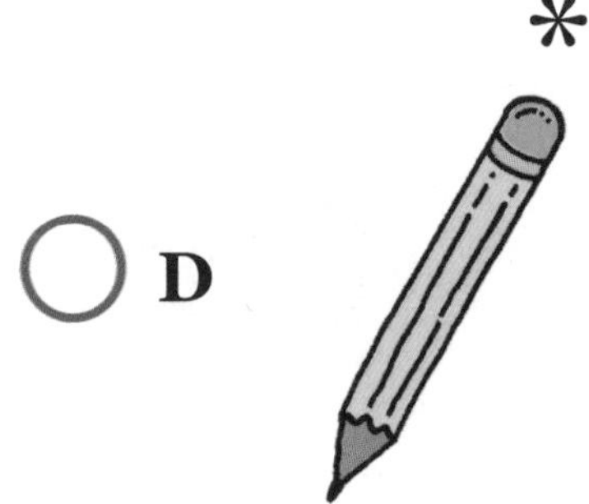

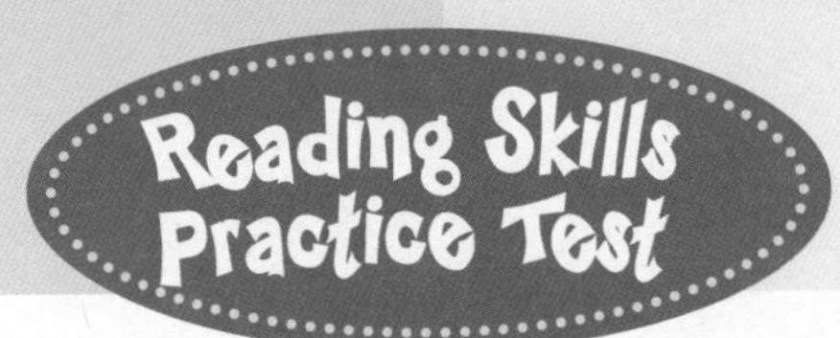

Color the bubble next to the correct answer.

5. Which picture shows a * to **left** of the dog?

- ○ A 
- ○ B
- ○ C 
- ○ D

6. Which event caused a fire?

- ○ A A candle fell onto a rug.
- ○ B Water was thrown on the fire.
- ○ C Firefighters arrived at the scene.
- ○ D Smokey the bear ran away.

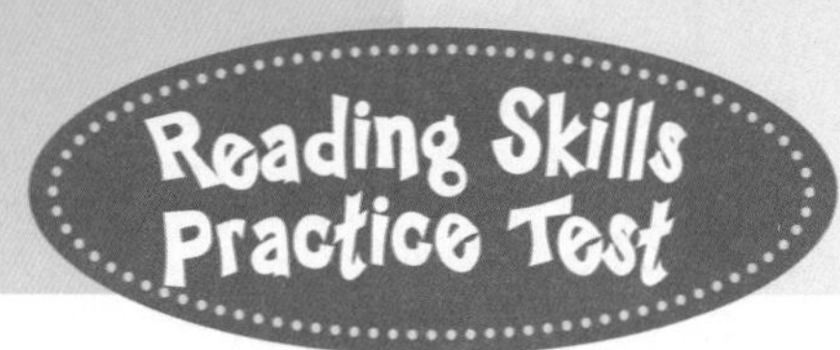

Color the bubble next to the correct answer.

7. Which event caused Carl to miss the bus?

- ○ **A** Carl was waiting for the bus.
- ○ **B** Carl did not have school that day.
- ○ **C** Carl met his friend.
- ○ **D** Carl got out of bed late.

8. Which would you do **first** to grow a new plant?

- ○ **A** Water the soil.
- ○ **B** Put soil in a pot.
- ○ **C** Wait for the seed to grow.
- ○ **D** Put a seed in the soil.

Numbers 1 to 20

In this book, your child reviews numbers 1 to 10 and is introduced to numbers 11 to 20. The number concepts will get your child ready for addition and subtraction.

What to do
Read the directions on each page with your child. Then have your child complete the activities. Review them together. Praise your child for a job well done!

Keep on going!
Go on a nature walk with your child. Have him or her collect items, such as rocks, leaves, flowers, shells, pine cones and other objects you see along the way. At home, have your child group the same objects together and count them. Ask which group has the most and which has the least.

Count the ● or ▲ in each shape in the picture. Use the matching color to fill in each shape.

6 = yellow　　7 = green　　8 = brown
9 = red　　10 = blue

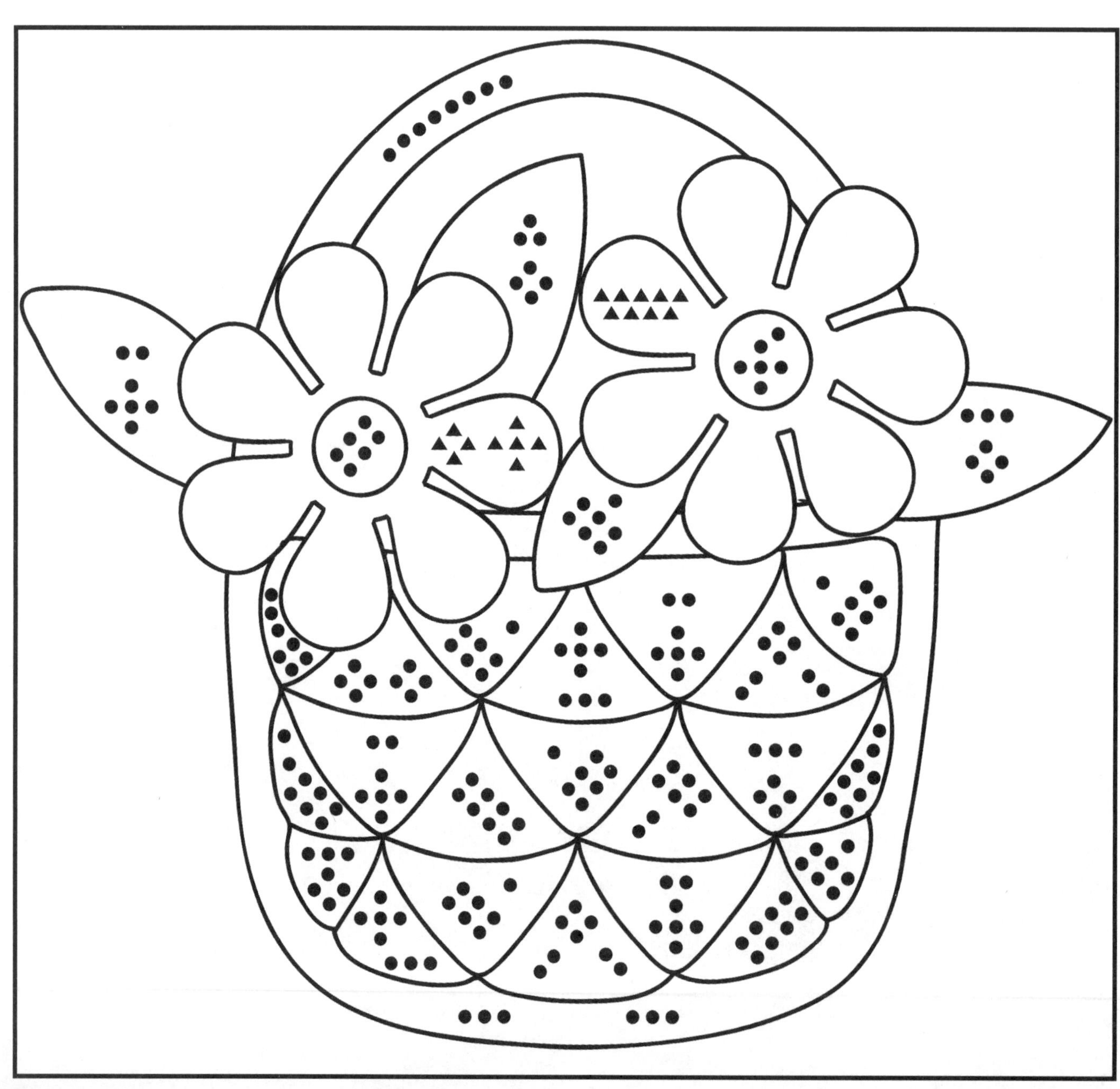

Count the dots in the boxes. Then color the matching number word in the picture.

•	= green	• •	= yellow	⁙	= blue
• • •	= red	∷	= purple		

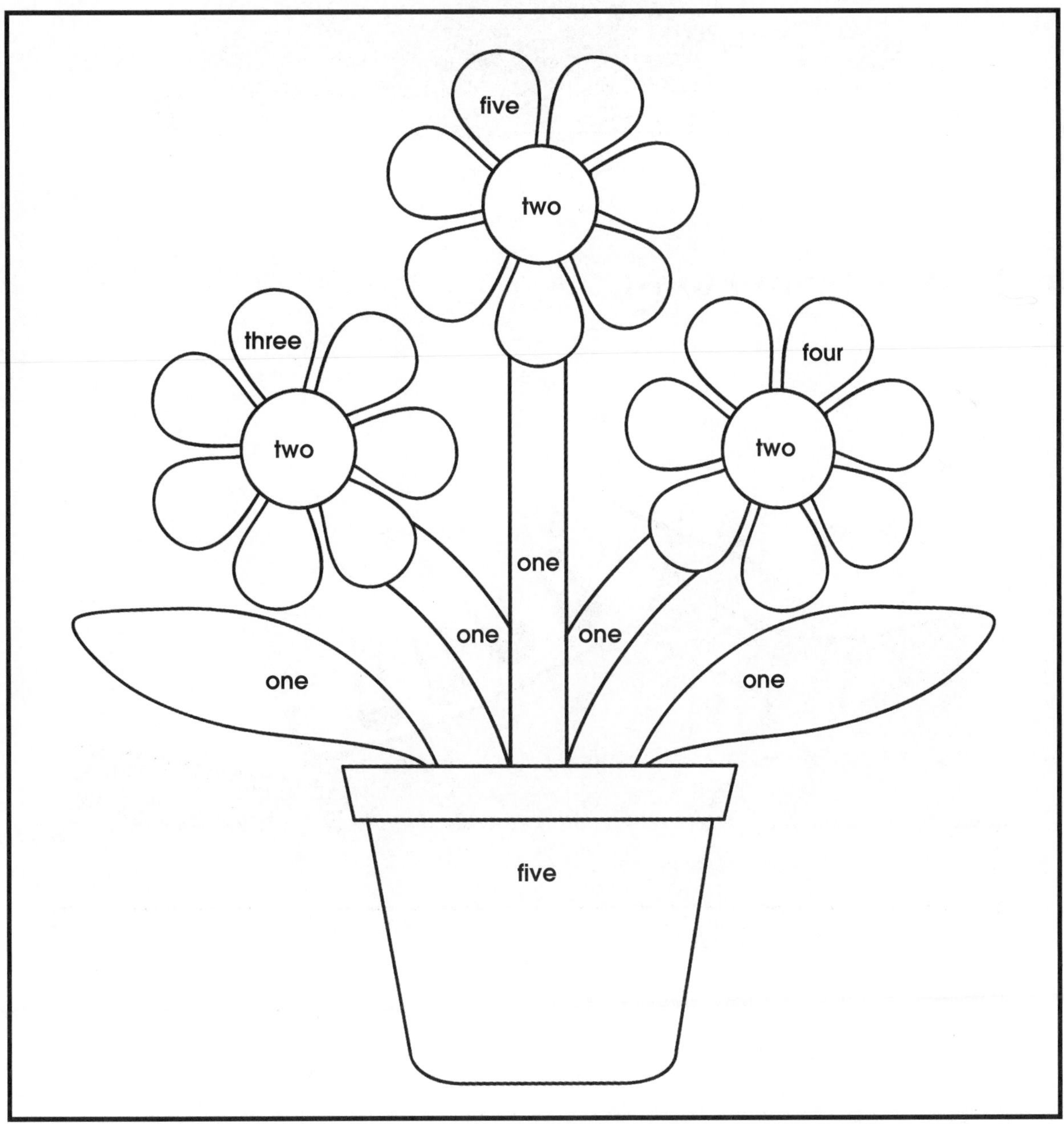

Date: ______________

Write the missing numbers.

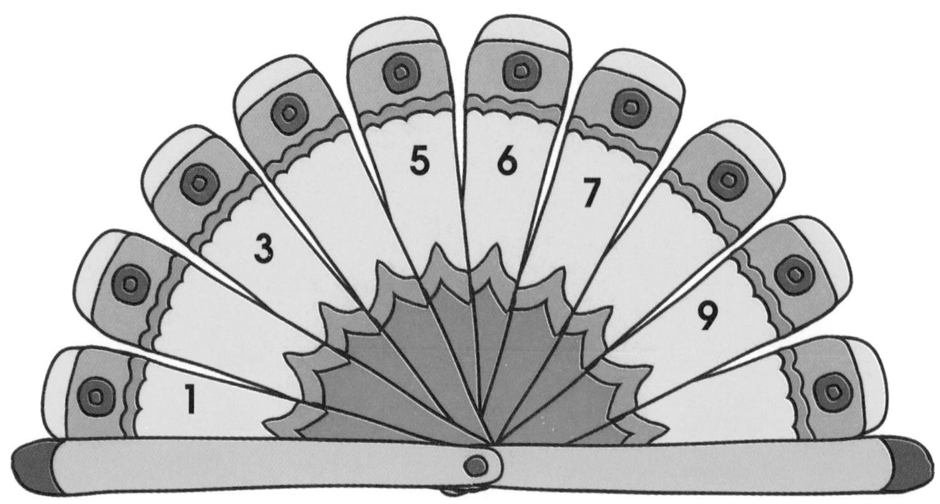

Join the dots from 1 to 10.

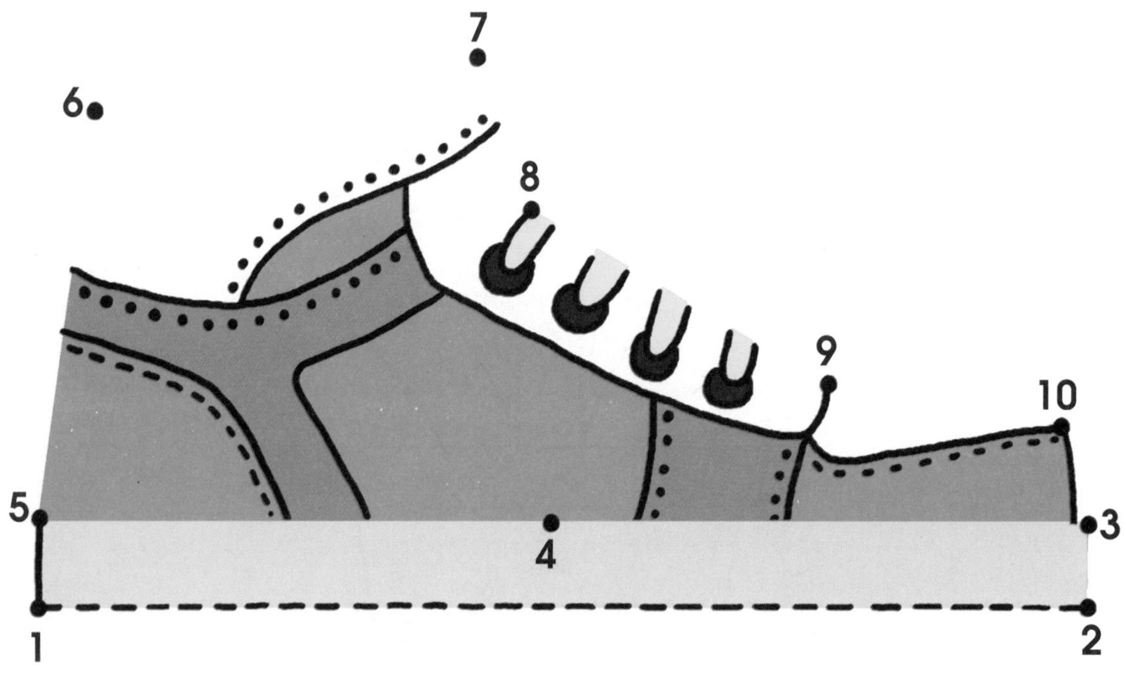

Date: ____________

Fill in the missing number words.

1.

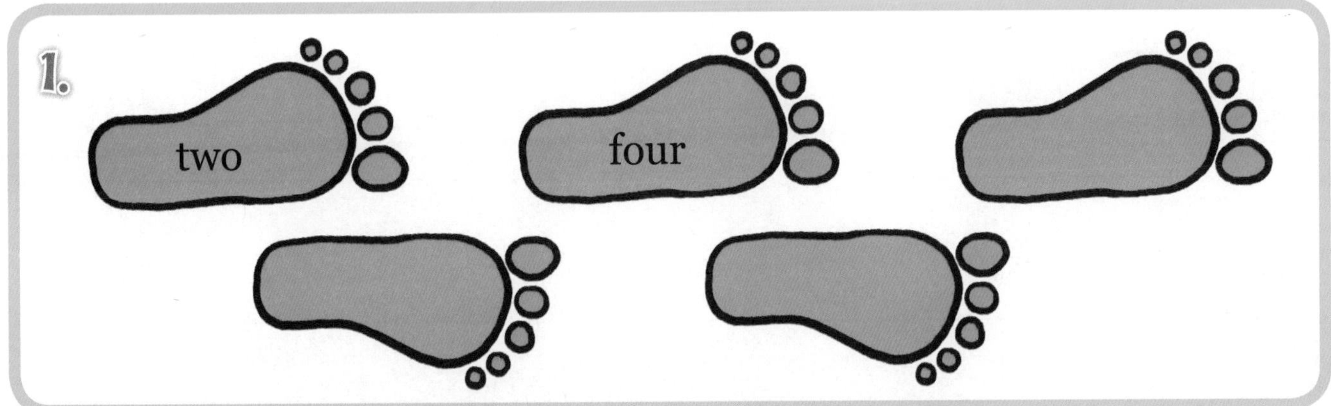

2.

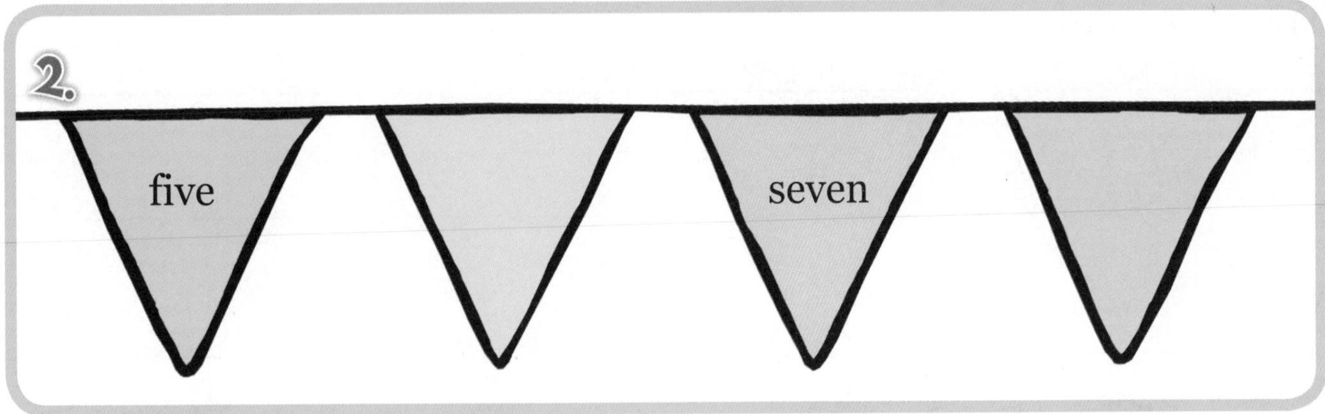

3.

Date: ______

Number Practice

Trace the number.

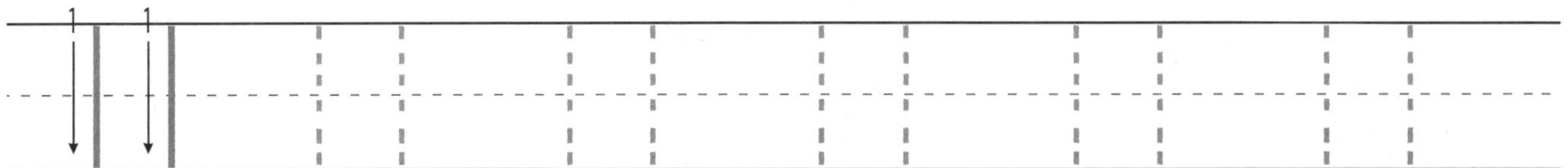

Write the number.

Trace the word.

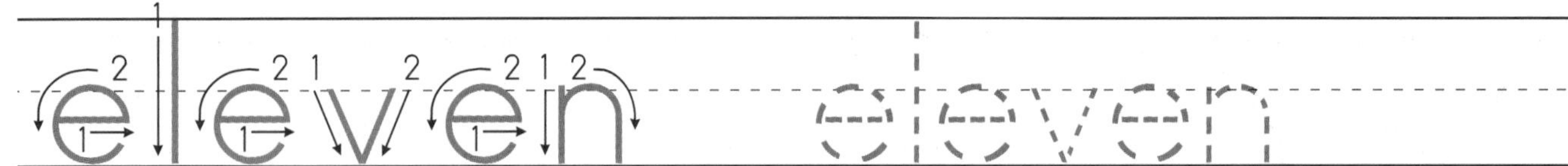

Write the word.

Number Hunt

Circle every number 11.

9	5	2	4	6	4	10	3	1	11
11	3	15	3	9	8	11	2	11	5
3	20	5	4	3	20	6	5	8	11
1	3	7	11	8	10	14	9	3	11

Date: ______________

11

eleven

1. **Draw** 11  in the candy jar.

Date: __________

11

eleven

1. **Draw** 11 ▢ on the building.

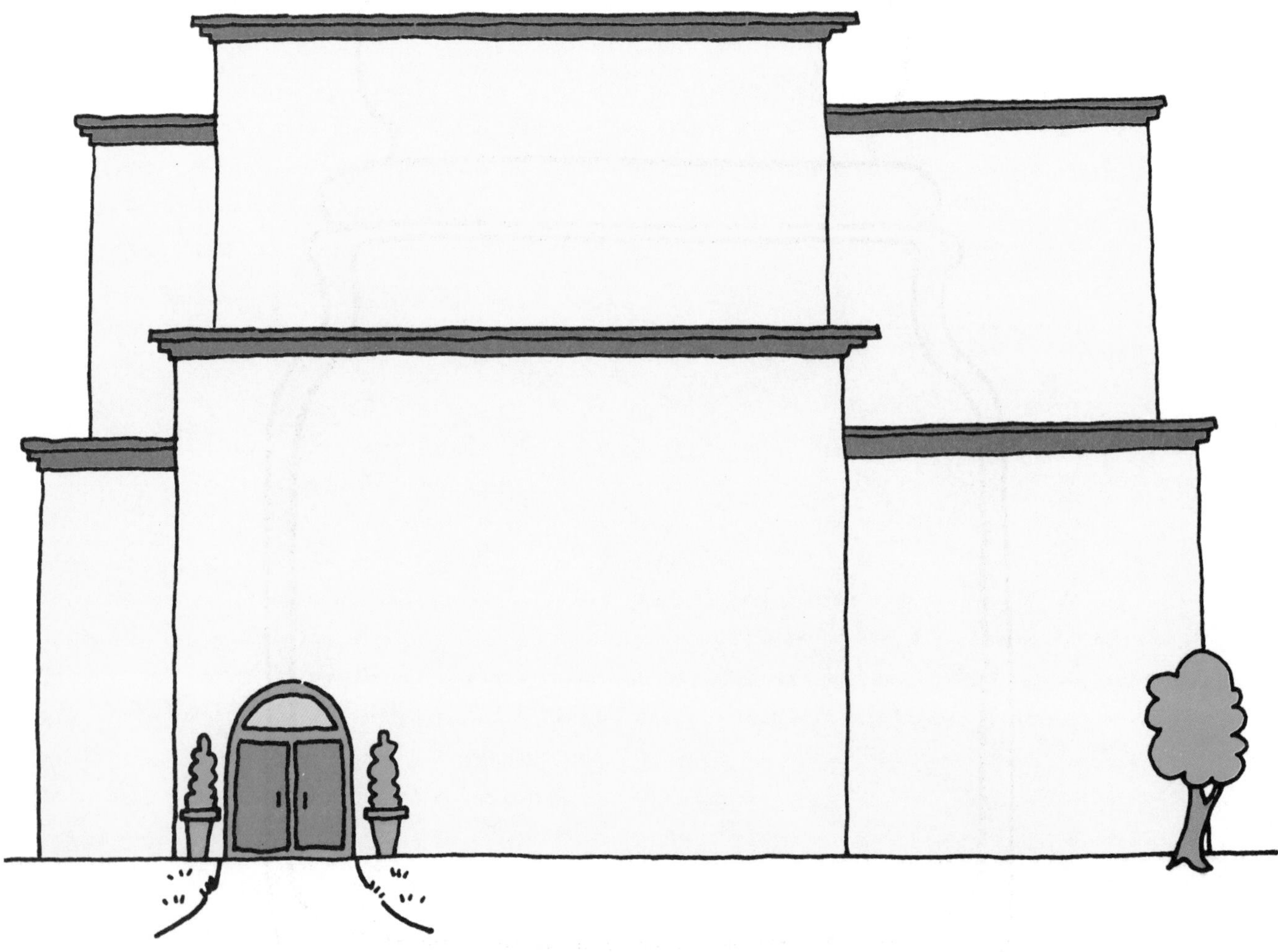

Date: ____________

Number Practice

Trace the number.

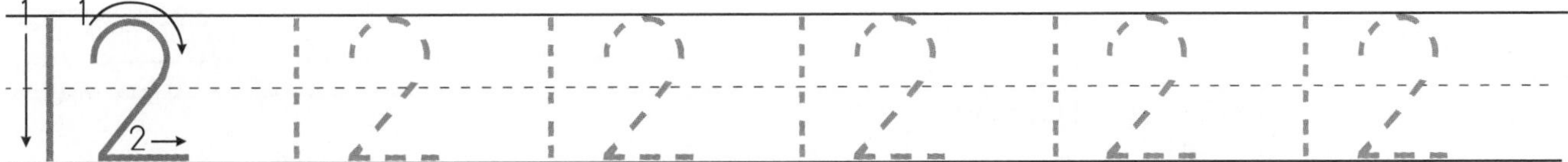

Write the number.

Trace the word.

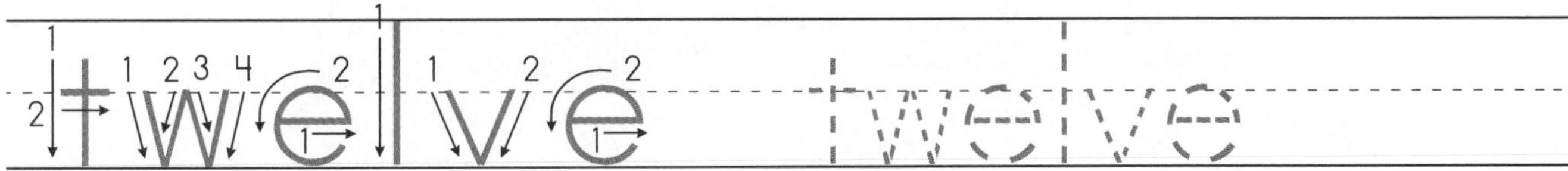

Write the word.

Number Hunt

Circle every number 12.

8	13	10	3	12	9	16	12	4	17
12	15	3	9	8	1	2	18	5	7
14	3	12	5	4	3	20	7	5	8
3	6	19	12	8	10	14	9	3	12

Date: ____________

12

twelve

1. **Draw** 12  on the tree.

Date: ______________

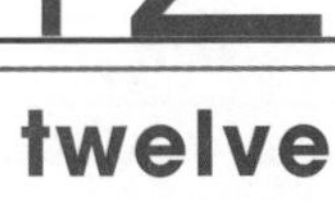

12

twelve

1. **Draw** 12 in the garden.

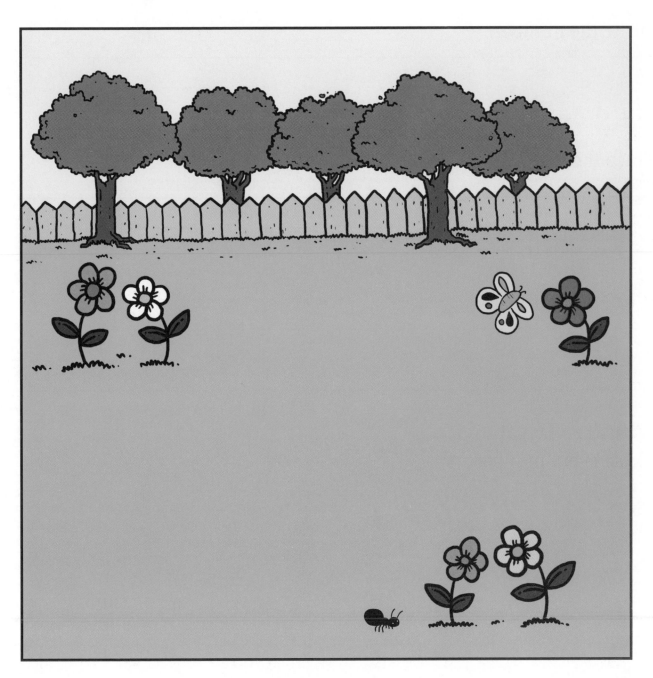

Number Practice

Trace the number.

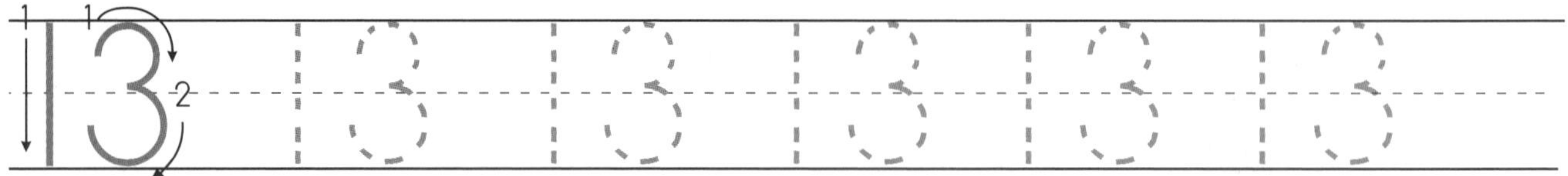

Write the number.

Trace the word.

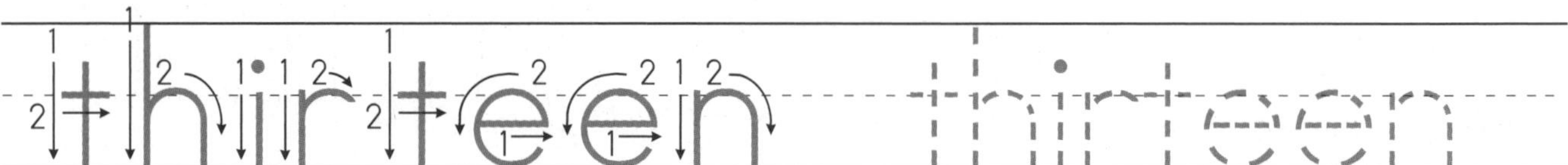

Write the word.

Number Hunt

Circle every number 13.

9	14	2	13	16	4	5	13	1	8
20	5	7	3	9	8	1	2	12	3
16	13	20	13	5	20	3	10	5	4
13	19	8	10	14	9	3	9	9	13

1. **Draw** 13  on the plate.

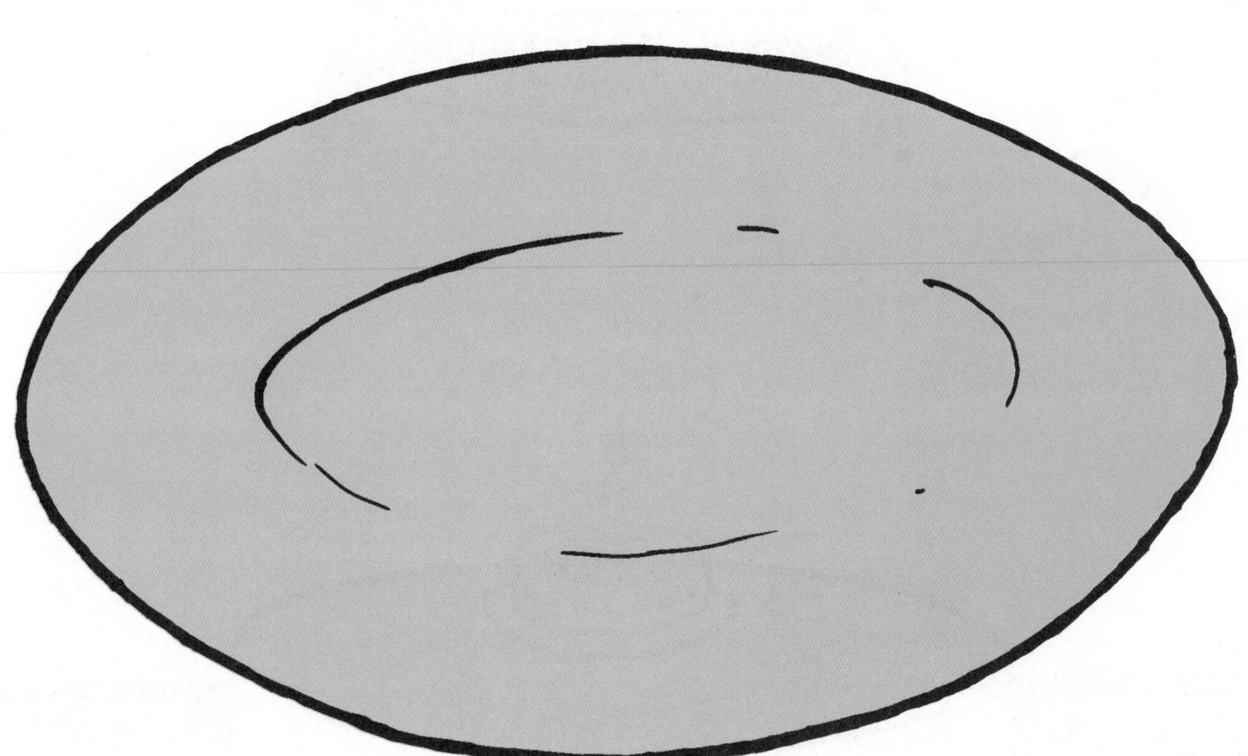

Date: ____________

13

thirteen

1. **Draw** 13 on the wall.

HAPPY BIRTHDAY

 Date: ____________

Number Practice

Trace the number.

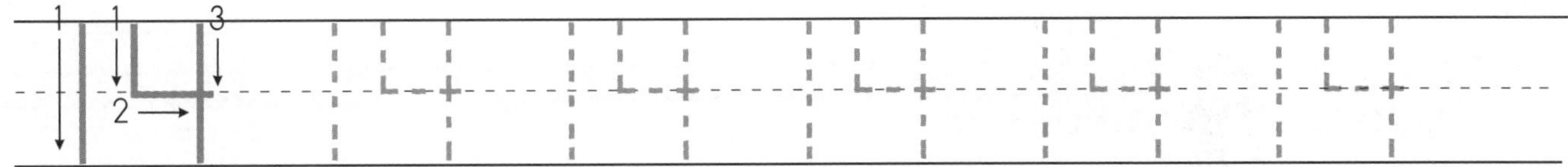

Write the number.

Trace the word.

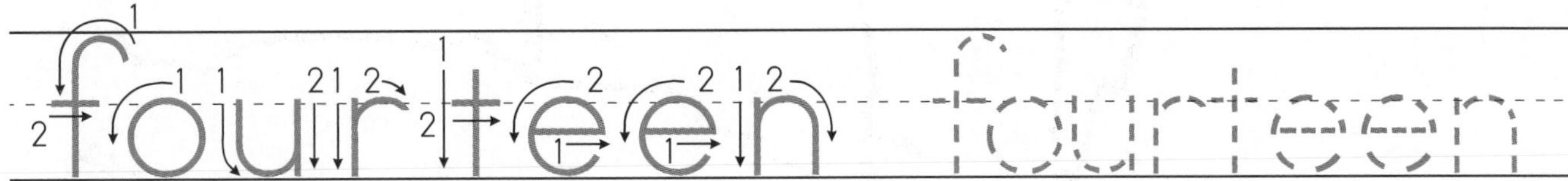

Write the word.

Number Hunt

Circle every number 14.

6	14	1	8	13	9	25	2	4	6
14	5	7	14	3	5	3	9	8	14
8	14	4	3	18	5	14	3	20	7
3	12	19	14	3	7	14	8	10	14

Date: ________________

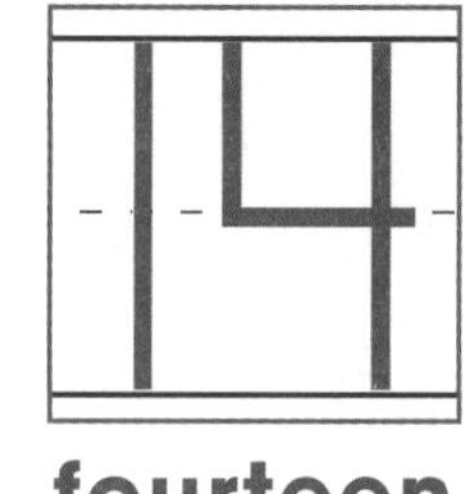

1. **Circle** 14  on the ice.

Date: ______________

14

fourteen

1. **Draw** 14 in the aquarium.

Date: ______

Number Practice

Trace the number.

Write the number.

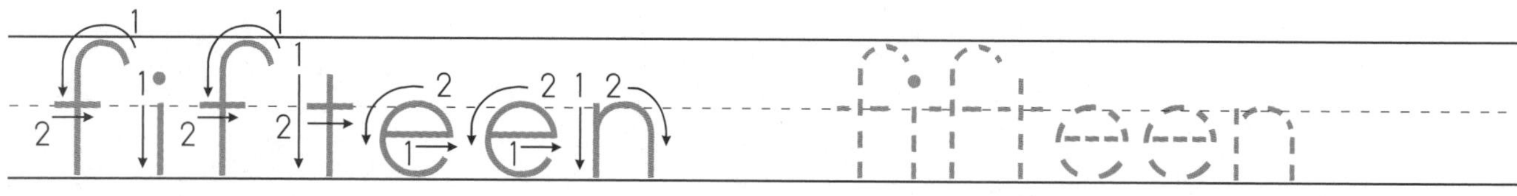

Write the word.

Number Hunt

Circle every number 15.

8	13	9	15	15	4	16	4	9	3
5	15	9	8	1	2	20	5	7	15
5	4	3	20	15	5	8	16	12	3
15	3	7	19	8	10	15	9	3	15

Date: ______________

1. **Circle** 15  in the barnyard.

Date: ______________

15
fifteen

1. **Draw** 15 (egg) in the nest .

Date: ____________

Number Practice

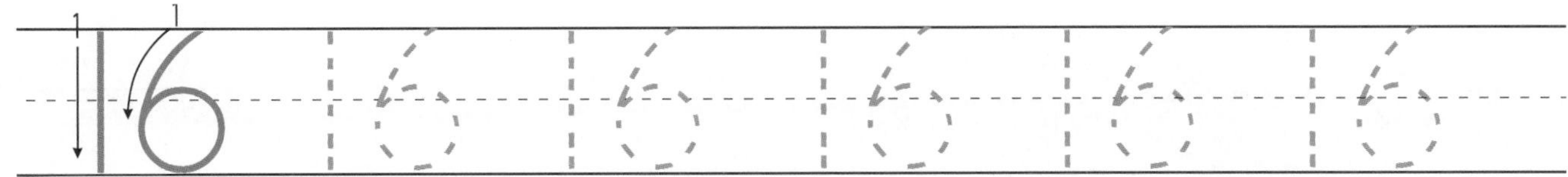

Write the number.

Trace the word.

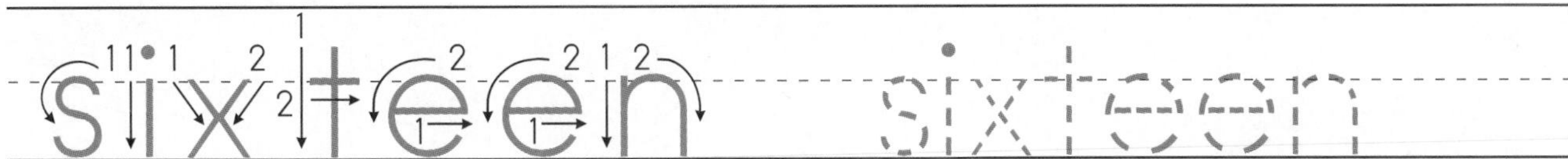

Write the word.

Number Hunt

Circle every number 16.

10	16	9	8	13	9	15	2	16	16
14	5	16	12	3	5	3	9	5	16
16	18	5	8	16	2	3	10	16	1
3	7	9	16	3	7	19	8	20	3

Date: ____________

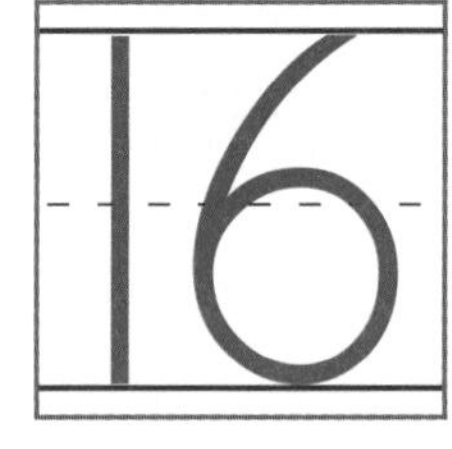
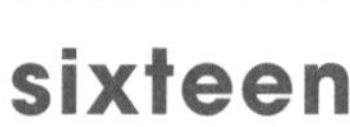

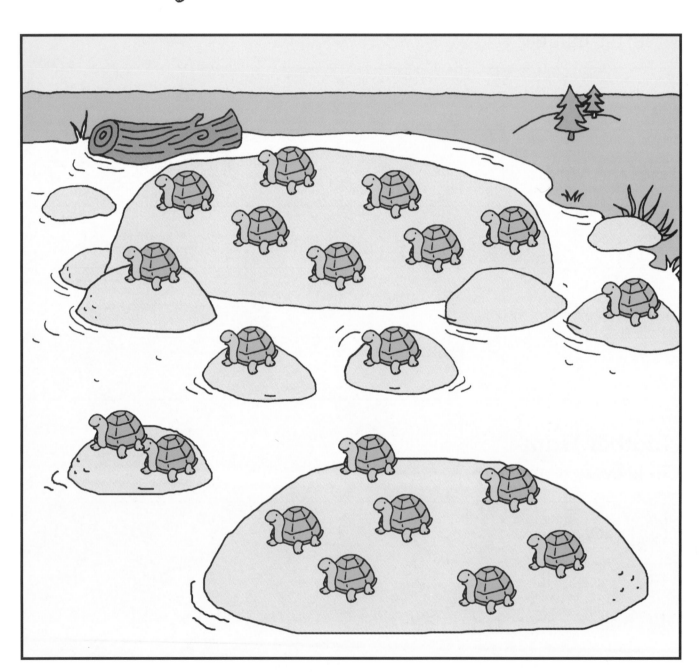

1. **Circle** 16 [turtle] on the rocks.

Date: ____________

16

sixteen

1. **Draw** 16 ▢ on the turtle's shell.

Date: ____________

Number Practice

Trace the number.

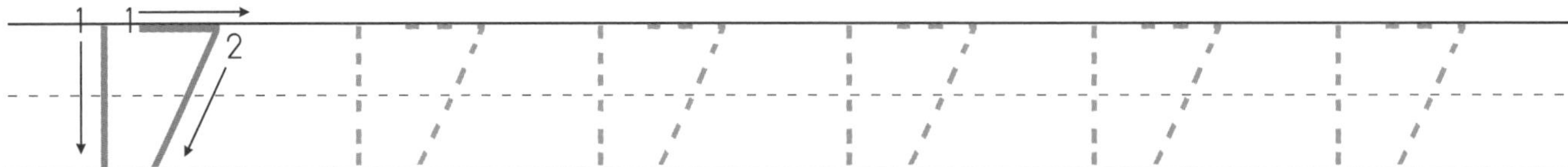

Write the number.

Write the word.

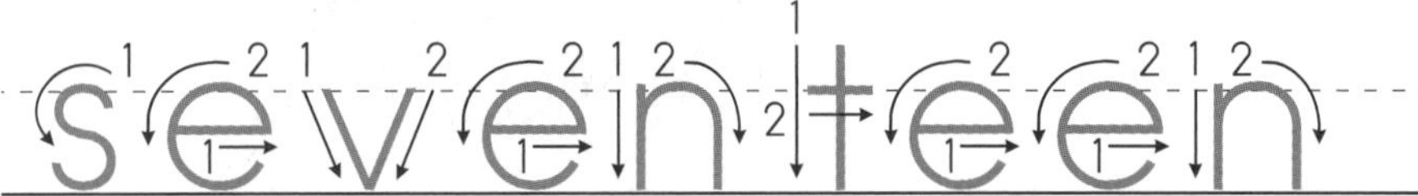

Number Hunt

Circle every number 17.

17	3	1	8	13	9	15	2	17	16
1	17	7	12	3	12	3	9	8	1
8	16	4	3	10	17	4	3	20	6
3	17	9	14	3	7	17	8	10	14

Date: ______________

17

seventeen

1. **Colour** 17  in the water.

Date: ____________

17

seventeen

1. **Draw** 17 on the beach.

Date: ____________

Number Practice

Trace the number.

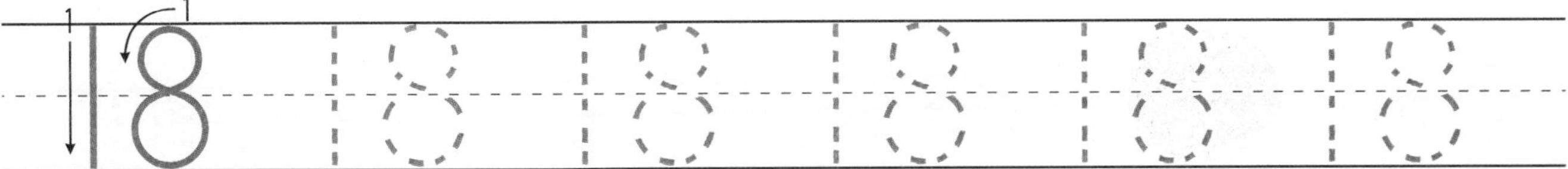

Write the number.

Trace the word.

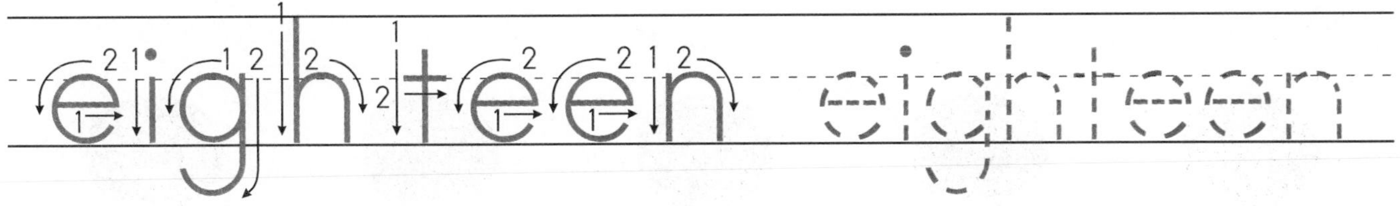

Write the word.

Number Hunt

Circle every number 18.

2	16	14	18	10	5	4	3	20	18
7	3	1	8	13	9	15	2	4	16
18	10	19	18	3	7	19	8	18	14
21	18	7	12	3	5	3	9	8	18

1. **Circle** 18 .

Date: ____________

18

eighteen

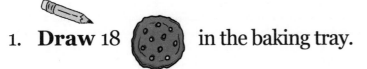

1. **Draw** 18 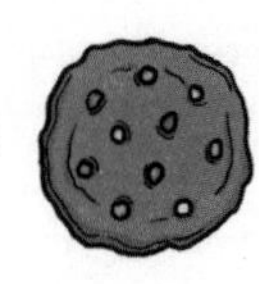 in the baking tray.

Date: ______

Number Practice

Trace the number.

Write the number.

Trace the word.

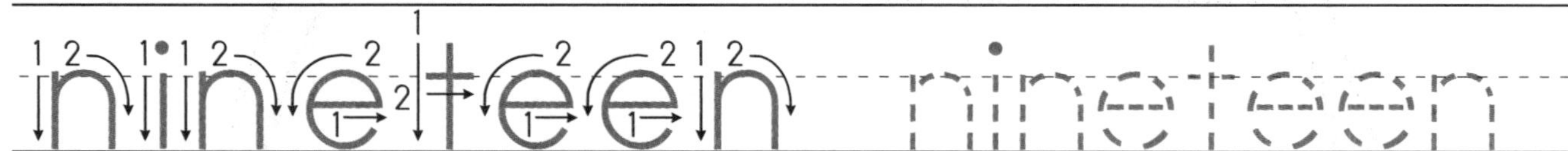

Write the word.

Number Hunt

Circle every number 19.

19	5	7	12	3	17	3	19	8	1
9	15	2	4	16	4	19	3	1	8
8	19	1	3	10	5	4	3	20	6
7	19	20	13	1	19	7	19	8	10

Date: ____________

nineteen

1. **Colour** 19  .

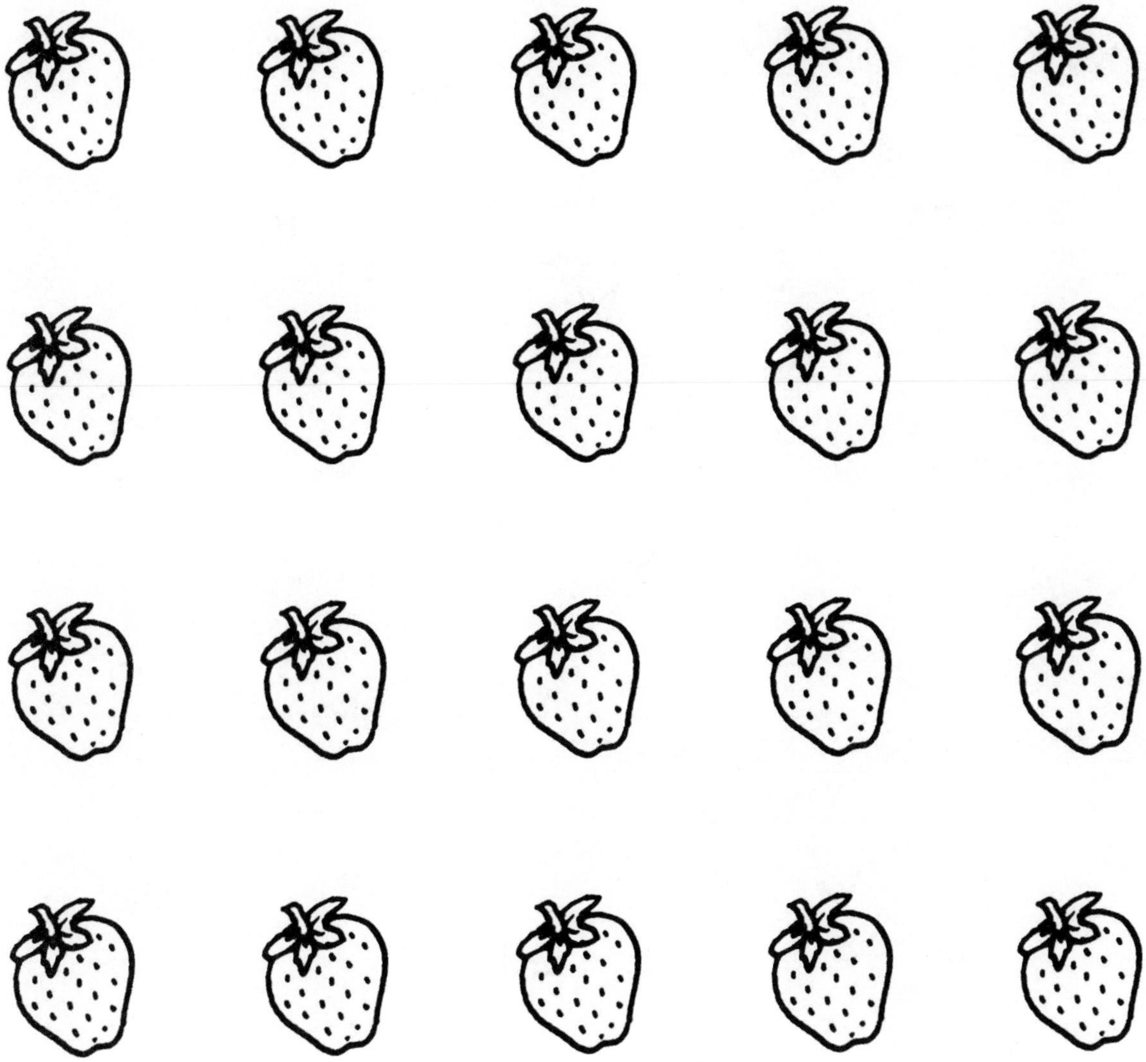

Date: ______________

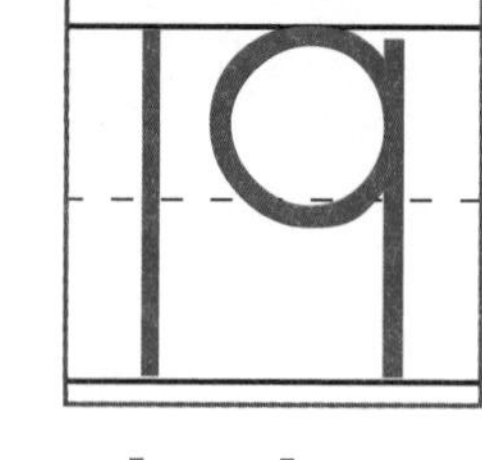

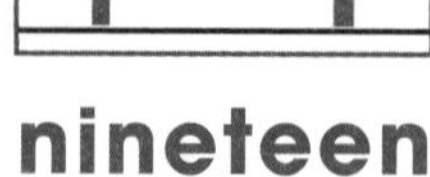

1. **Draw** 19 in the grass.

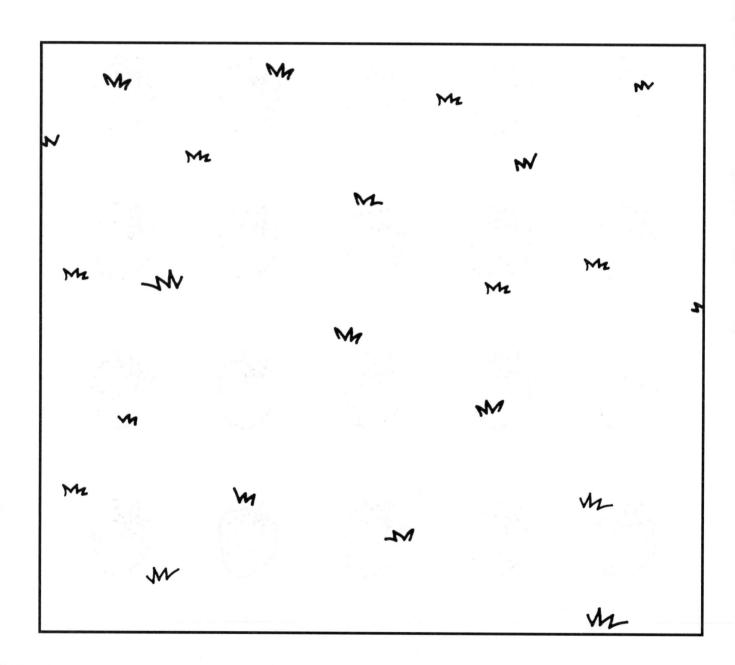

Date: ____________

Number Practice

Trace the number.

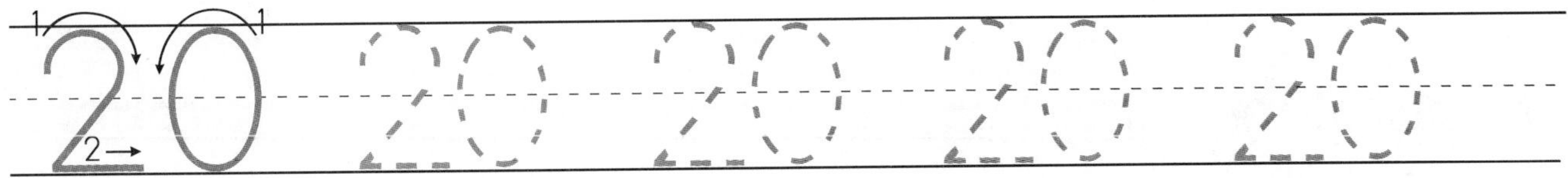

Write the number.

Trace the word.

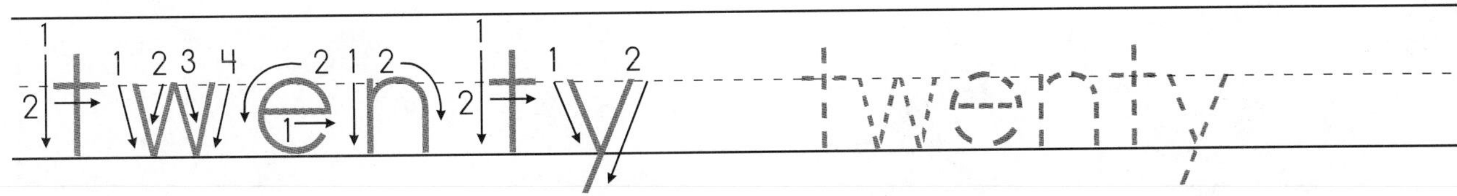

Write the word.

Number Hunt

Circle every number 20.

20	10	9	1	3	7	19	20	10	14
2	5	7	12	20	5	3	9	8	1
8	20	4	3	10	5	4	20	20	7
10	3	1	20	13	9	20	2	4	6

Date: ______________

1. **Circle** 20 dragonflies above the pond.

Date: ______________

20

twenty

1. **Draw** 20 [fish] swimming in the ocean.

Date: ____________

Count the flowers in each vase.
Circle the correct number.

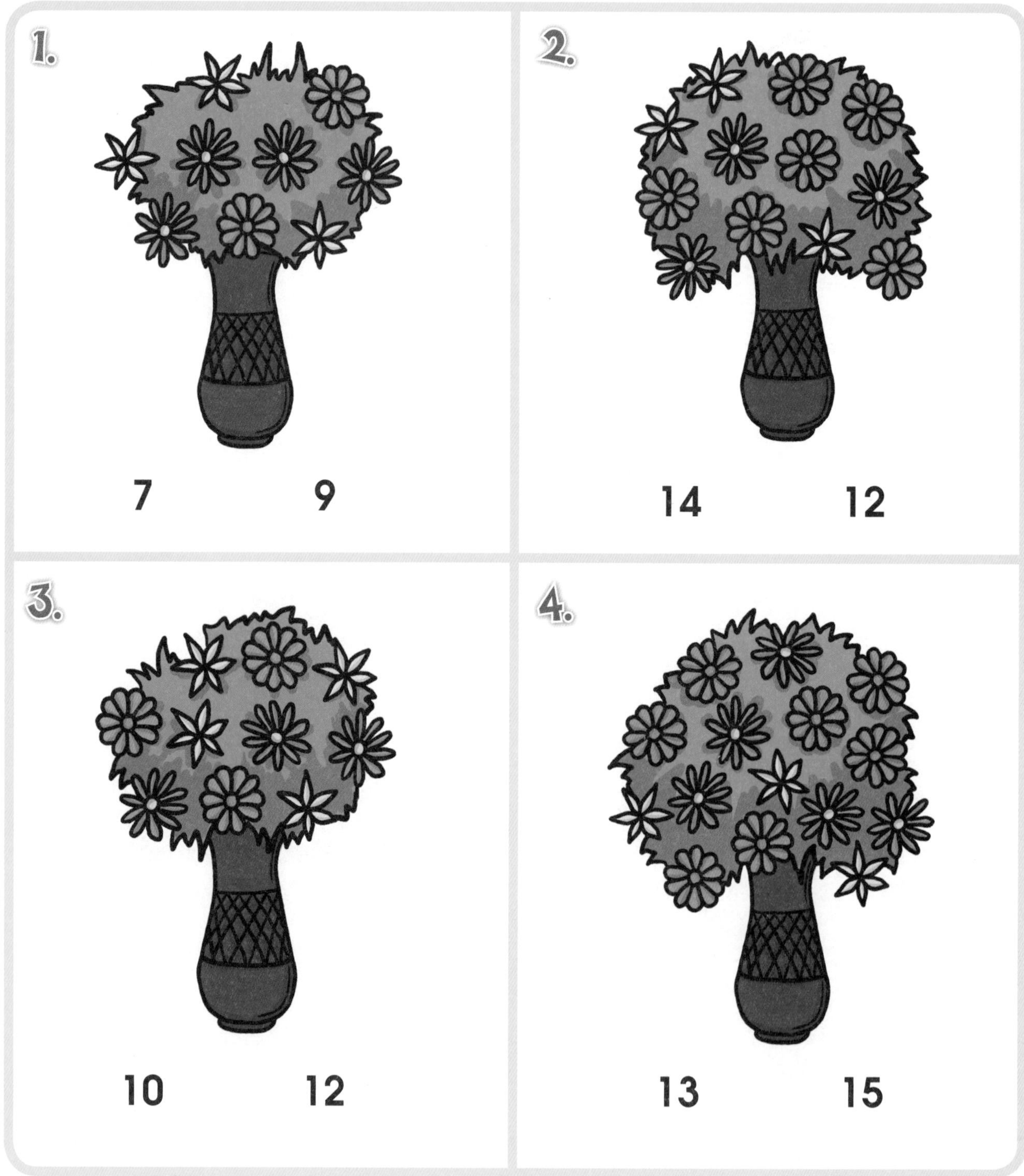

Date: ____________

Count the spots on each ladybug.
Circle the correct number word.

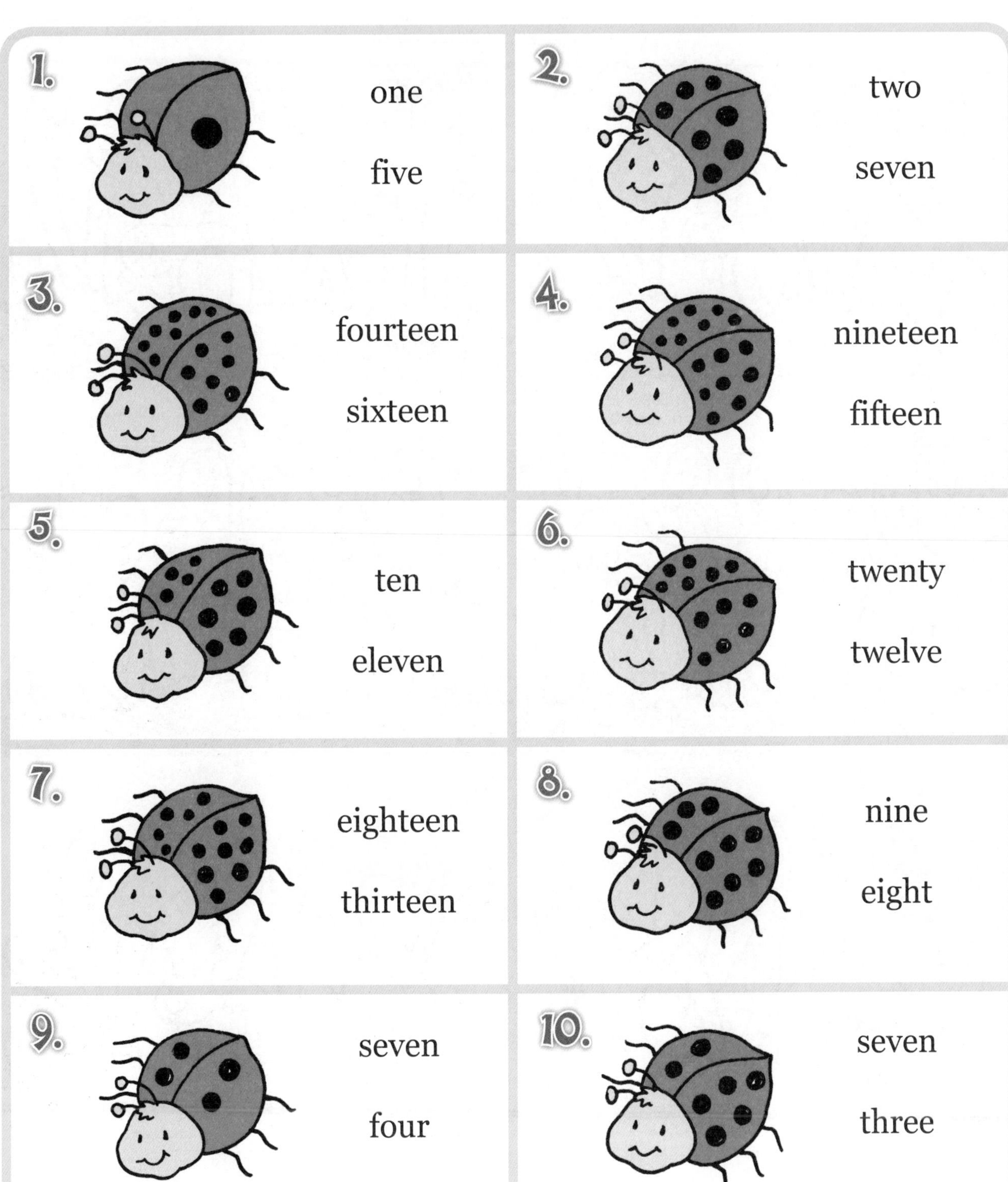

Date: ____________

Color each set of 11 earthworms.

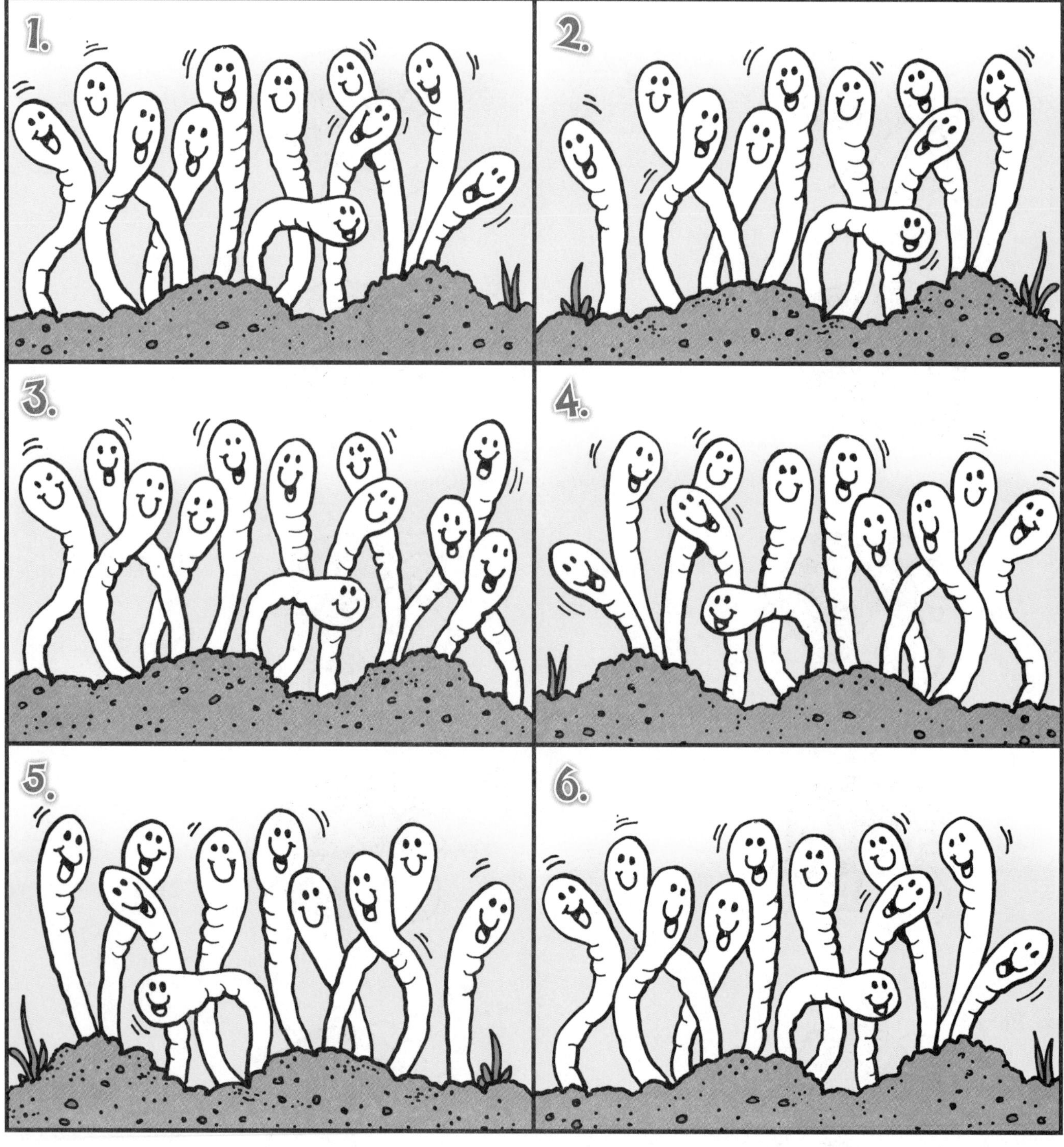

Date: ____________

Draw a circle around each shelf with 12 toys.

1. 

2. 

3. 

4. 

5. 

Date: ____________

Draw a circle around each group of 13 objects.

1. 

2. 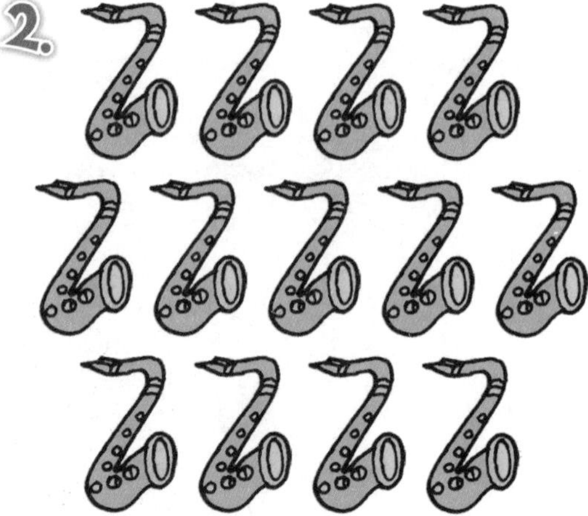

3. 

4. 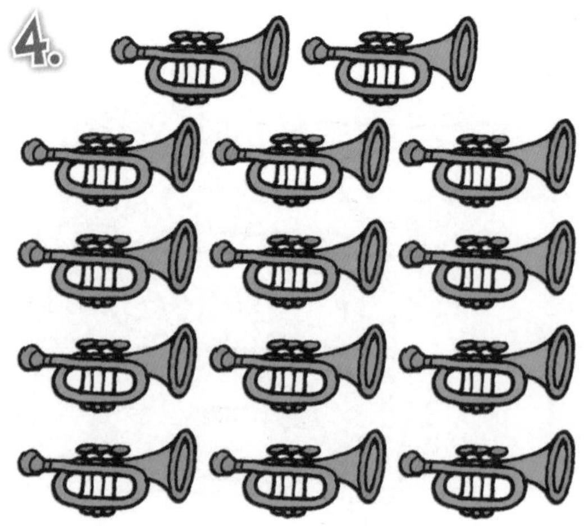

5. 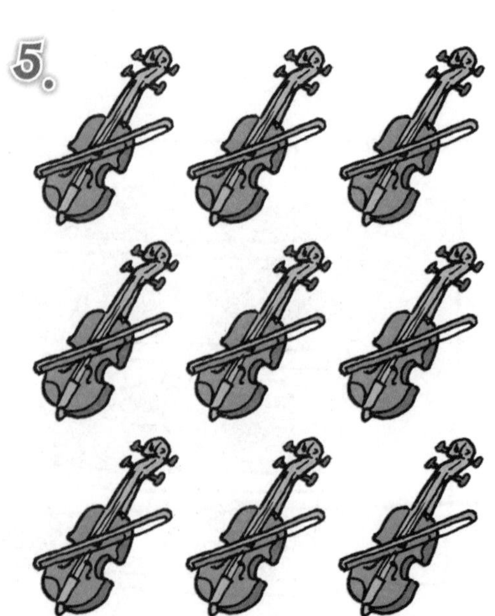

Date: ____________

Color each ball with 14 dots.

Date: ____________

Draw a circle around each group of 15 vegetables.

1.

2. 

3. 

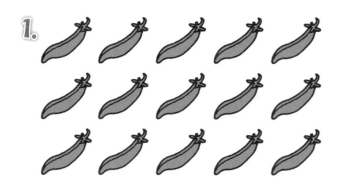

4. 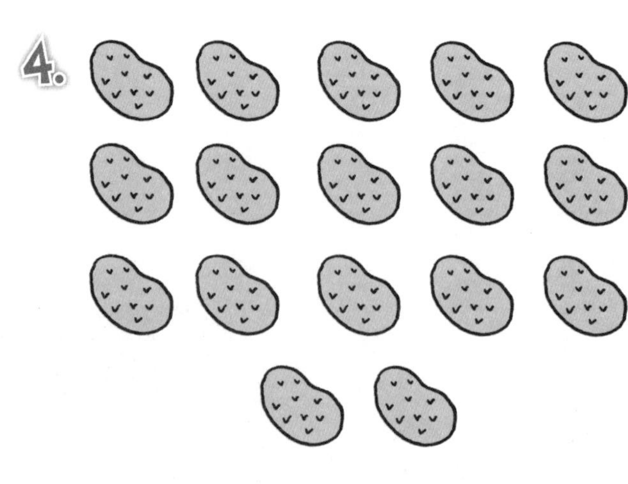

5. 

6. 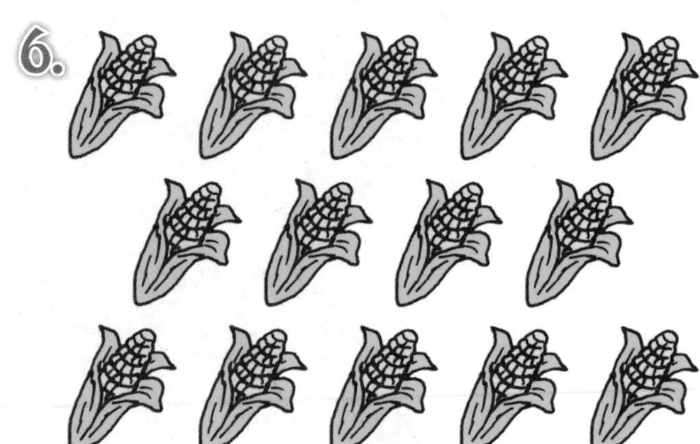

Date: ______________

Color each jar with 16 candies.

1.

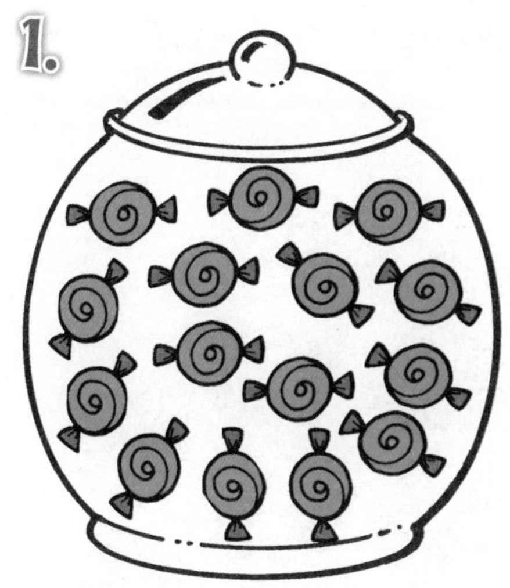

2.

3.

4.

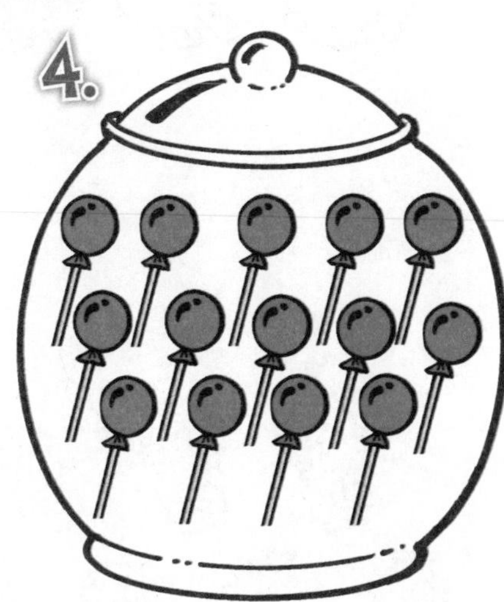

5.

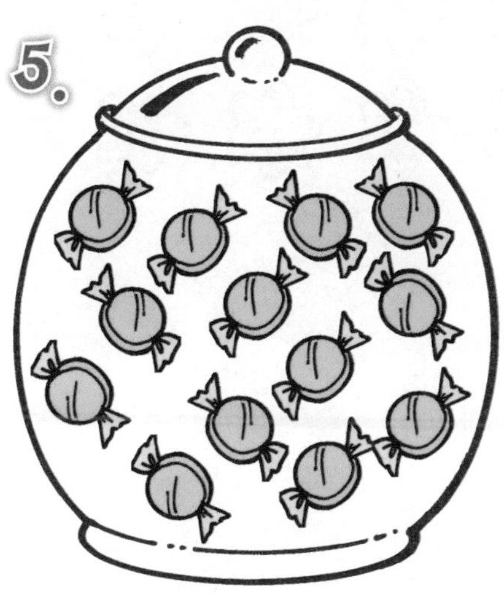

6.

Date: ____________

Draw a circle around each group of 17 sea animals.

1.

2.

3.

4.

 Date: ____________

Circle 18 stars in each box.

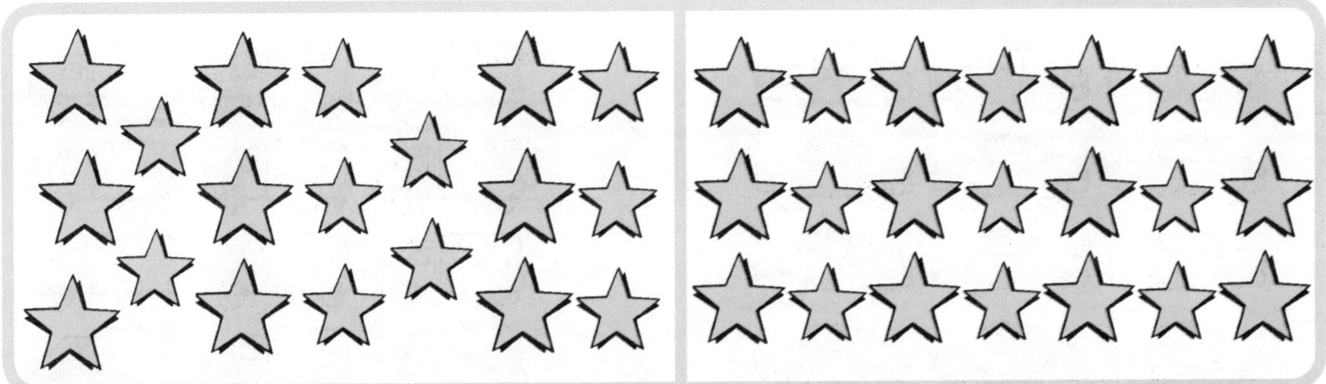

Draw more stars to make 18 stars.

Count the planets. Write the number.

Date: ____________

Draw a circle around each group of 19 vehicles.

1.

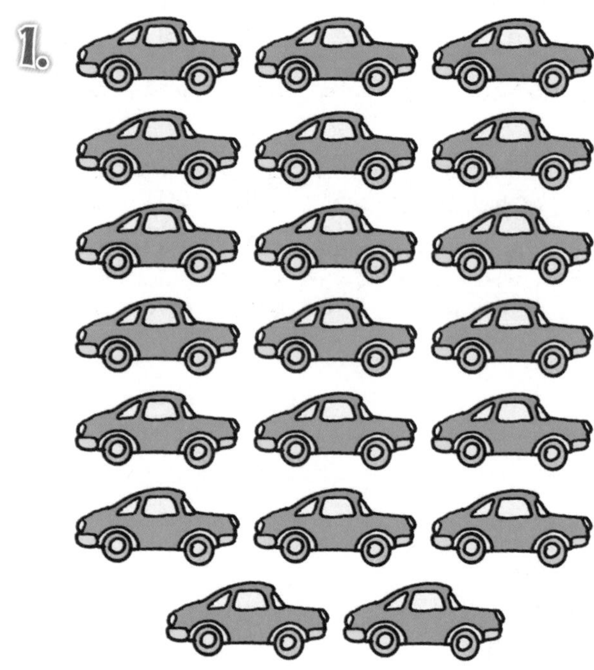

2.

3.

4.

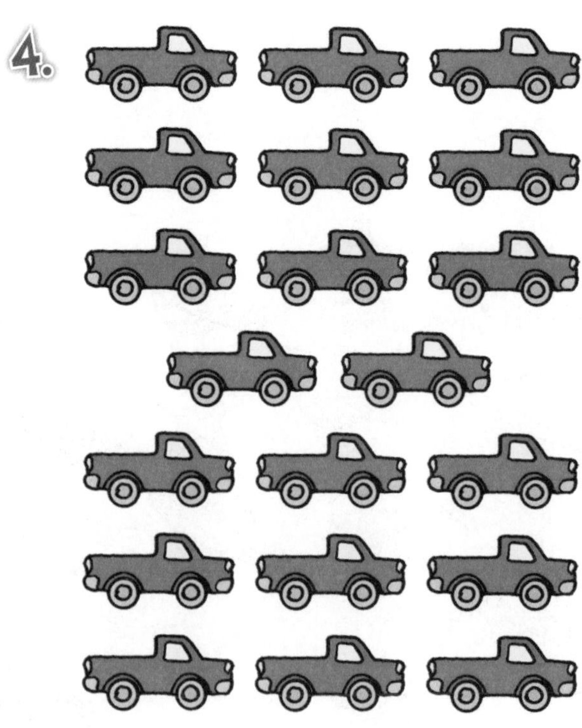

Date: ____________

Count the marbles. Circle the number that tells how many. Color each group with 20 marbles.

1.

18 19 20

2.
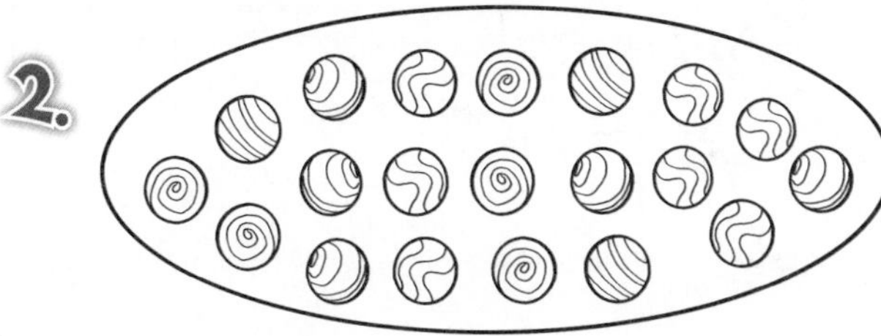

18 19 20

3.

18 19 20

4.
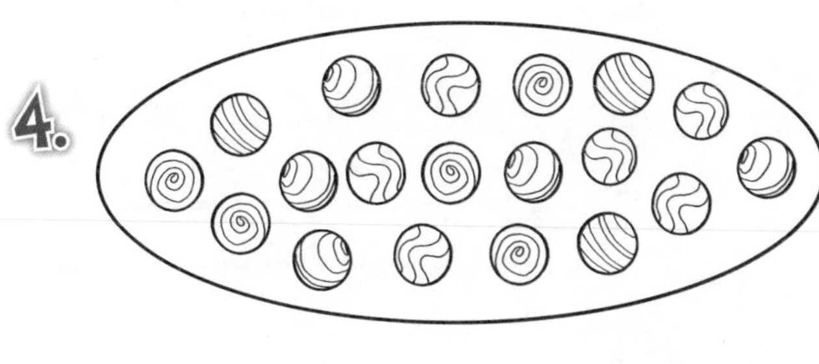

18 19 20

5.

18 19 20

6.
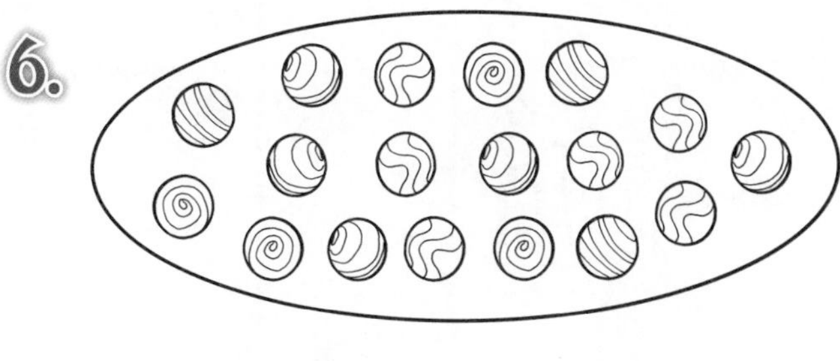

18 19 20

Color.

11 = yellow
12 = black
13 = blue
14 = white
15 = orange
16 = green
17 = red
18 = purple
19 = brown
20 = pink

Date: ____________

Color.

eleven = yellow
twelve = black
thirteen = blue
fourteen = peach
fifteen = orange
sixteen = green
seventeen = purple
eighteen = brown
nineteen = pink
twenty = red

Date: ____________

Join the dots from 1 to 20.

Date: ____________

Find the petrol station by joining the numbers in the correct order from 1 to 20.

Date: ________

Fill in the missing numbers of the houses.

11 | ___ | 15 | ___

12 | ___ | ___ | 18

What pattern do you see in the house numbers?

Date: ______________

Write the number words for 1 to 20 on the trail.

one

Find and color 20 butterflies in the picture.

Date: ____________

Color the bows on the tails to match the number above each kite.

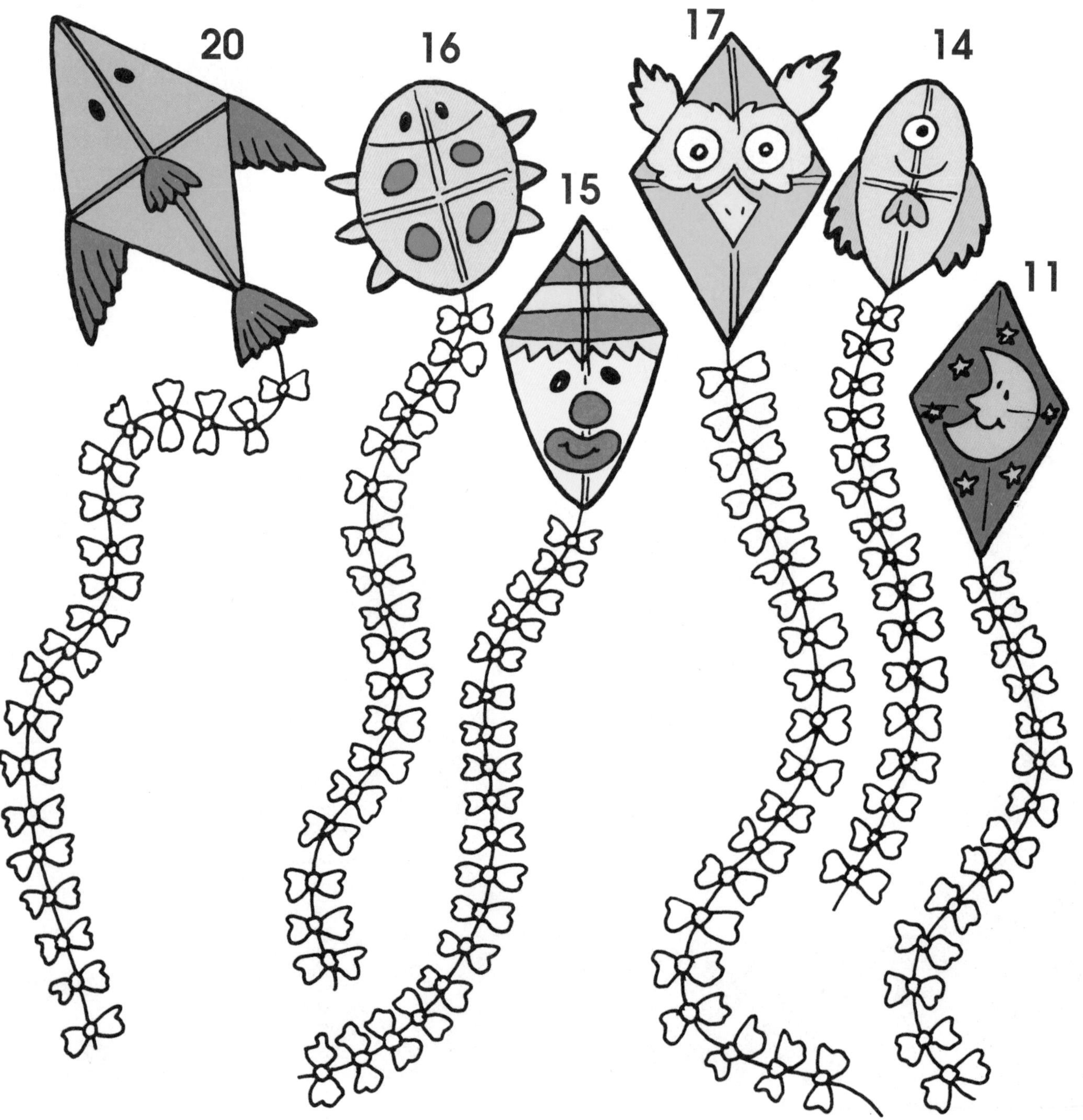

Date: ______________

Count. Write how many.

1.

2.

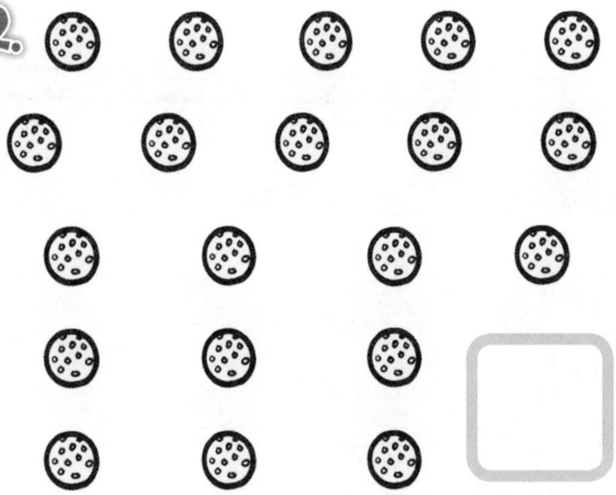

3.

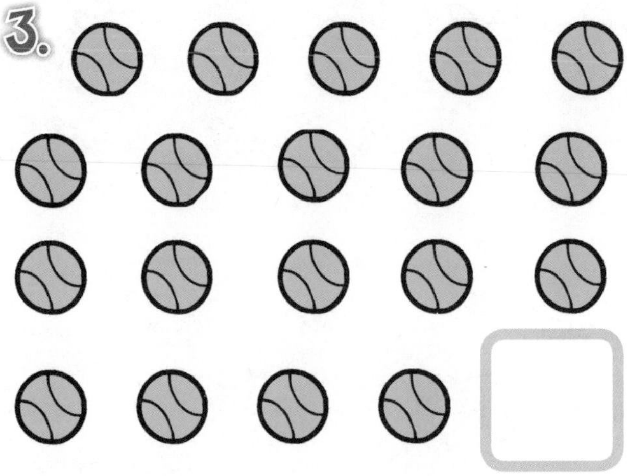

4.

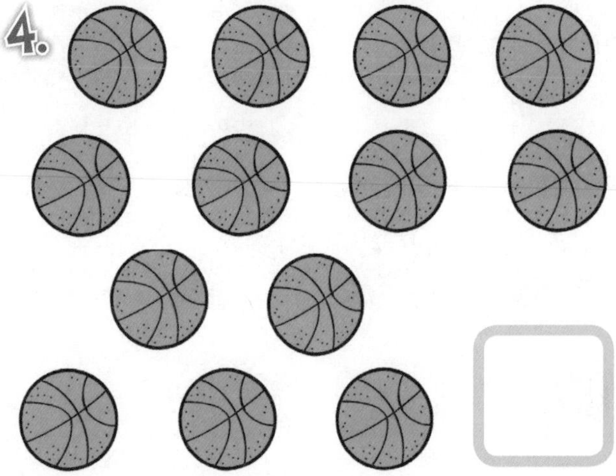

5.

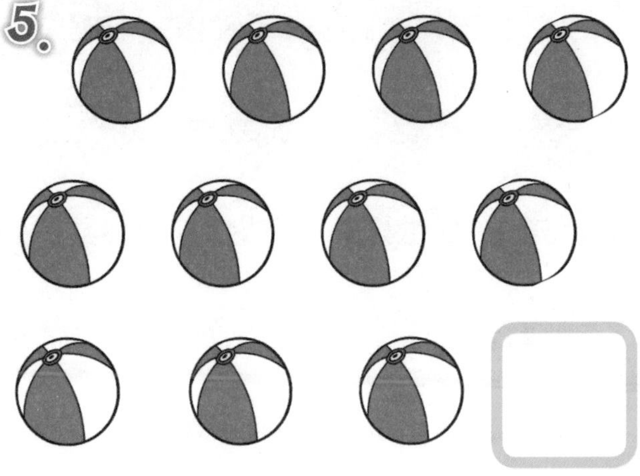

6.

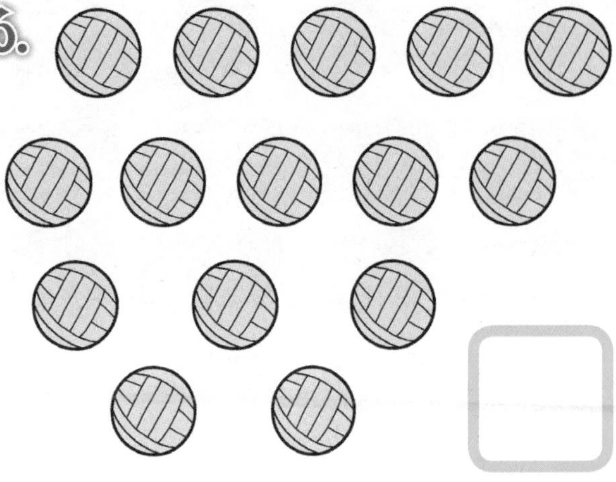

Date: ____________

Count. Write how many.

Date: ______________

Count. Color each group of 20 objects.

Write how many.

Date: ____________

Count. Then match.

• eighteen

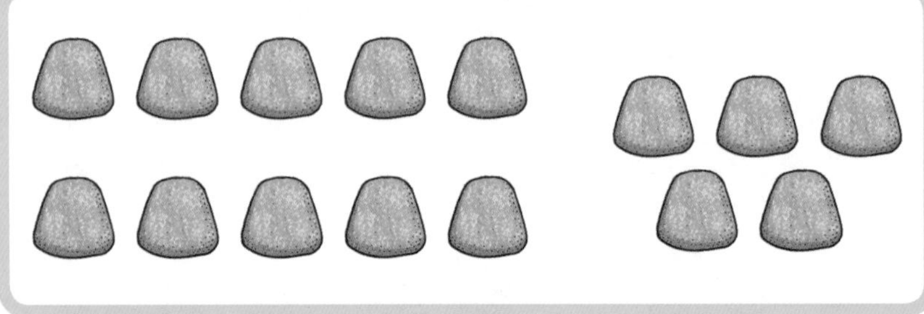

• fifteen

• thirteen

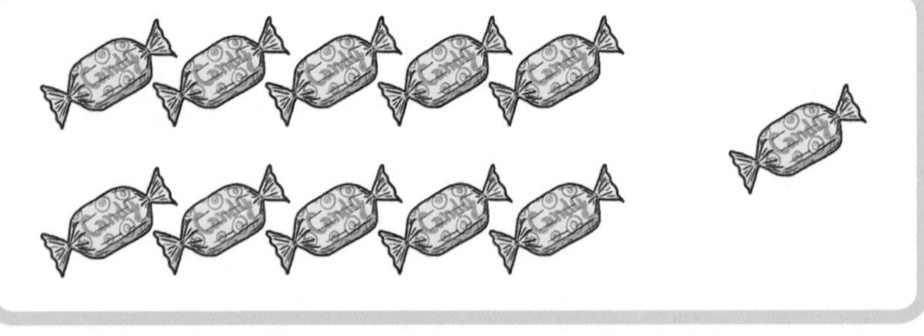

• eleven

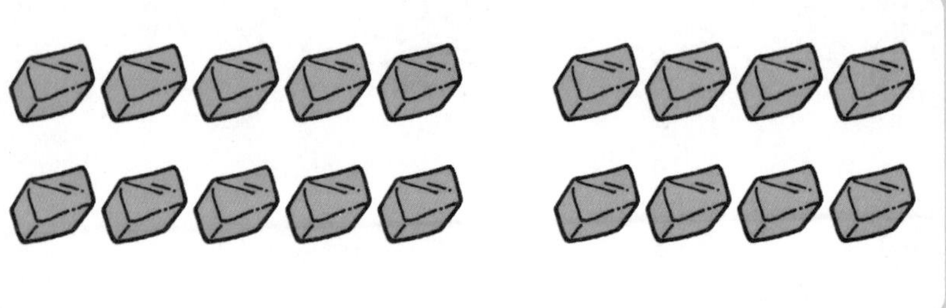

• nineteen

Date: _______________

Draw a line to match equal groups.

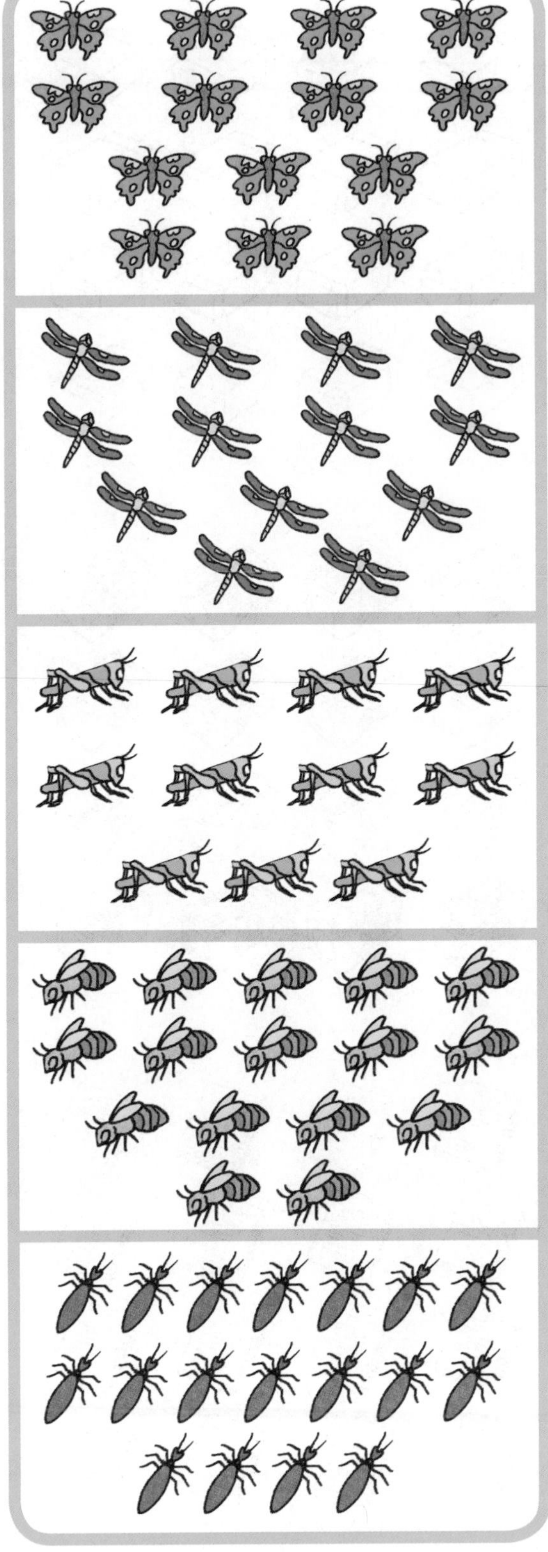

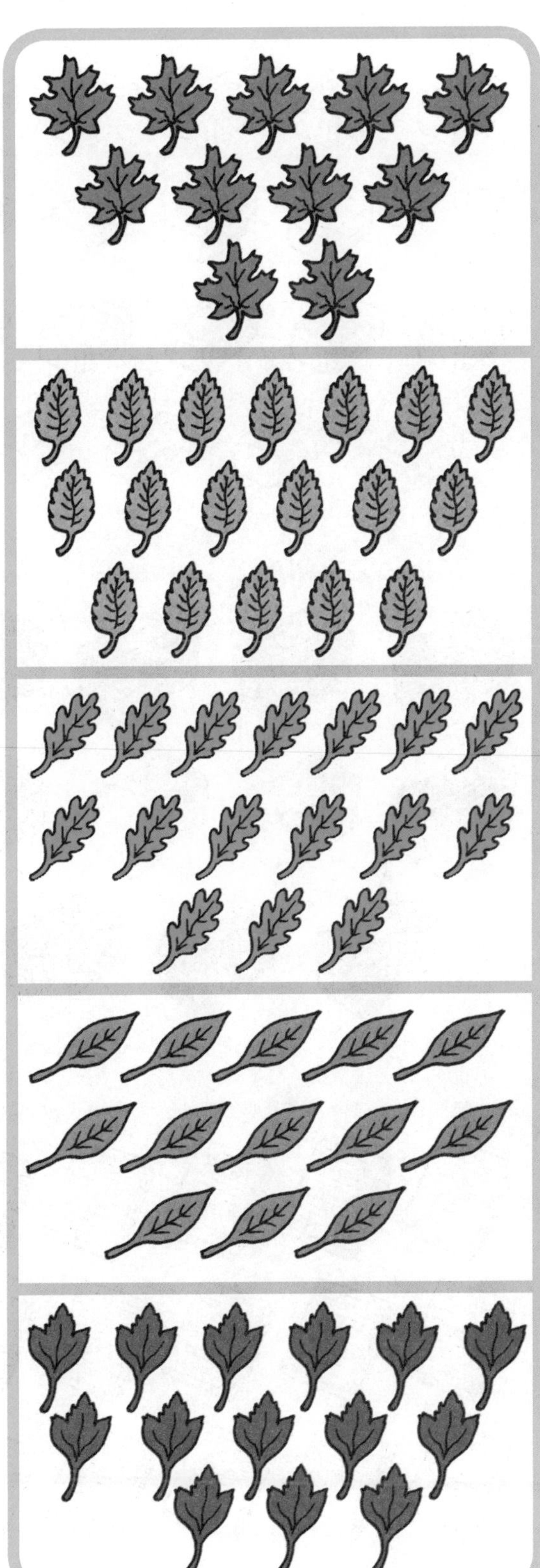

Date: ____________

Color the correct number of objects to form equal groups.

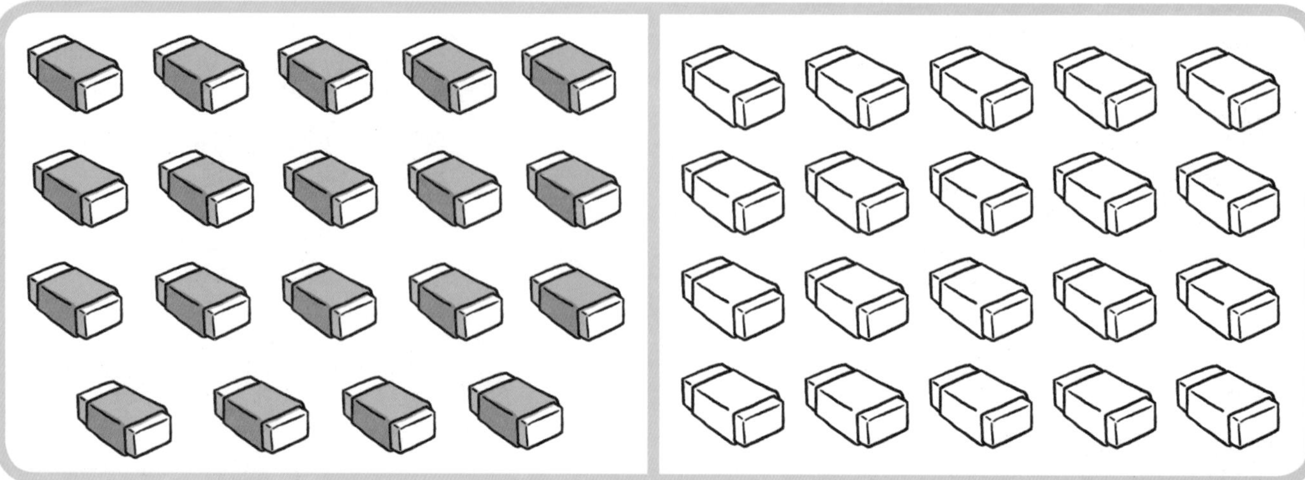

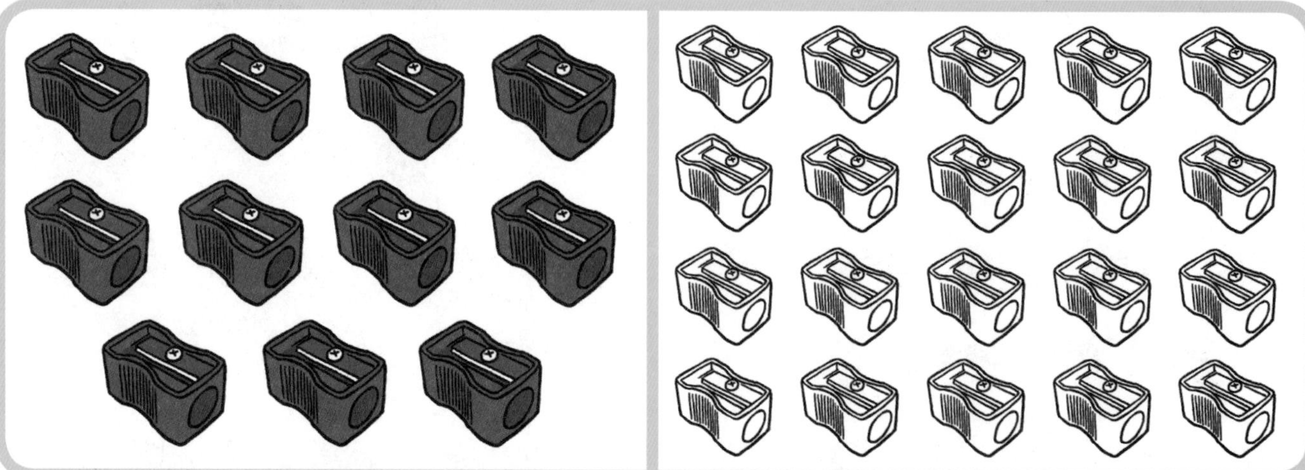

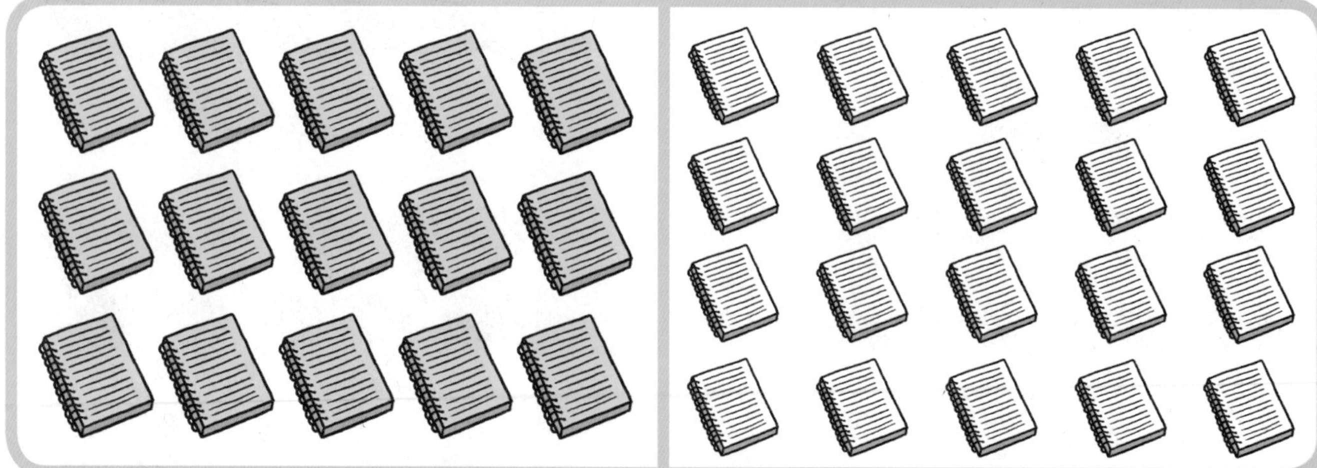

Date: ____________

Add the correct number of food items to form equal groups.

Example

Date: ____________

Color the giraffe with more spots in each picture.

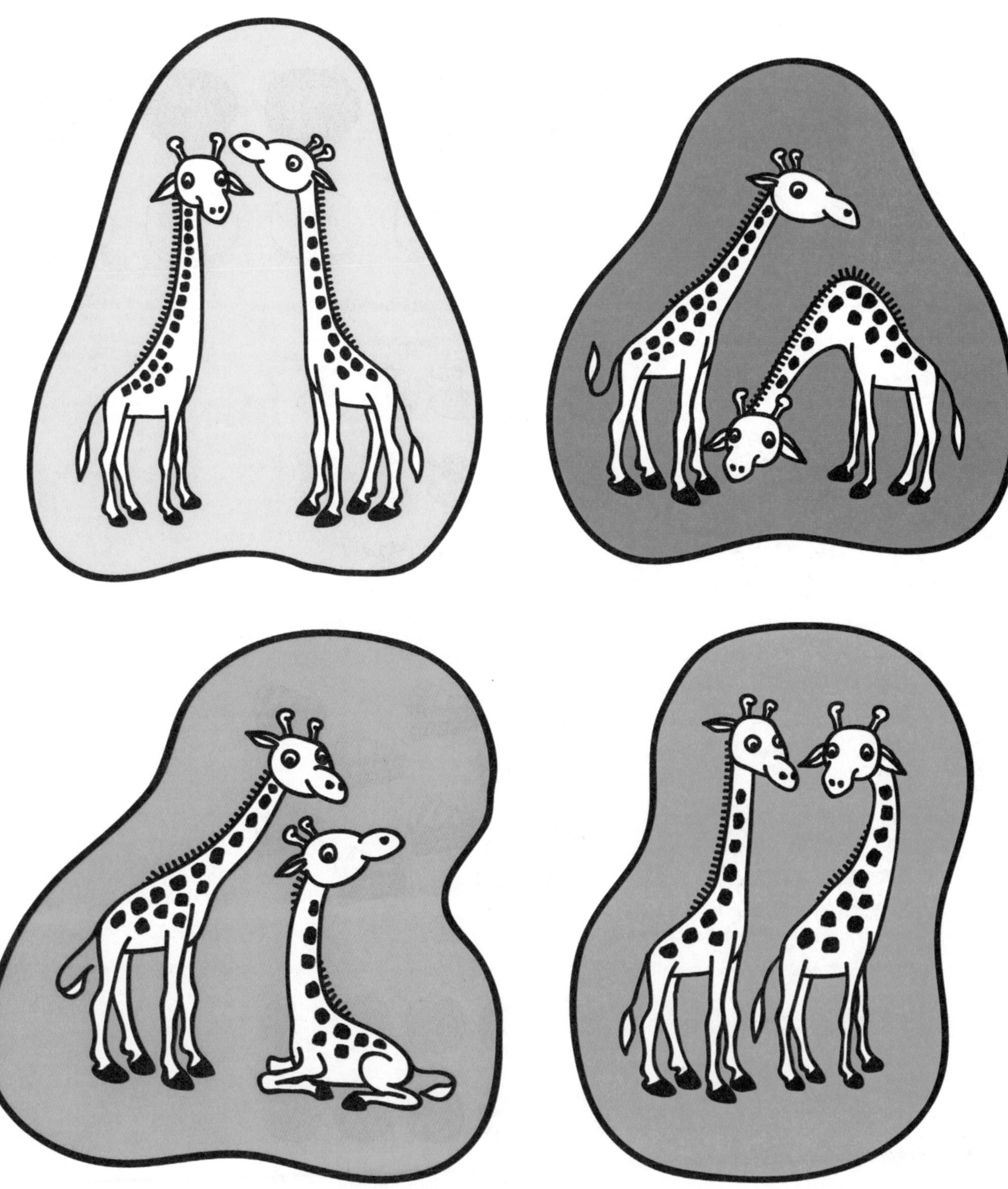

Date: ____________

Circle the correct number of vehicles.

Example

More than 15

More than 11

More than 19

More than 12

Date: ____________

Circle the one with less in each box.

1.

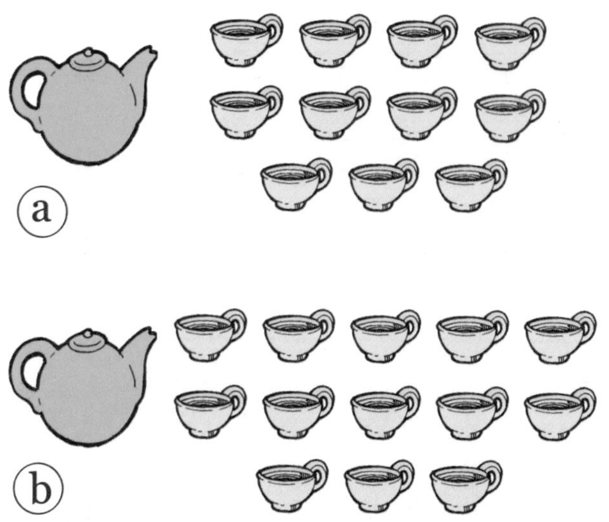

a

b

2.

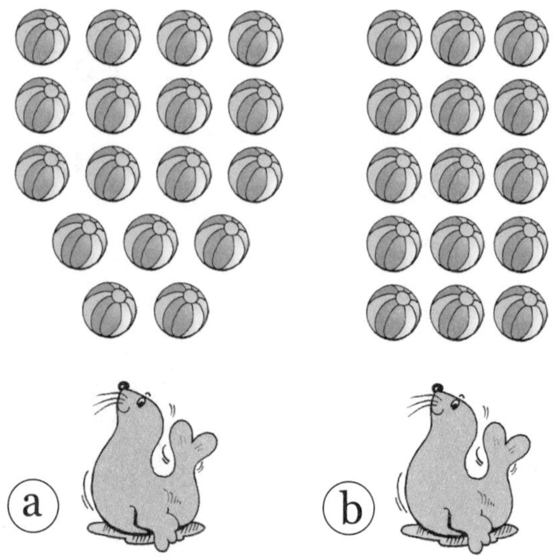

a

b

3.

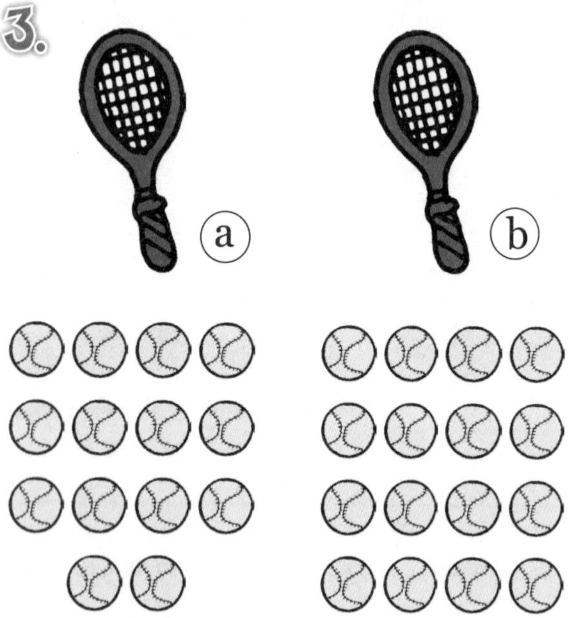

a

b

4.

a

b

Date: ____________

Color the correct number of objects.

Example

Less than 16

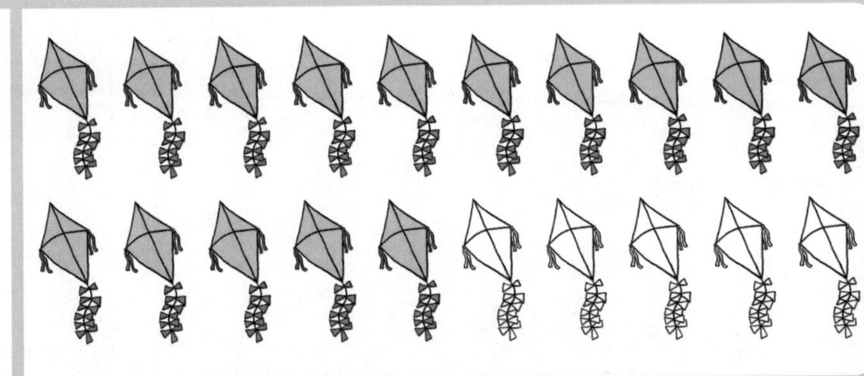

Less than 12

Less than 19

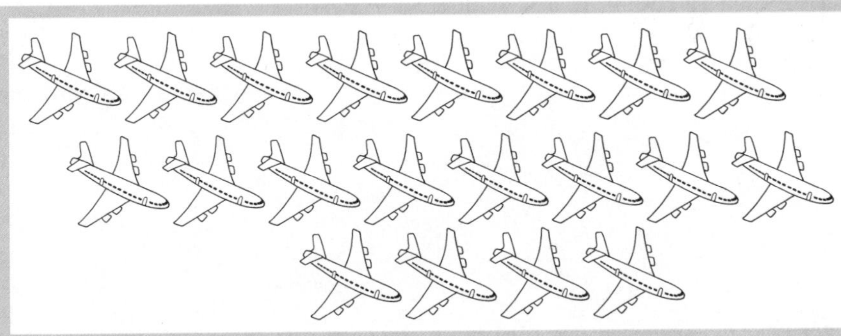

Less than 15

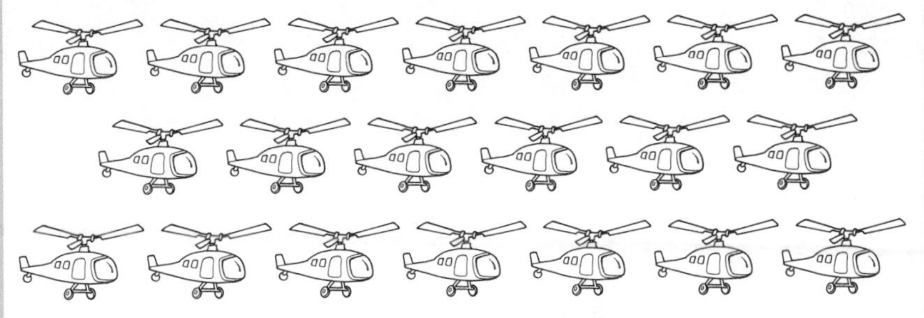

Count and write the number of each group.

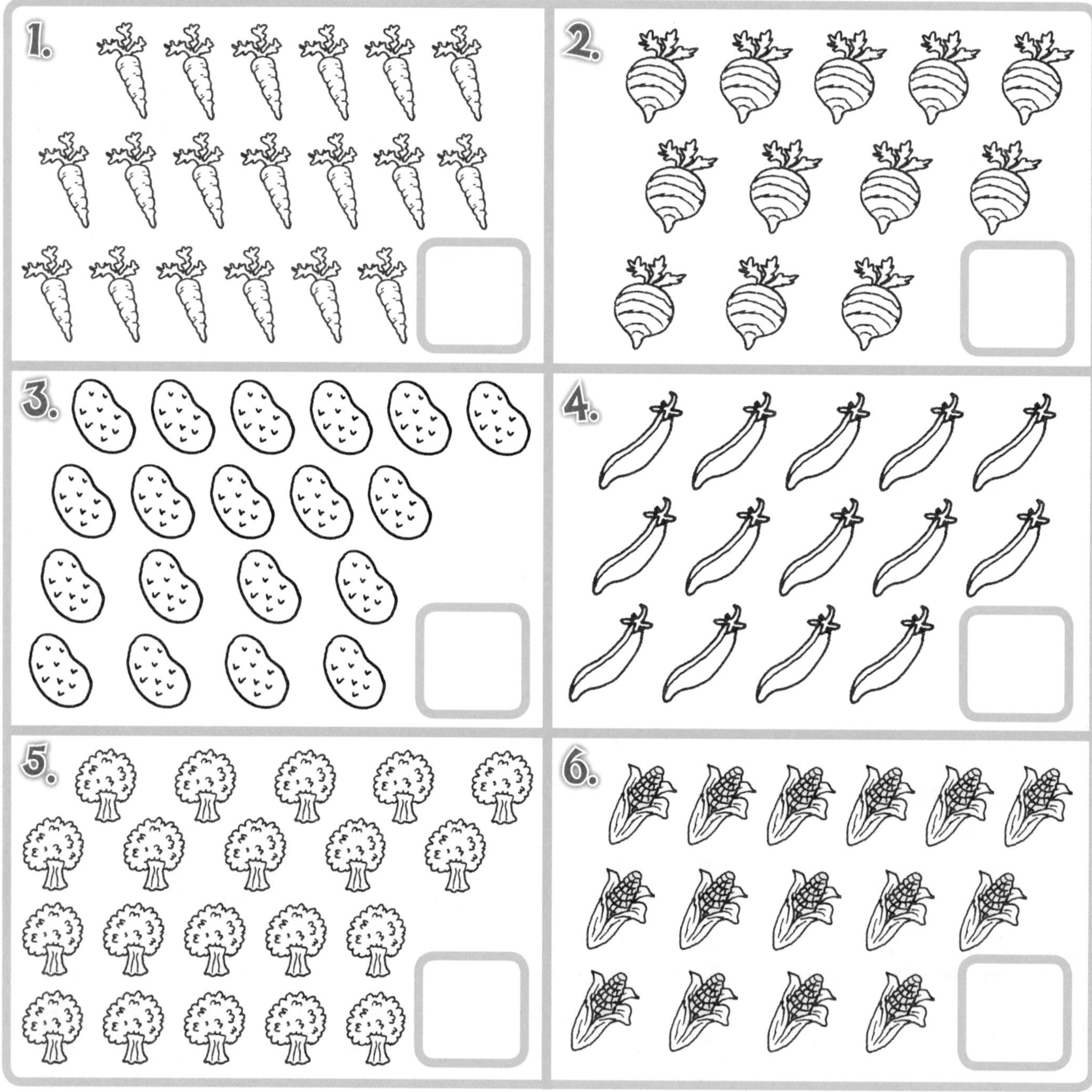

Color the group with the most number of vegetables green.
Color the group with the least number of vegetables red.

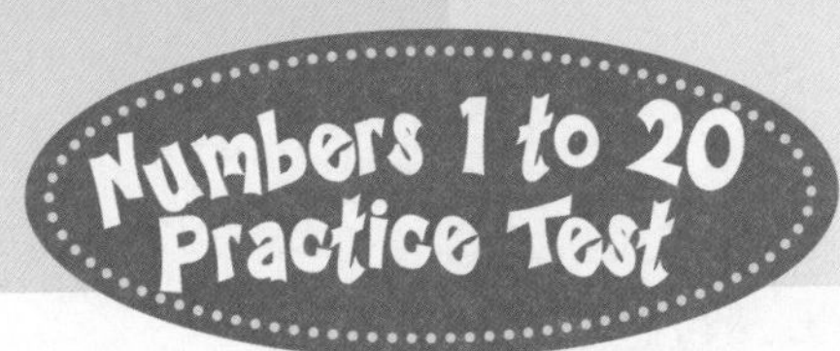

Color the bubble next to the correct answer.

1. Which number word comes after twelve?

○ **A** fifteen　　○ **C** thirteen

○ **B** twenty　　○ **D** eleven

2. Which number word comes before fourteen?

○ **A** nineteen　　○ **C** thirteen

○ **B** eleven　　○ **D** sixteen

3. Which number word comes after seventeen?

○ **A** twelve　　○ **C** fifteen

○ **B** eighteen　　○ **D** nineteen

4. Which number word comes before nineteen?

○ **A** eleven　　○ **C** fourteen

○ **B** seventeen　　○ **D** eighteen

Color the bubble next to the correct answer.

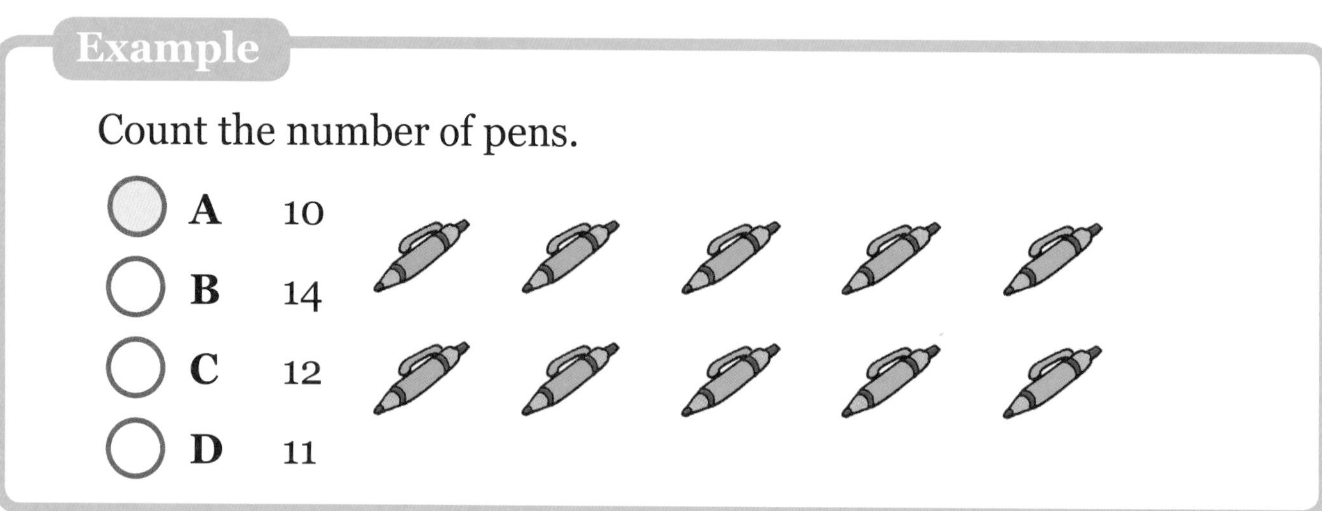

Example

Count the number of pens.

- A 10
- B 14
- C 12
- D 11

5. Count the number of backpacks.

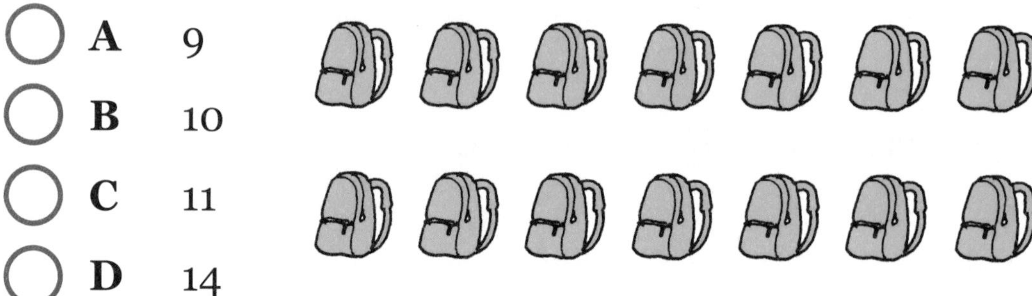

- A 9
- B 10
- C 11
- D 14

6. Count the number of crayons.

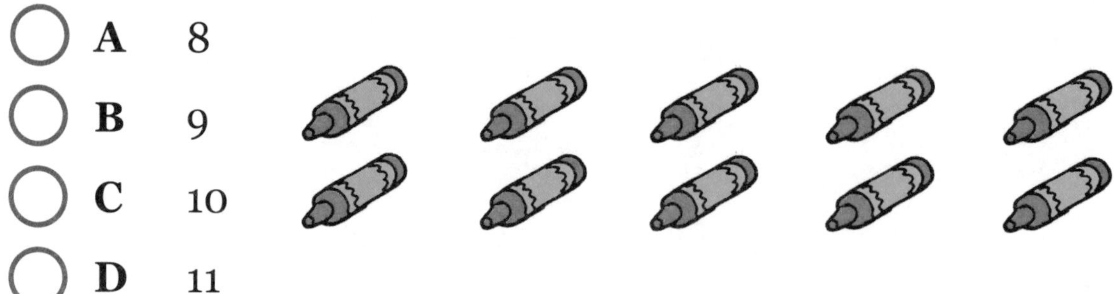

- A 8
- B 9
- C 10
- D 11

Color the bubble next to the correct answer.

7. Count the number of strawberries.

○ A 17
○ B 18
○ C 19
○ D 20

8. Count the number of pears.

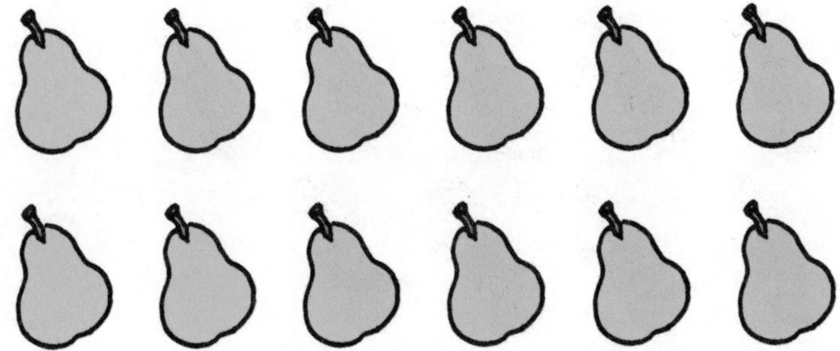

○ A 12
○ B 13
○ C 14
○ D 15

Color the bubble next to the correct answer.

9. Count the number of trumpets.

○ **A** 13
○ **B** 12
○ **C** 11
○ **D** 10

10. Count the number of violins.

○ **A** 15
○ **B** 16
○ **C** 17
○ **D** 18

Color the bubble next to the correct answer.

11. Which group has **more than 15**?

○ A 

○ B 

○ C 

○ D 

12. Which group has **less than 18?**

○ A 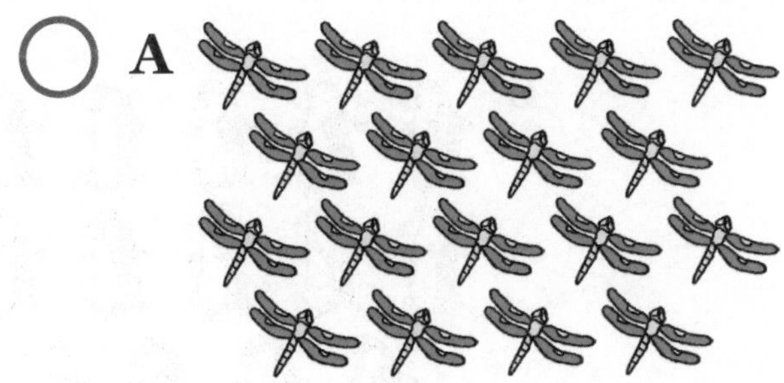

○ B 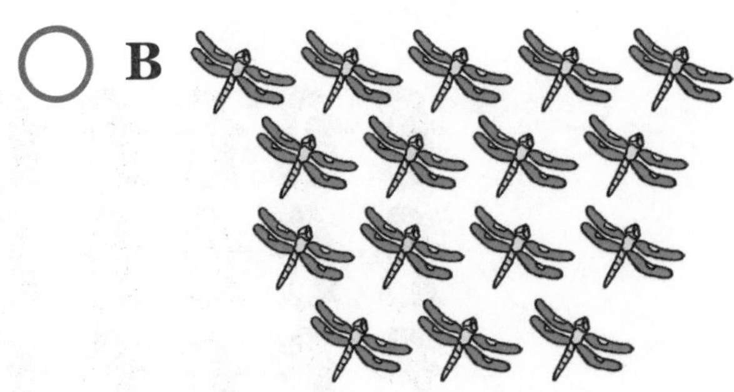

○ C 

○ D 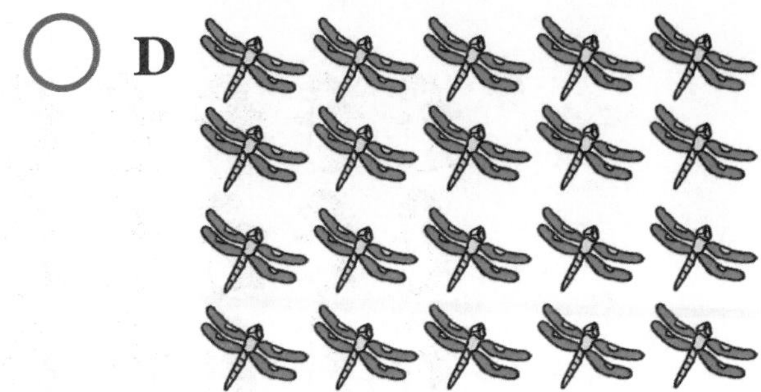

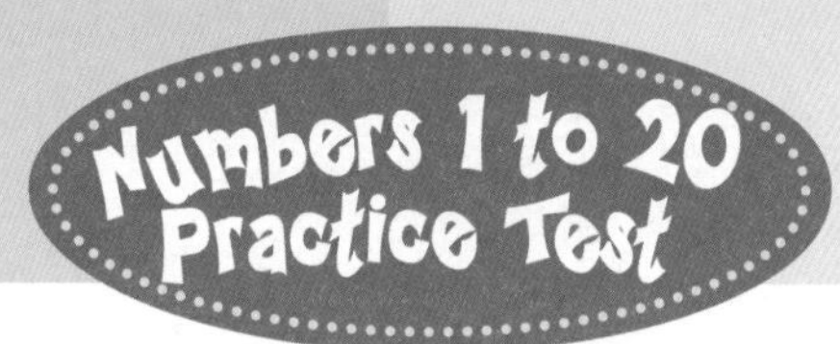

Color the bubble next to the correct answer.

13. Which group has **the most** number of seashells?

○ A 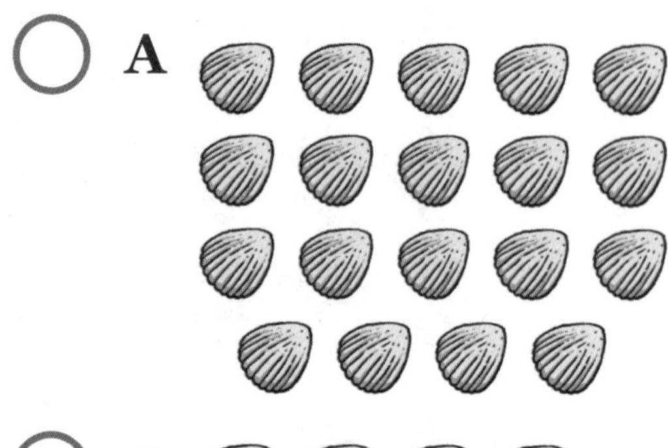

○ B 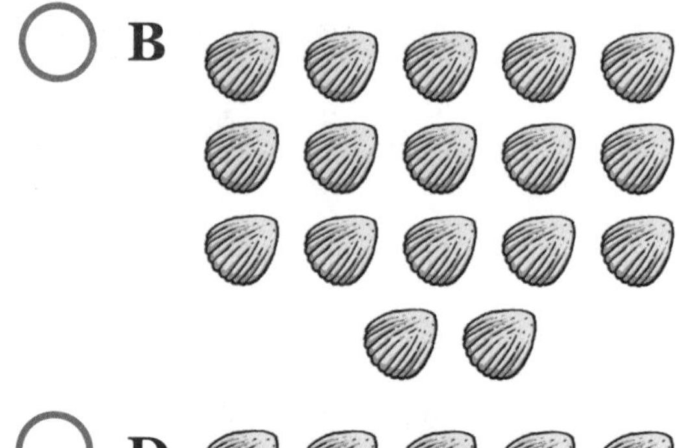

○ C 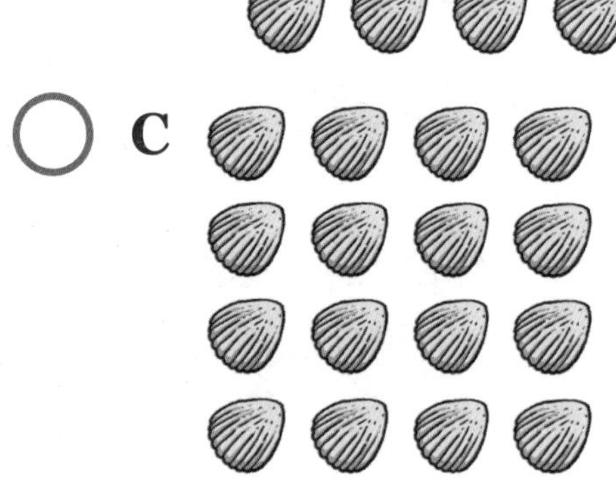

○ D 

14. Which group has **the least** number of penguins?

○ A

○ B

○ C

○ D

Shapes and Patterns

In this section, your child will identify a variety of shapes. Recognizing shapes helps children develop geometry skills. Your child will also learn to identify the sequence of objects in patterns and to anticipate which object comes next in the pattern.

What to do
Review the directions on each page with your child. Then, have your child name the shapes on each page. Next, make your child complete the patterns on the pattern pages.

Keep on going!
Have your child identify the many shapes he or she sees around the home or while shopping. Then together, draw the shapes on paper. Cut them out and create different patterns.

Date: ____________

Color the pictures. Say the words.

	circle
	square
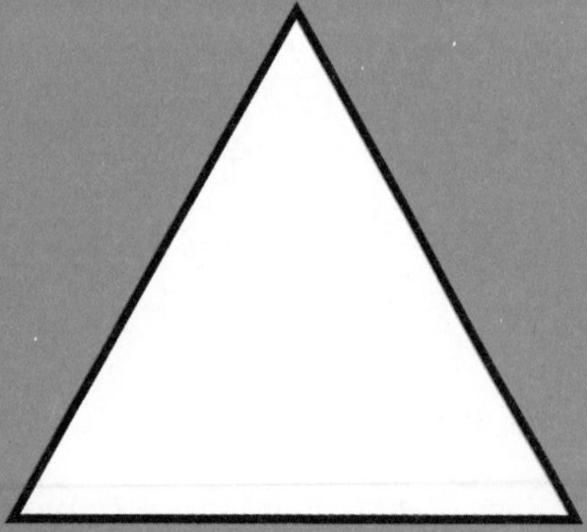	triangle

Date: ____________

Color the pictures. Say the words.

	rectangle
	star
	diamond

Date: ____________

Color the pictures. Say the words.

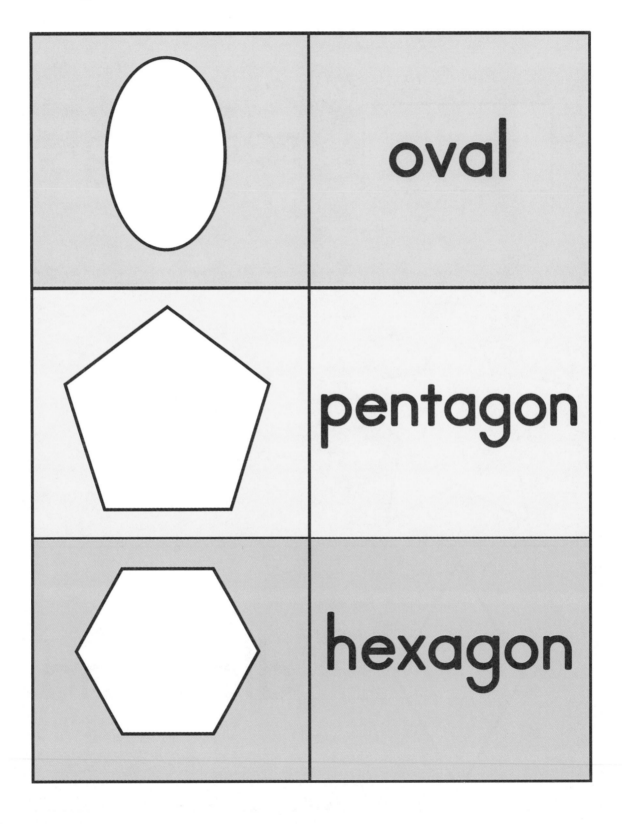

	oval
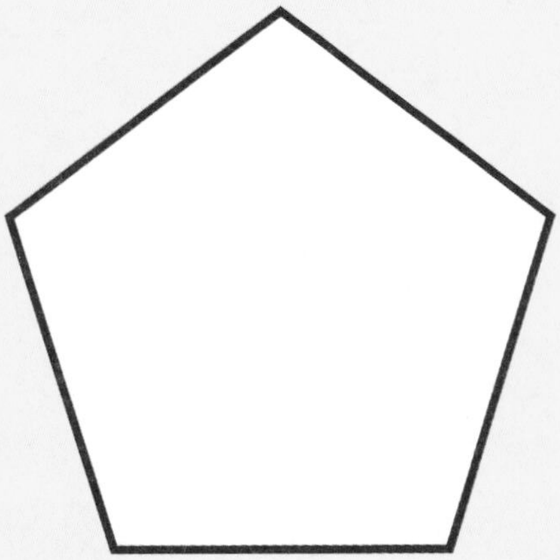	pentagon
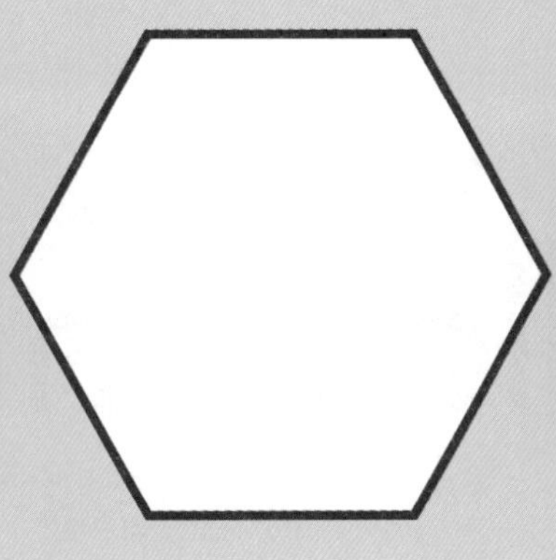	hexagon

Date: ____________

Color the circles red. Color the squares blue.

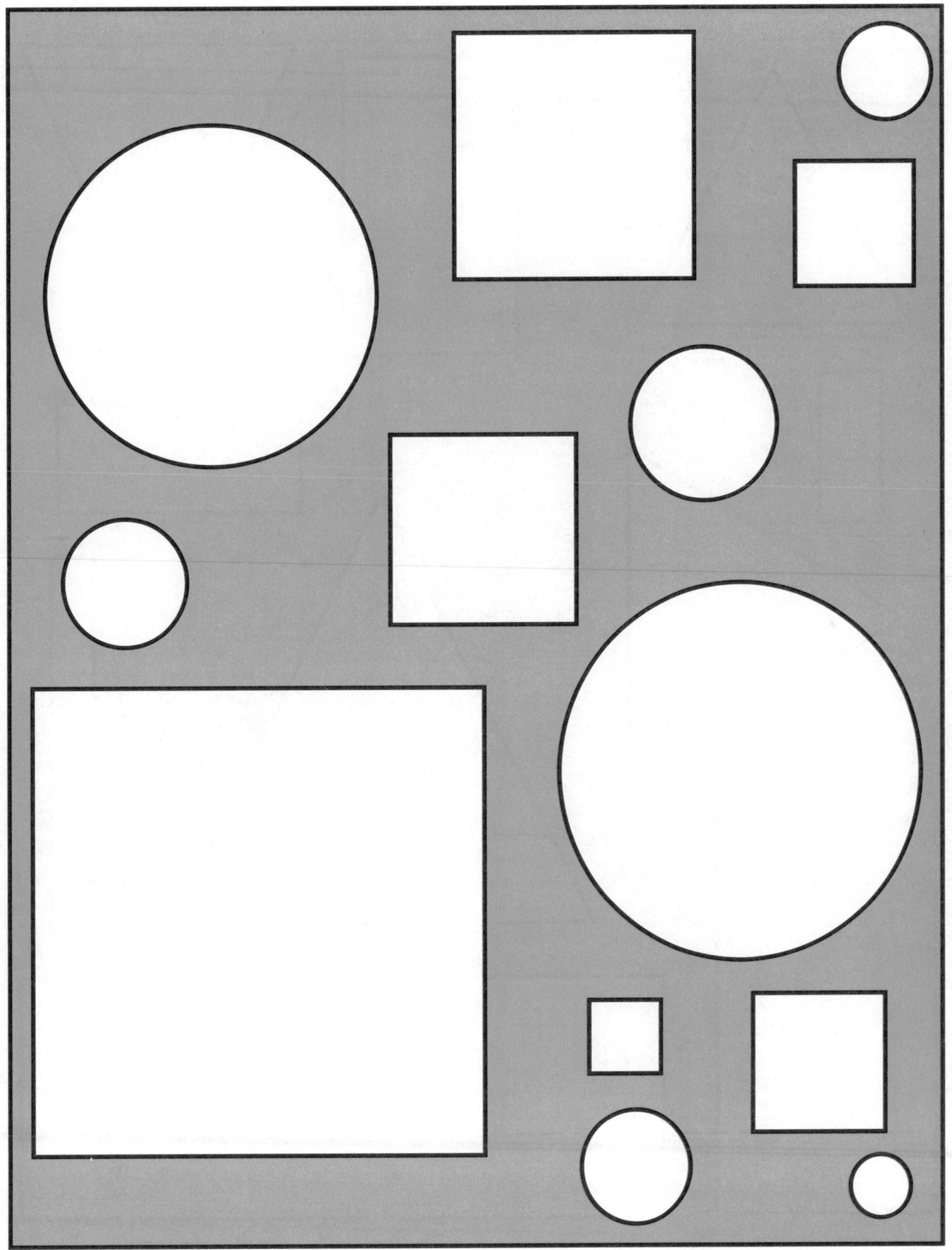

Date: ____________

Color the triangles orange. Color the rectangles green.

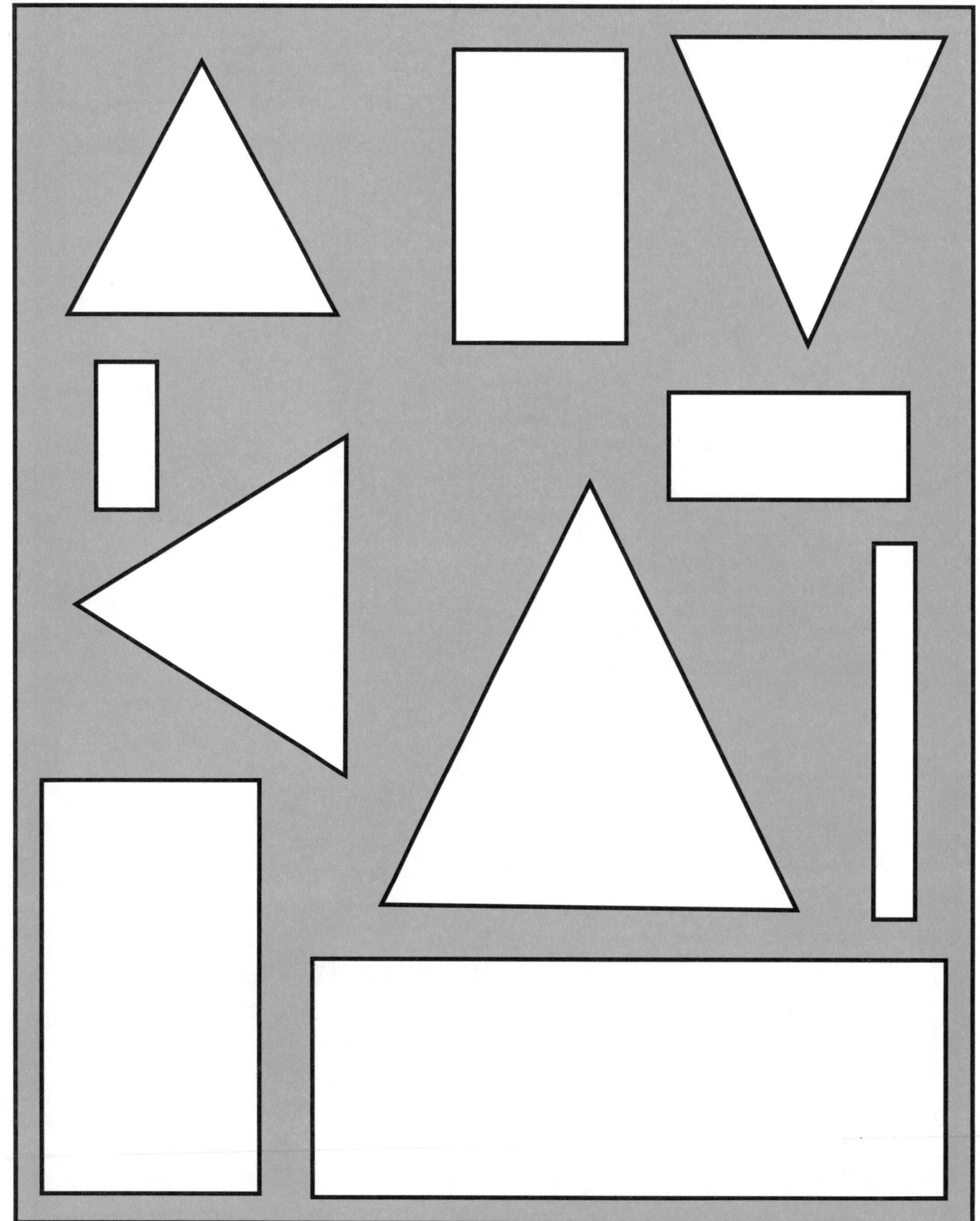

Date: ____________

Color the diamonds purple. Color the ovals yellow.

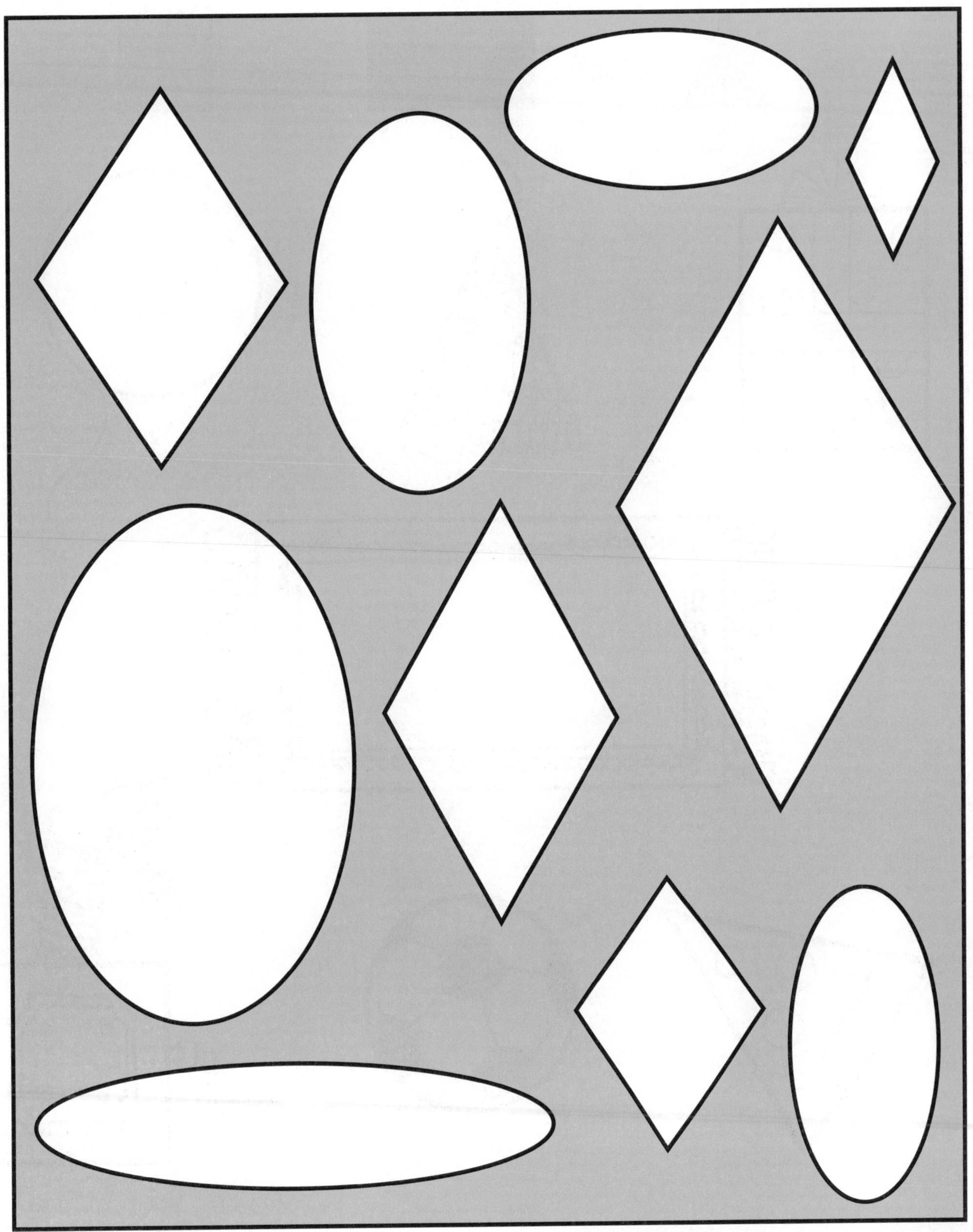

Date: ____________

Color.

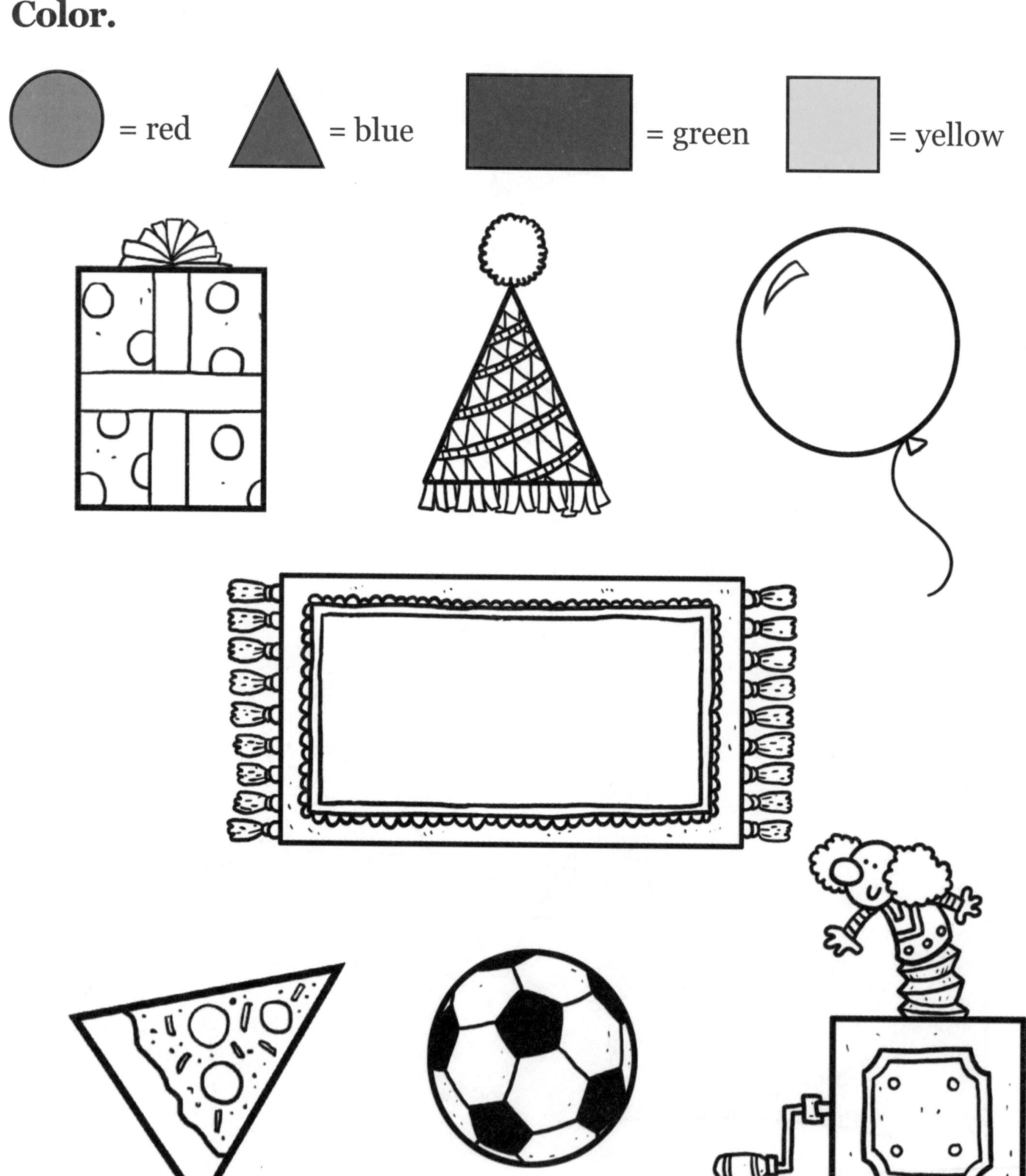

Date: __________

Color.

Date: ______________

Draw lines to match the shapes and objects.

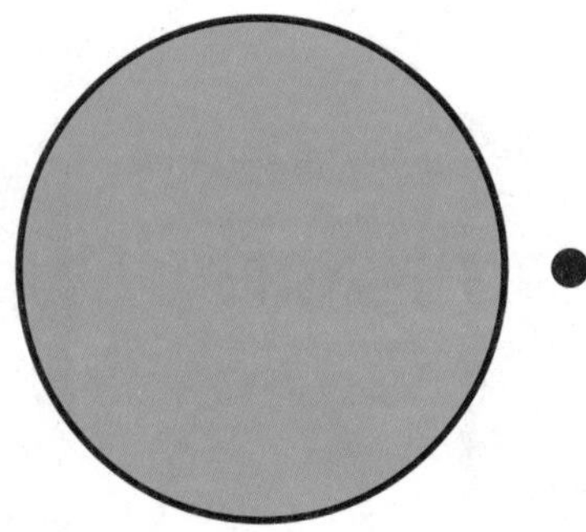

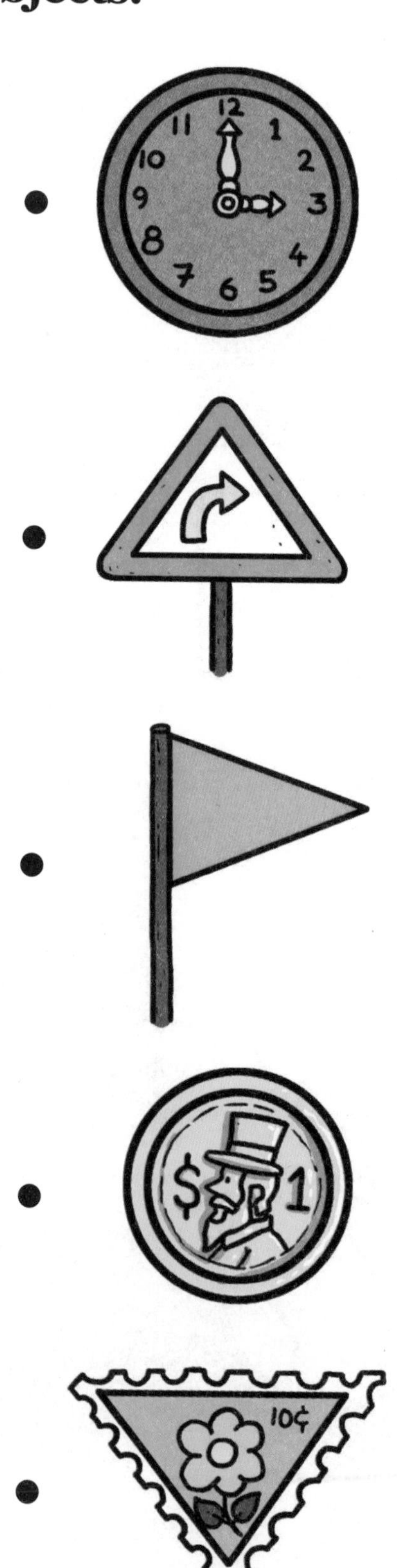

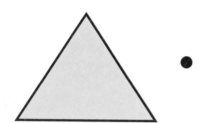

Date: ____________

Draw lines to match the shapes and objects.

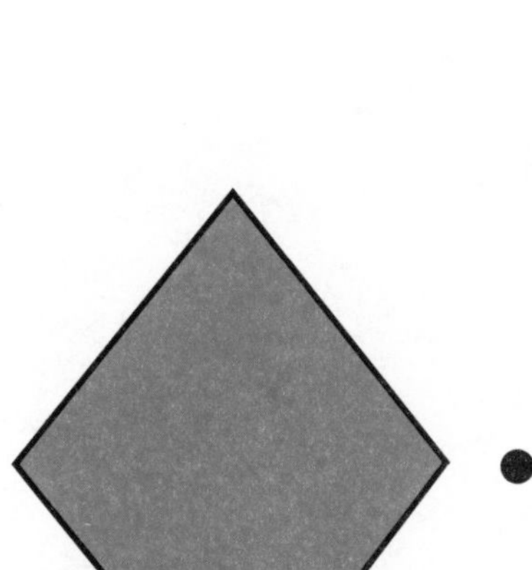

Date: ___________

Trace and color the stars.

Date: ______________

Color the stars.

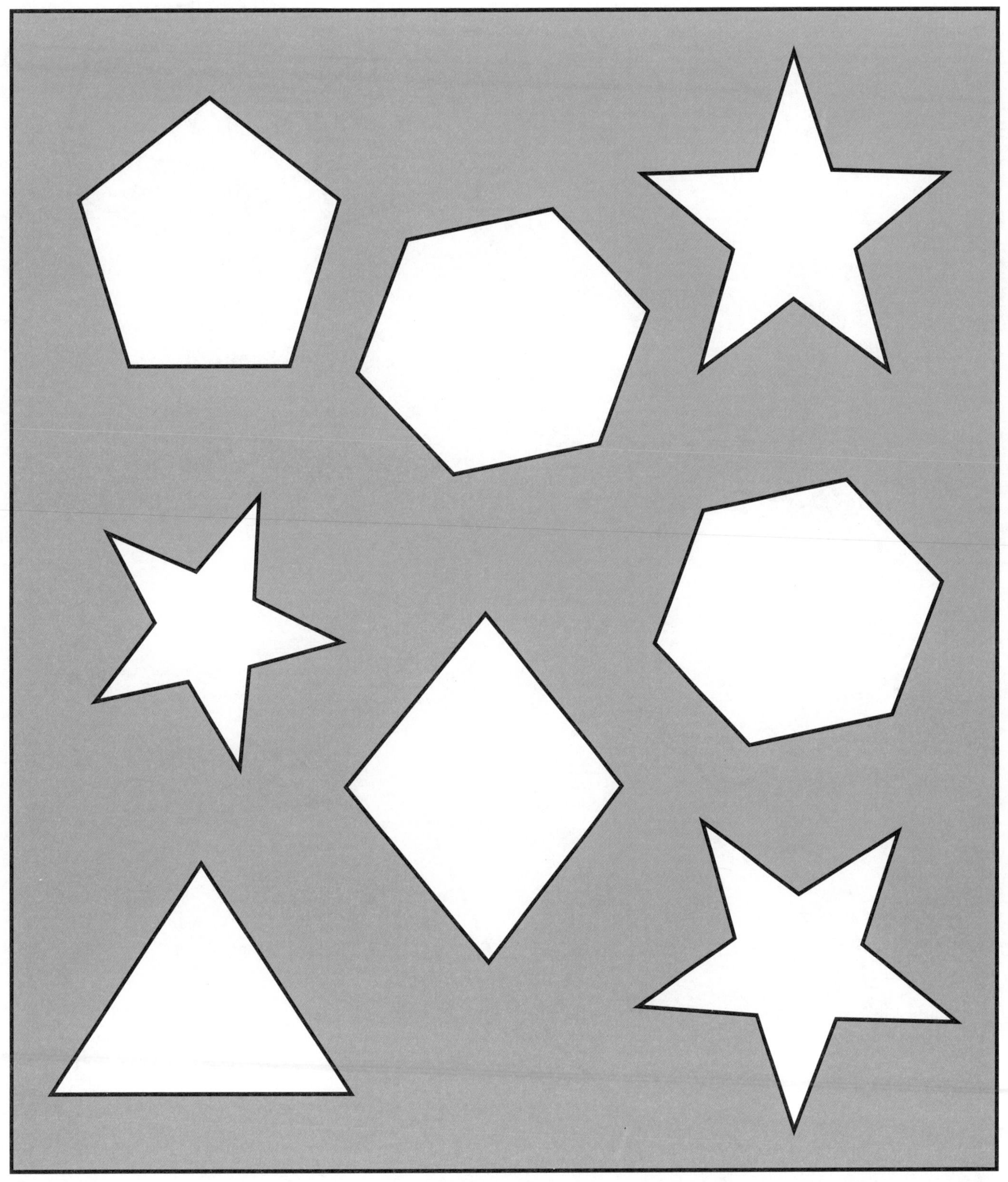

Date: ______________

Trace and color the pentagons.

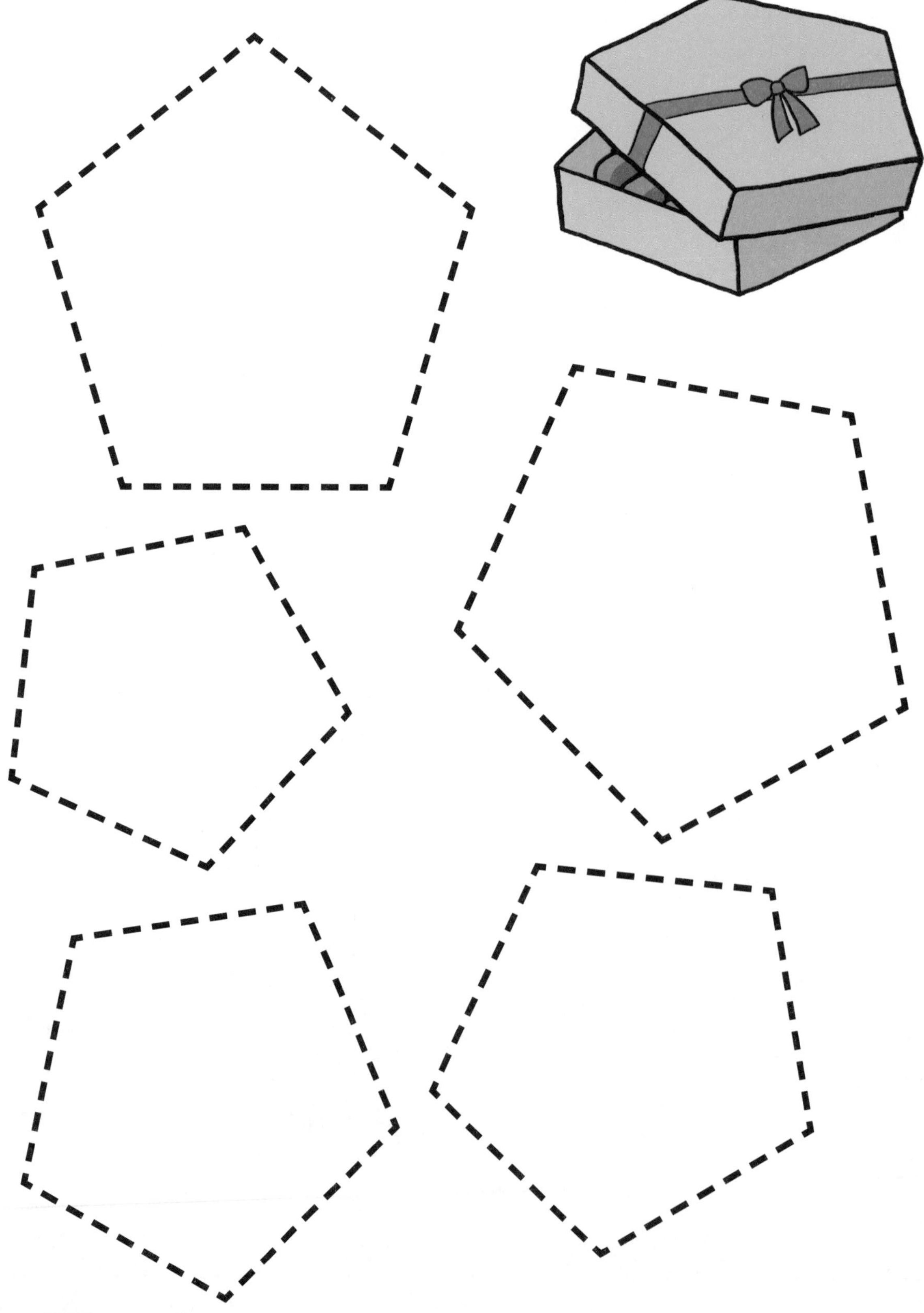

Date: ____________

Color the pentagons.

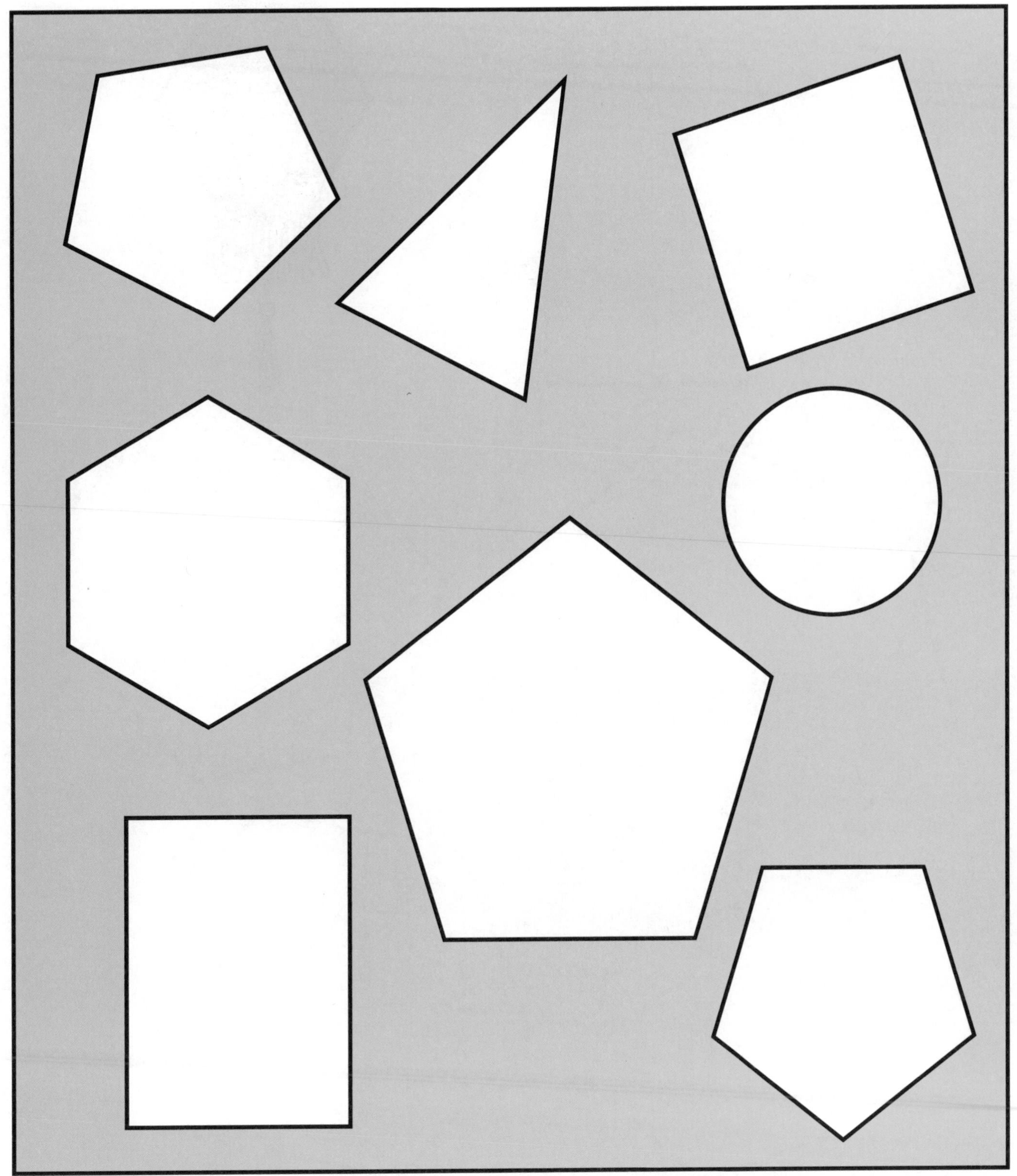

Date: ____________

Trace and color the hexagons.

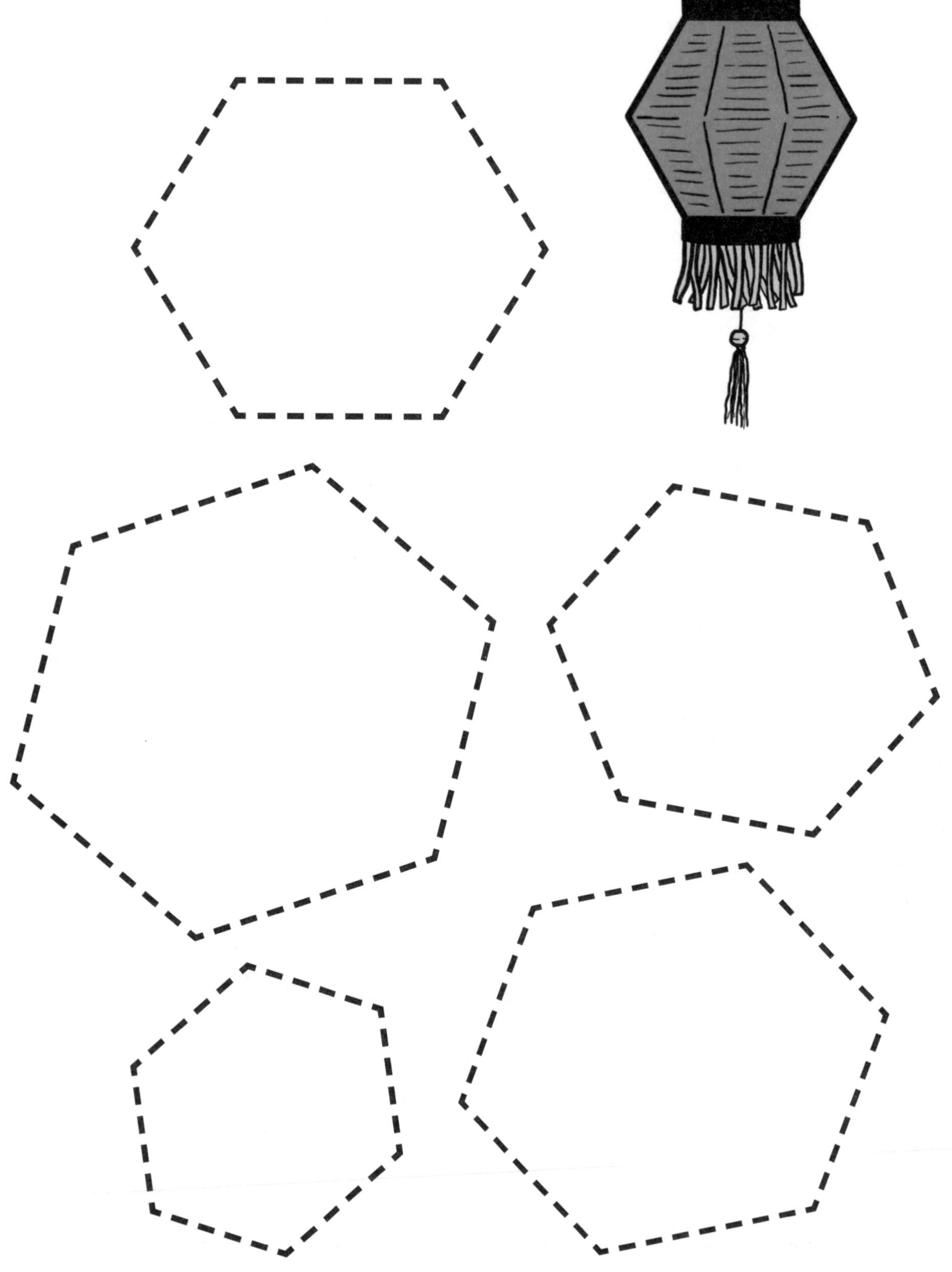

Date: ____________

Color the hexagons.

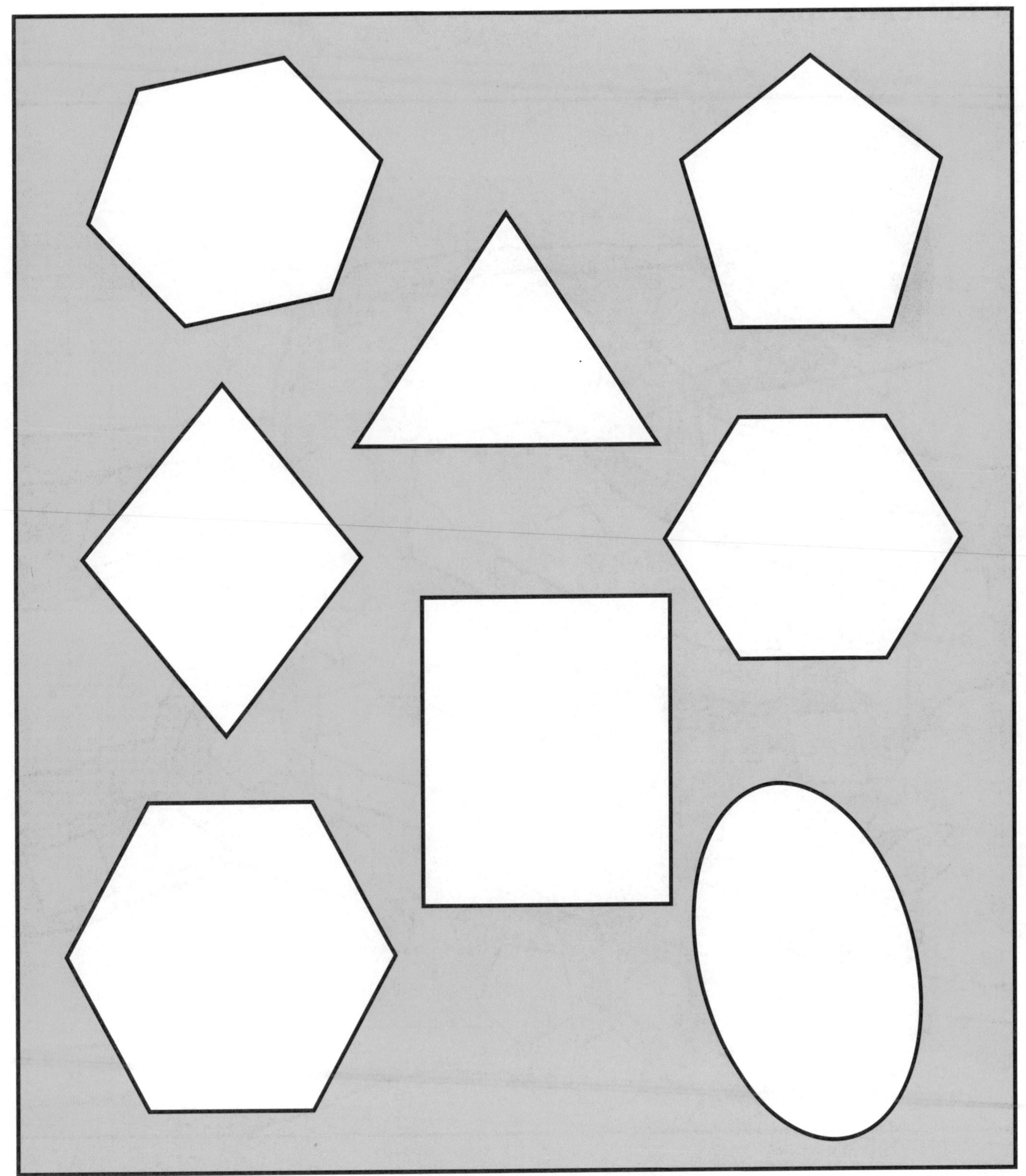

Date: ____________

Help the penguin find its food. Color all the stars, pentagons and hexagons.

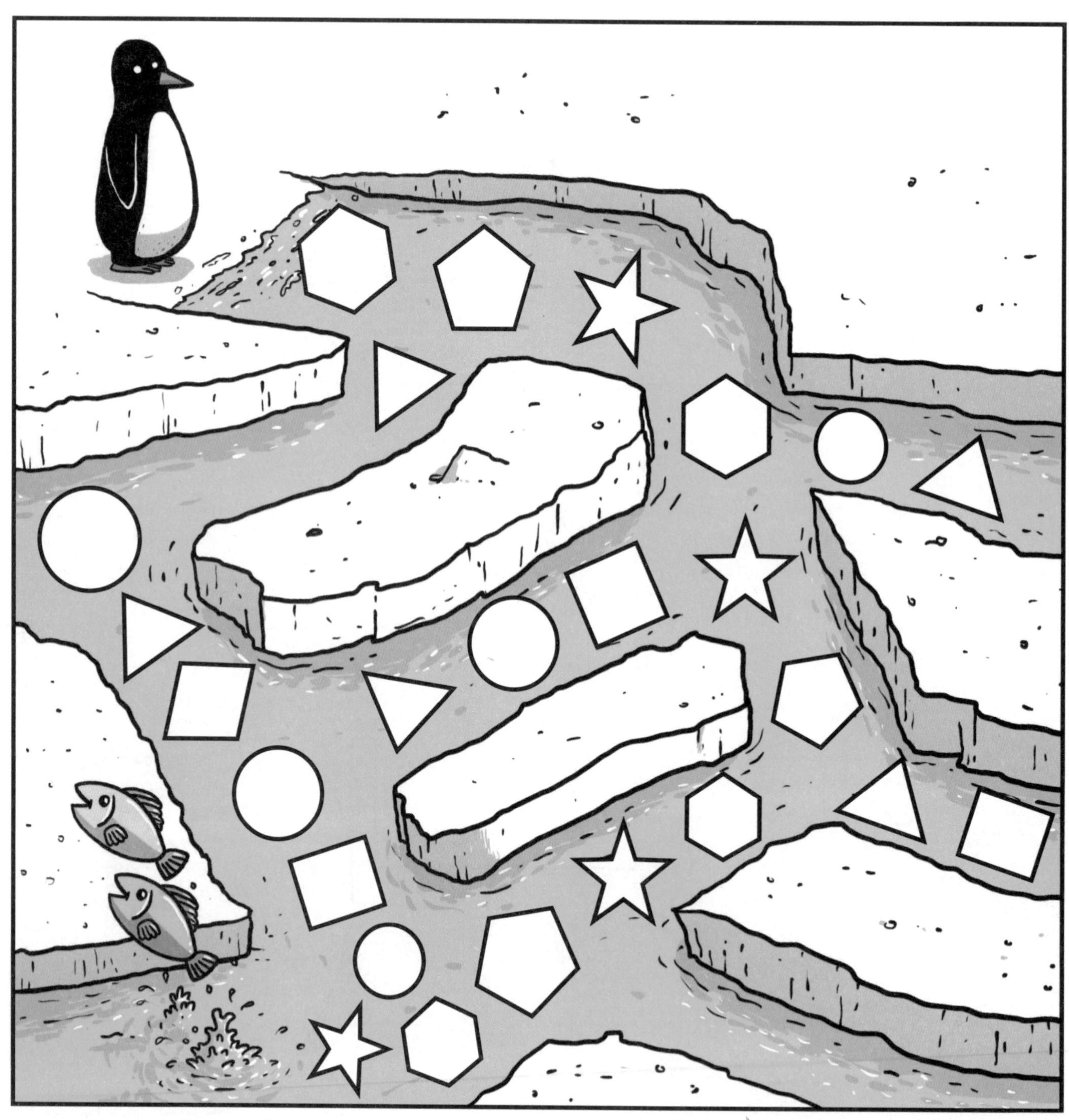

Date: ____________

Put an X on the shape that does not belong in each row.

1. 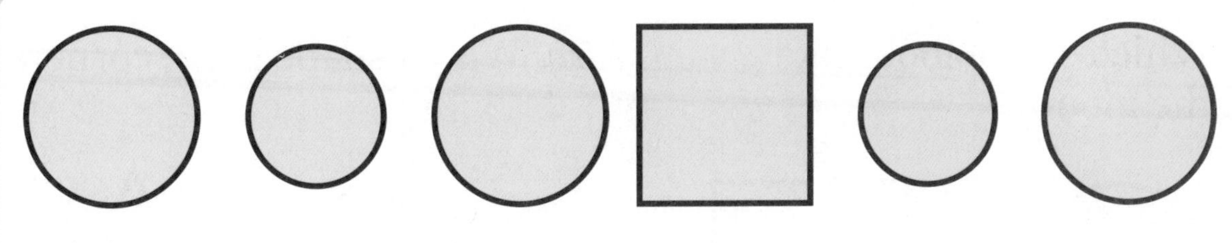

2. 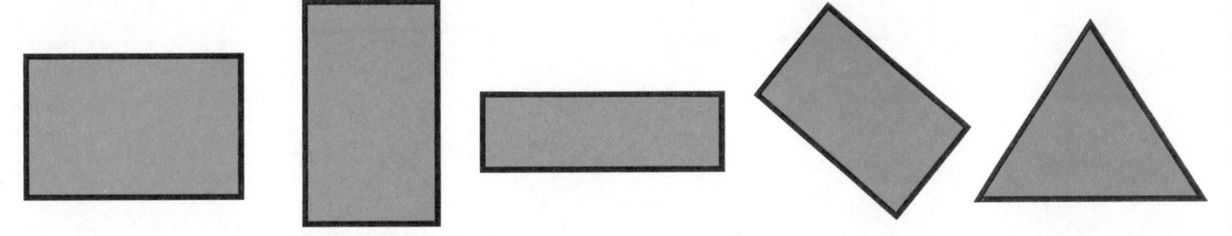

3. 

4. 

5. 

Date: ____________

Color the correct shape for each question.

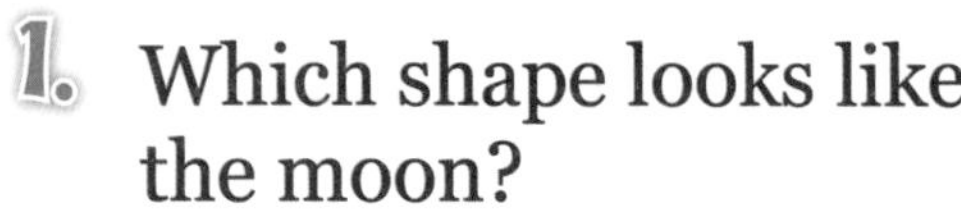

1. Which shape looks like the moon?

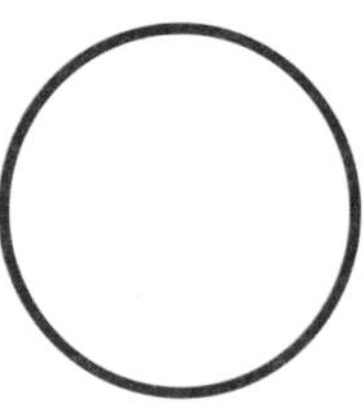

2. Which shape looks like an egg?

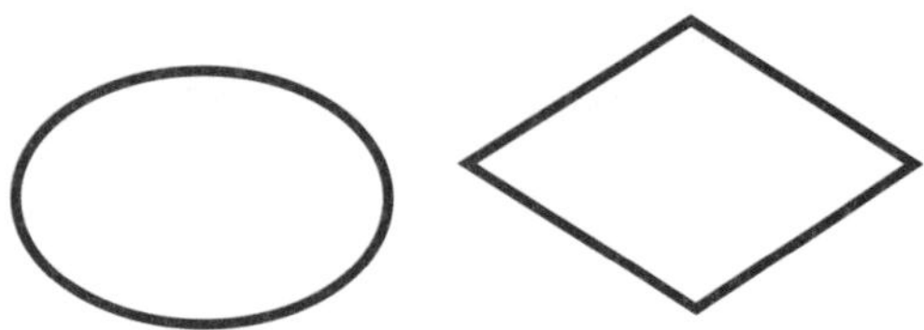

3. Which shape has 5 sharp points?

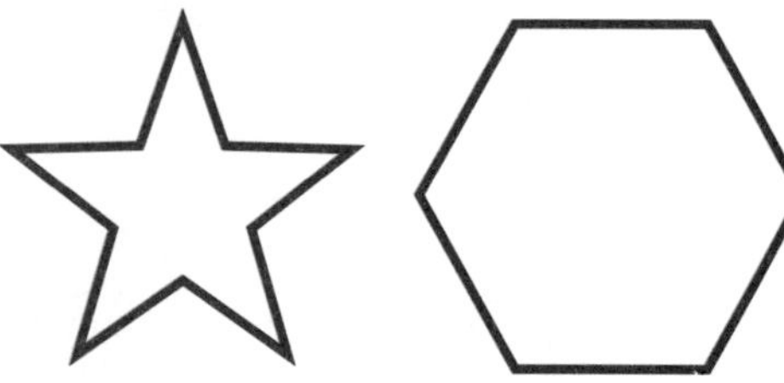

4. Which shape has 3 corners?

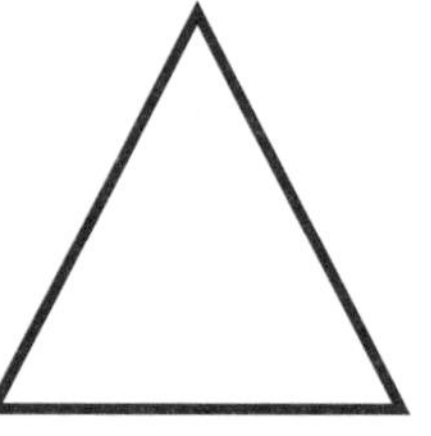

5. Which shape has 6 sides?

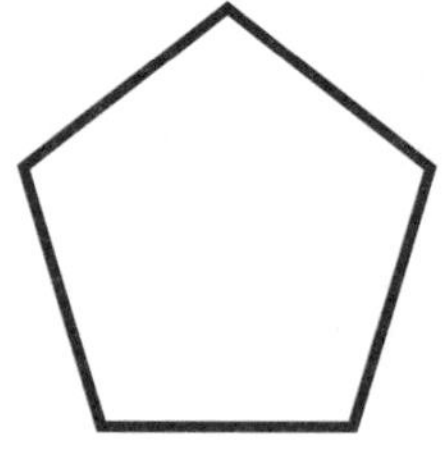
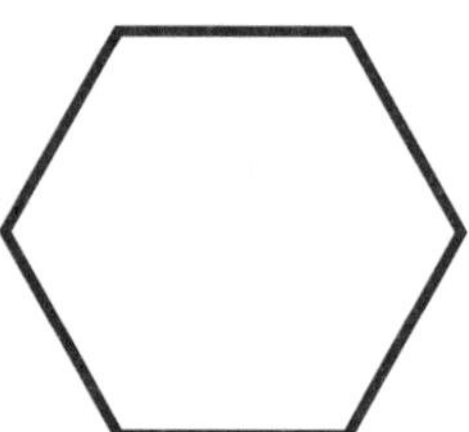

6. Which shape has 4 corners?

Date: ______________

Draw lines to match the sentences and shapes.

1. It has 4 sides and 4 corners. •

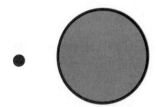

2. It has 3 sides and 3 corners. •

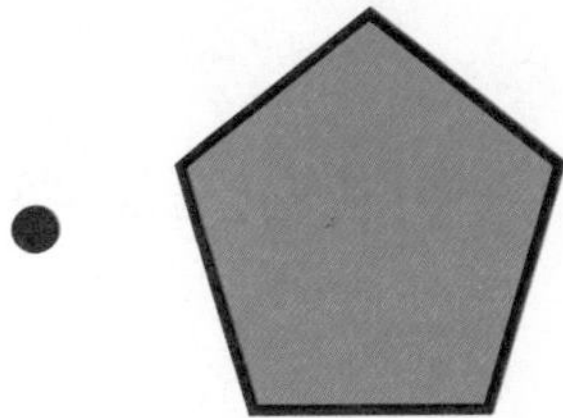

3. It has no sides and no corners. •

4. It has 5 sides and 5 corners. •

5. It has 6 sides and 6 corners. •

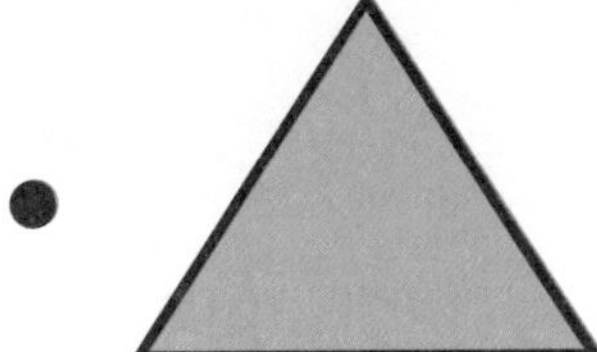

Date: __________

Draw lines to match the shapes and shape names.

1. triangle ●　　　　● 

2. circle ●　　　　● 

3. hexagon ●　　　　● 

4. oval ●　　　　● 

5. pentagon ●　　　　● 

Date: ____________

Color. ◆ = purple ⬠ = yellow ▲ = orange

▬ = green ★ = blue ⬬ = red

Date: ____________

Color. 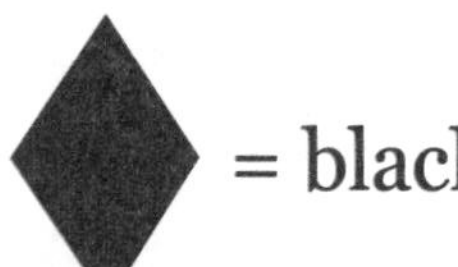 = black 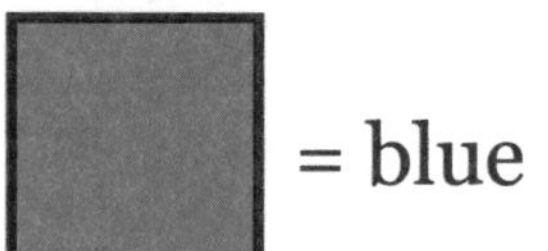 = blue 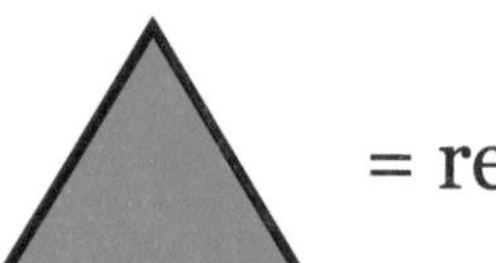 = red

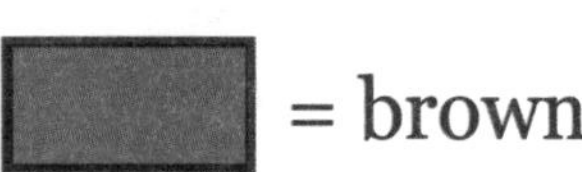 = brown = green 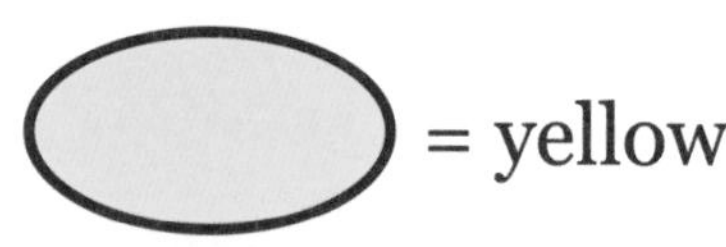 = yellow

= orange 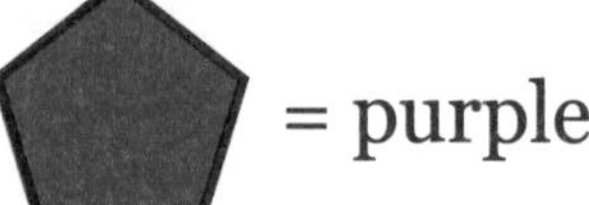 = purple 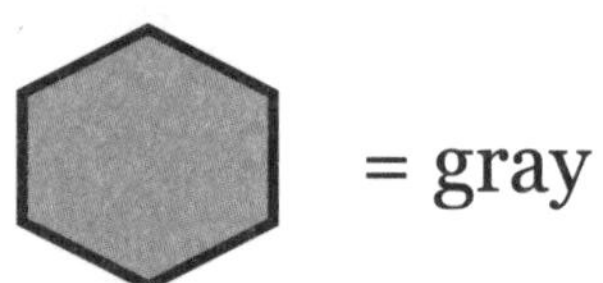 = gray

Date: ____________

Draw the correct shape in each circle to match the shapes on each shelf.

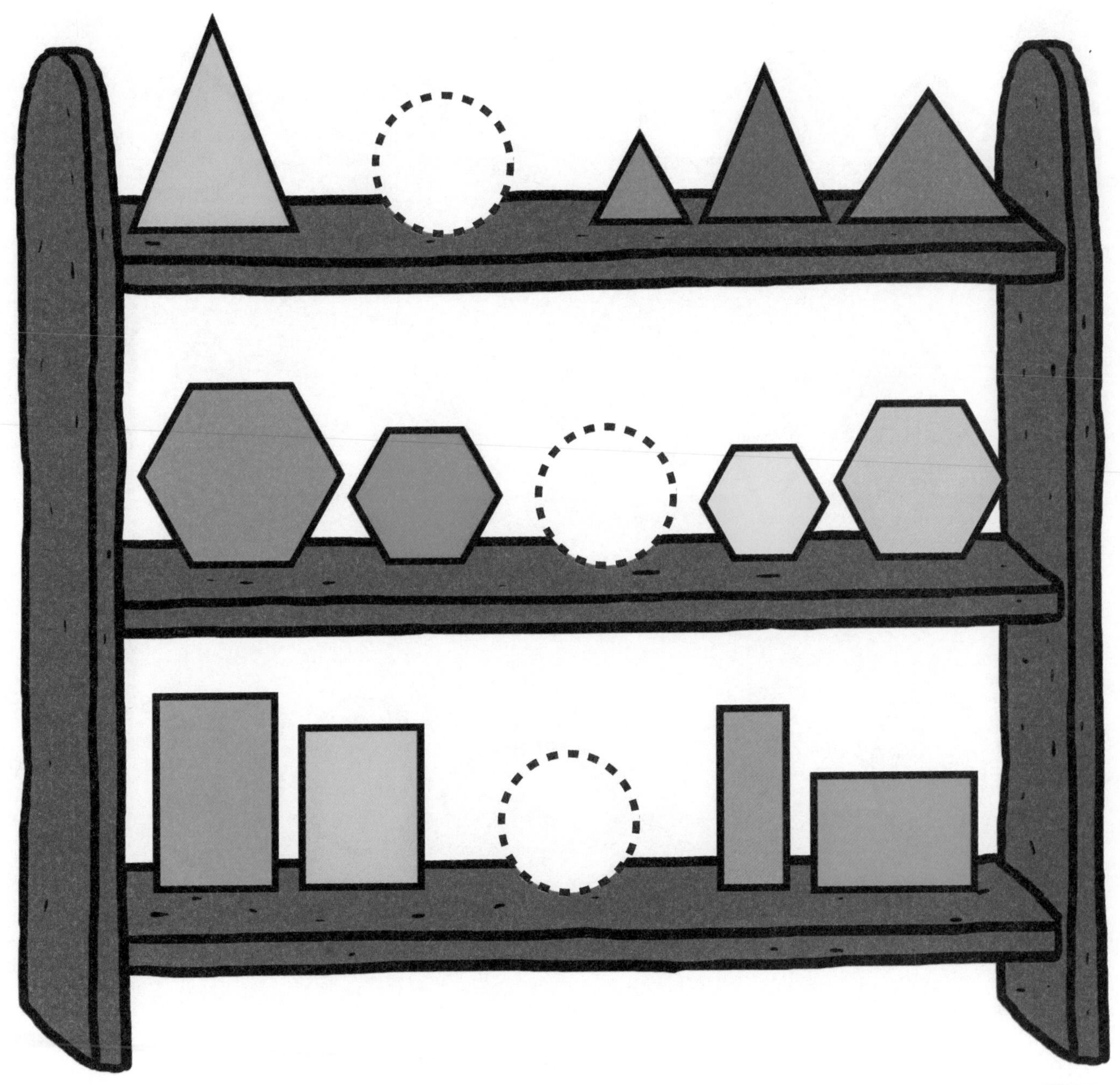

Date: ____________

Draw the correct shape in each circle to match the shapes on each shelf.

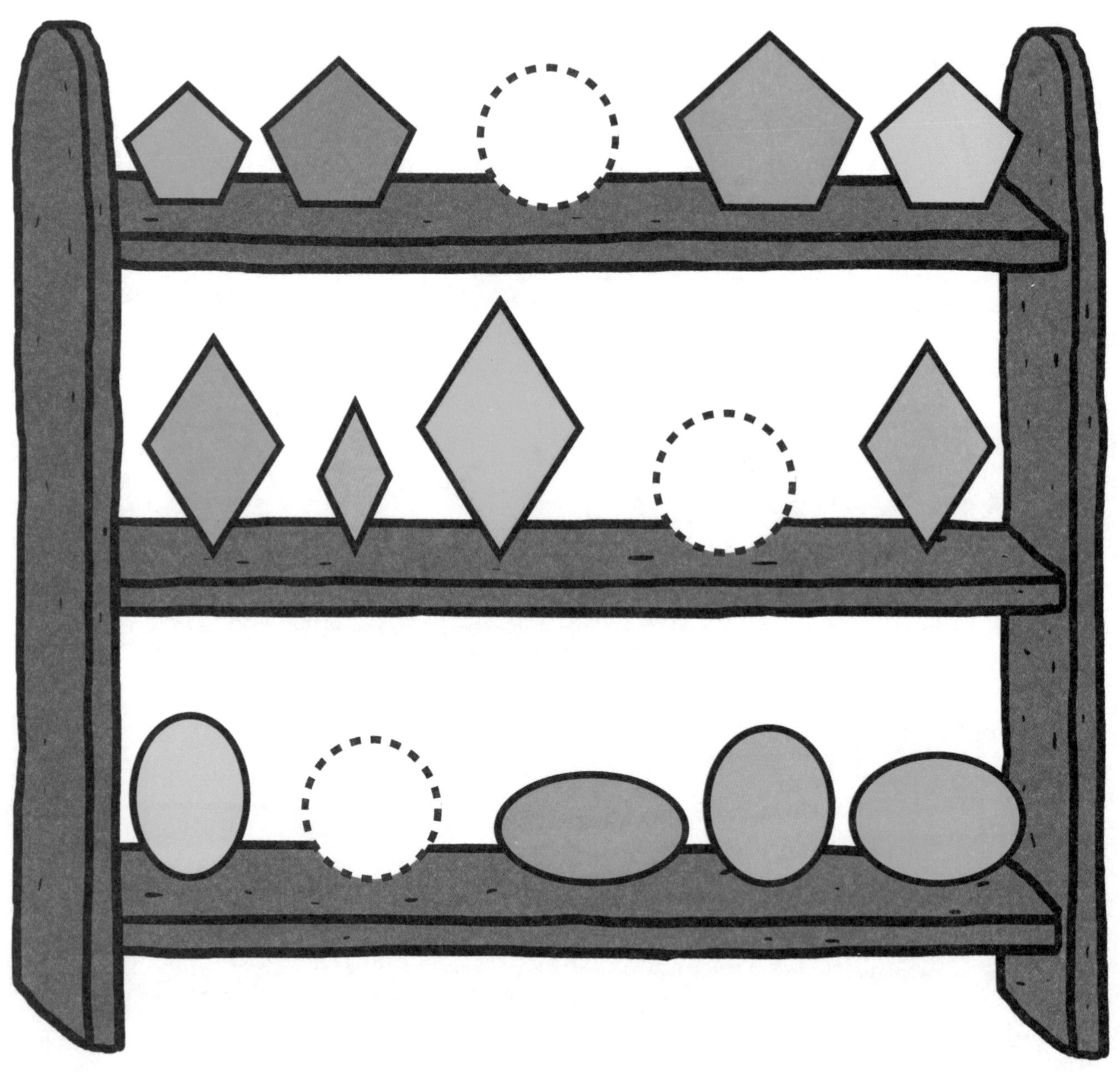

Date: ____________

Draw the correct shape on each tray.

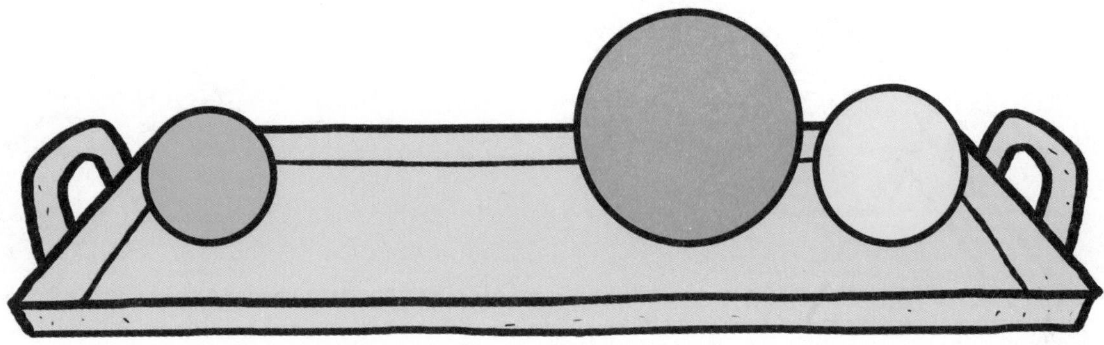

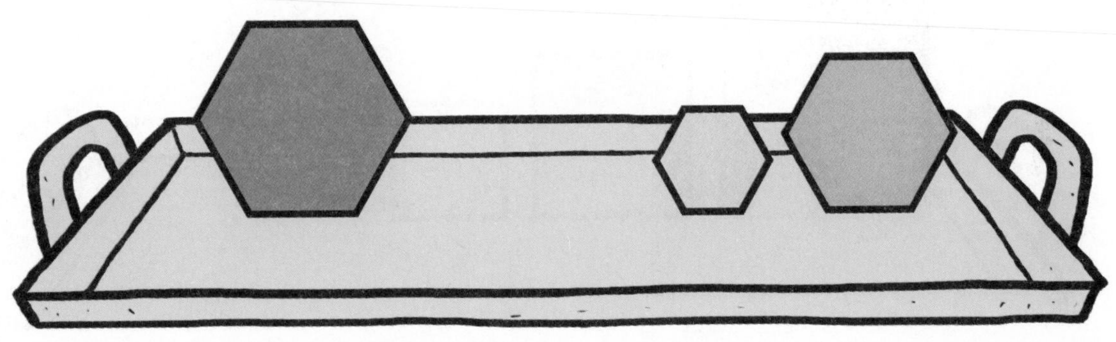

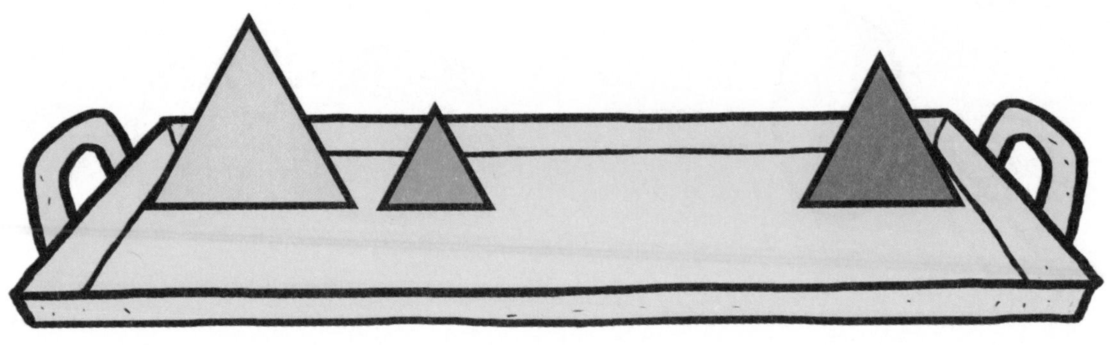

Date: ____________

Draw the correct shape on each tray.

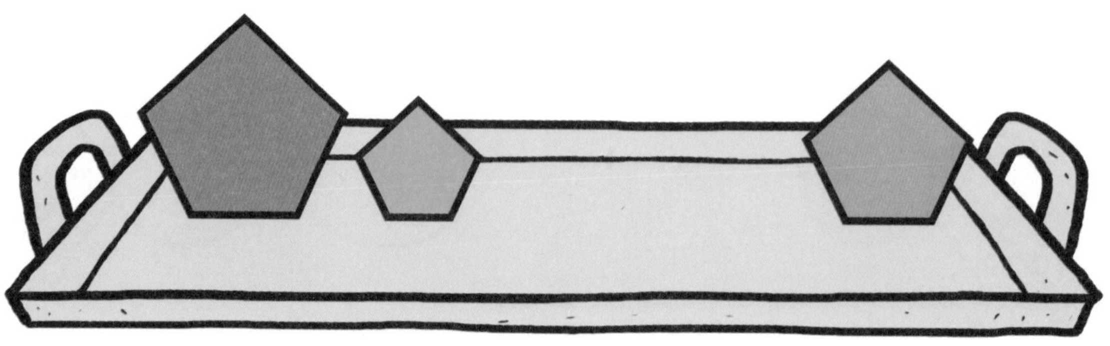

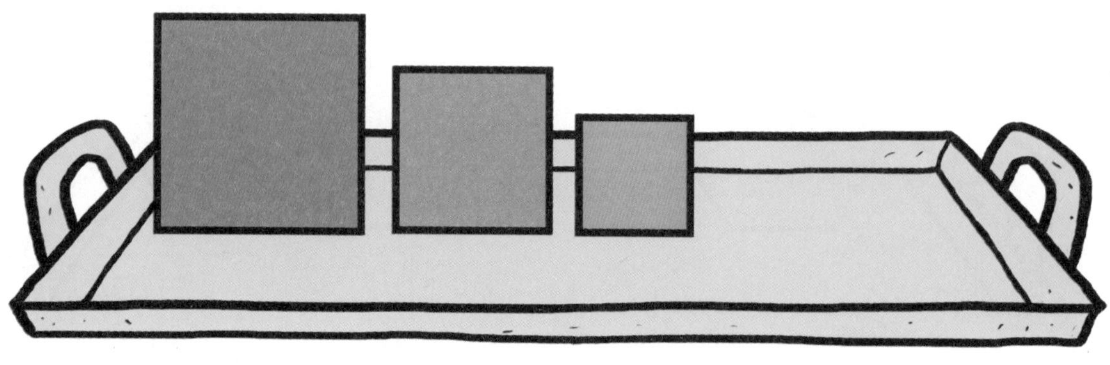

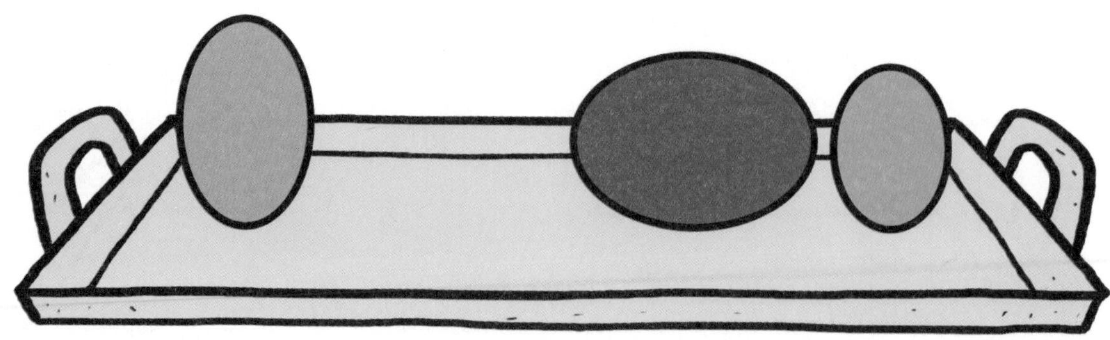

Date: ____________

1. **Trace** the dotted line in the shape to form two triangles.

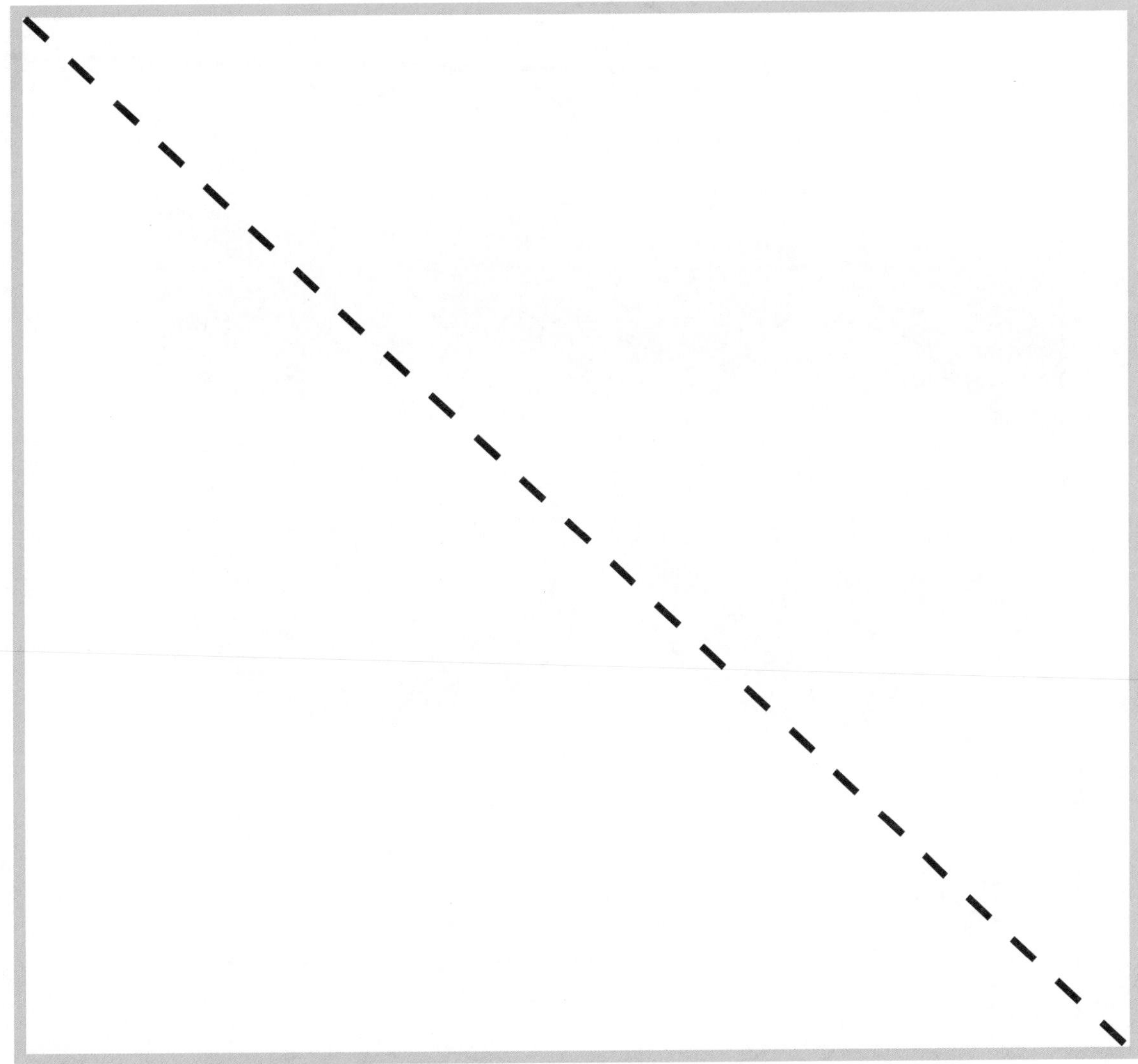

2. **Color** one of the triangles red.

3. **Draw** a line in the white triangle to make 2 smaller white triangles.

4. **Color** one of the smaller white triangles blue.

Date: ____________

Trace and color the shapes to make the two pictures look the same.

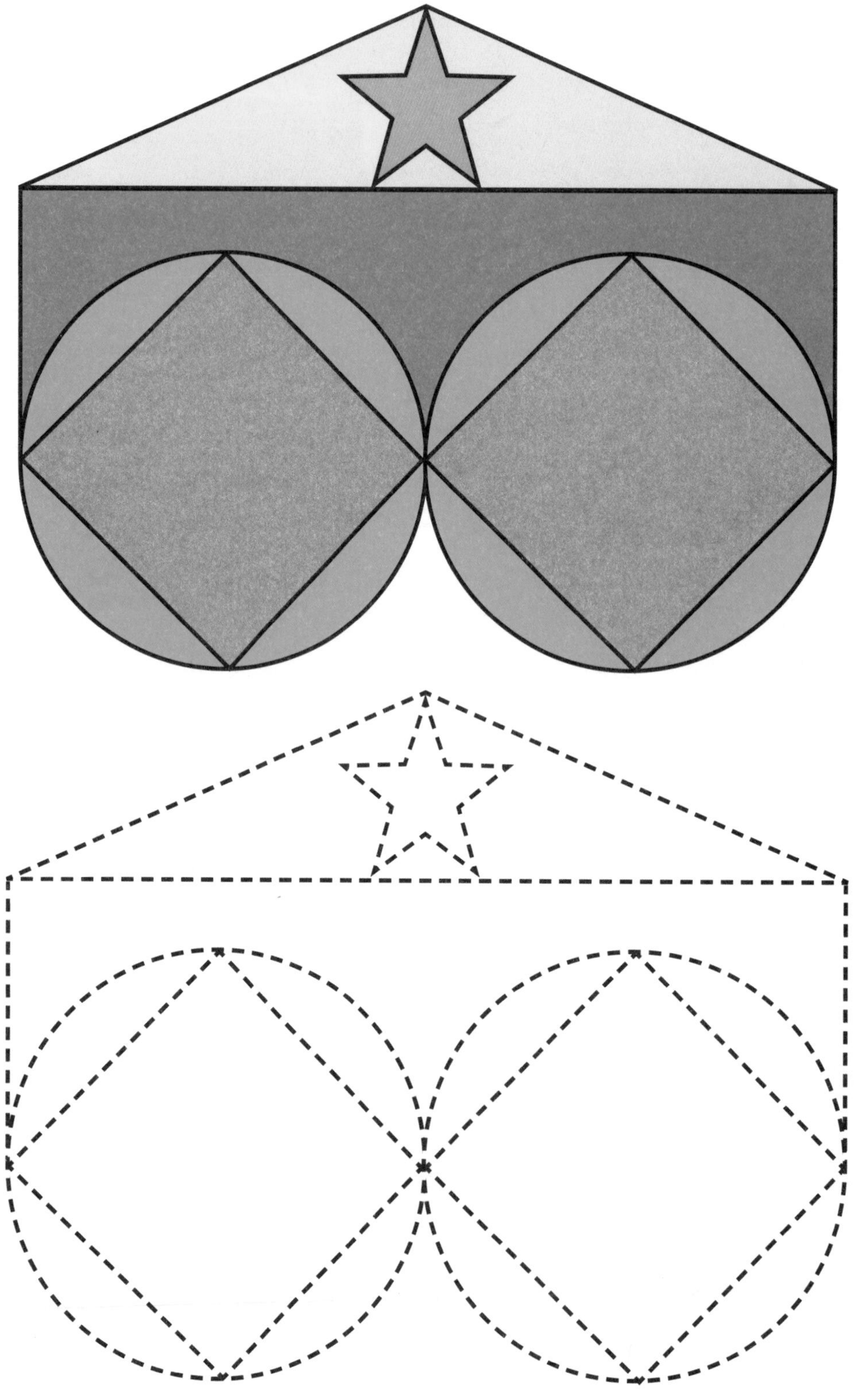

Date: ______________

Trace and color the shapes to make the two pictures look the same.

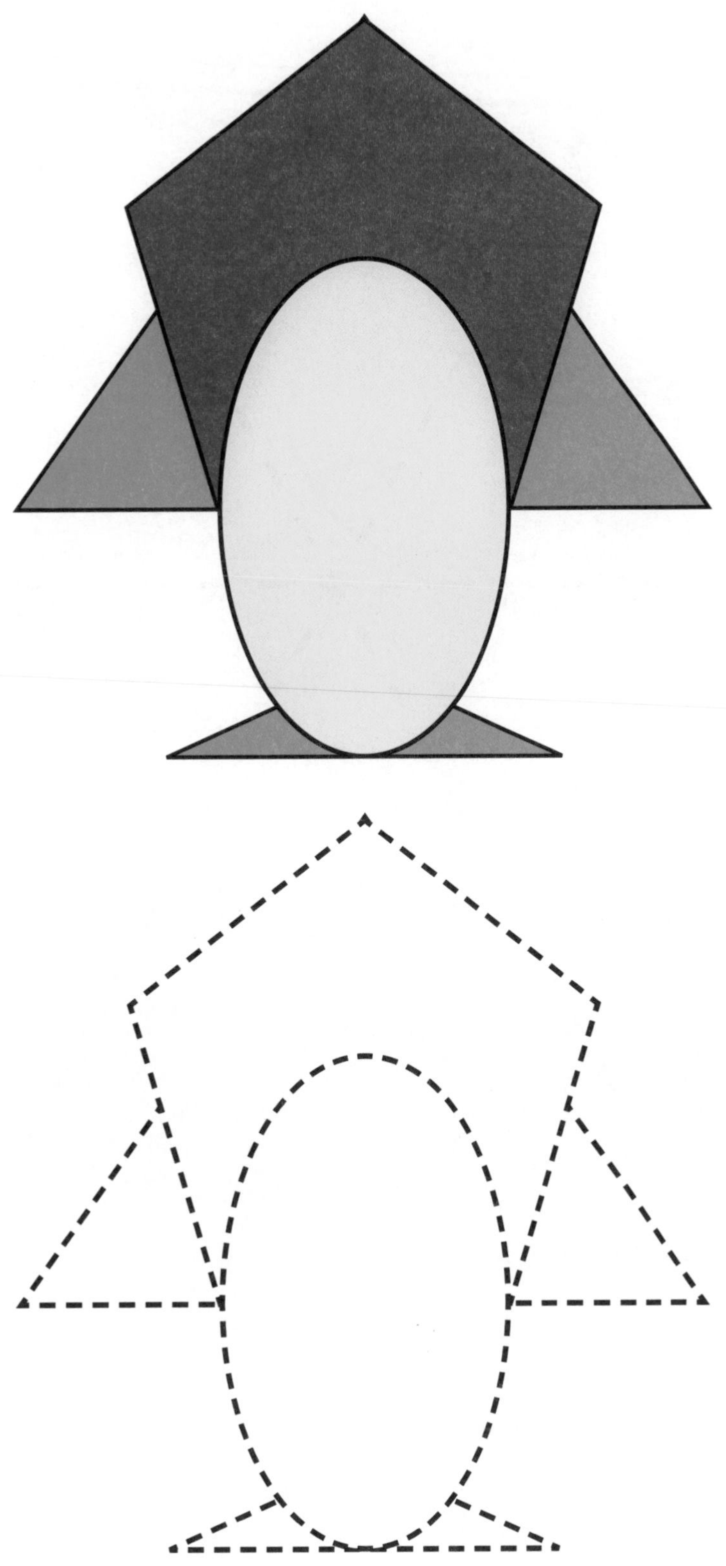

Date: ____________

1. **Trace** the dotted line in the shape to form triangles.

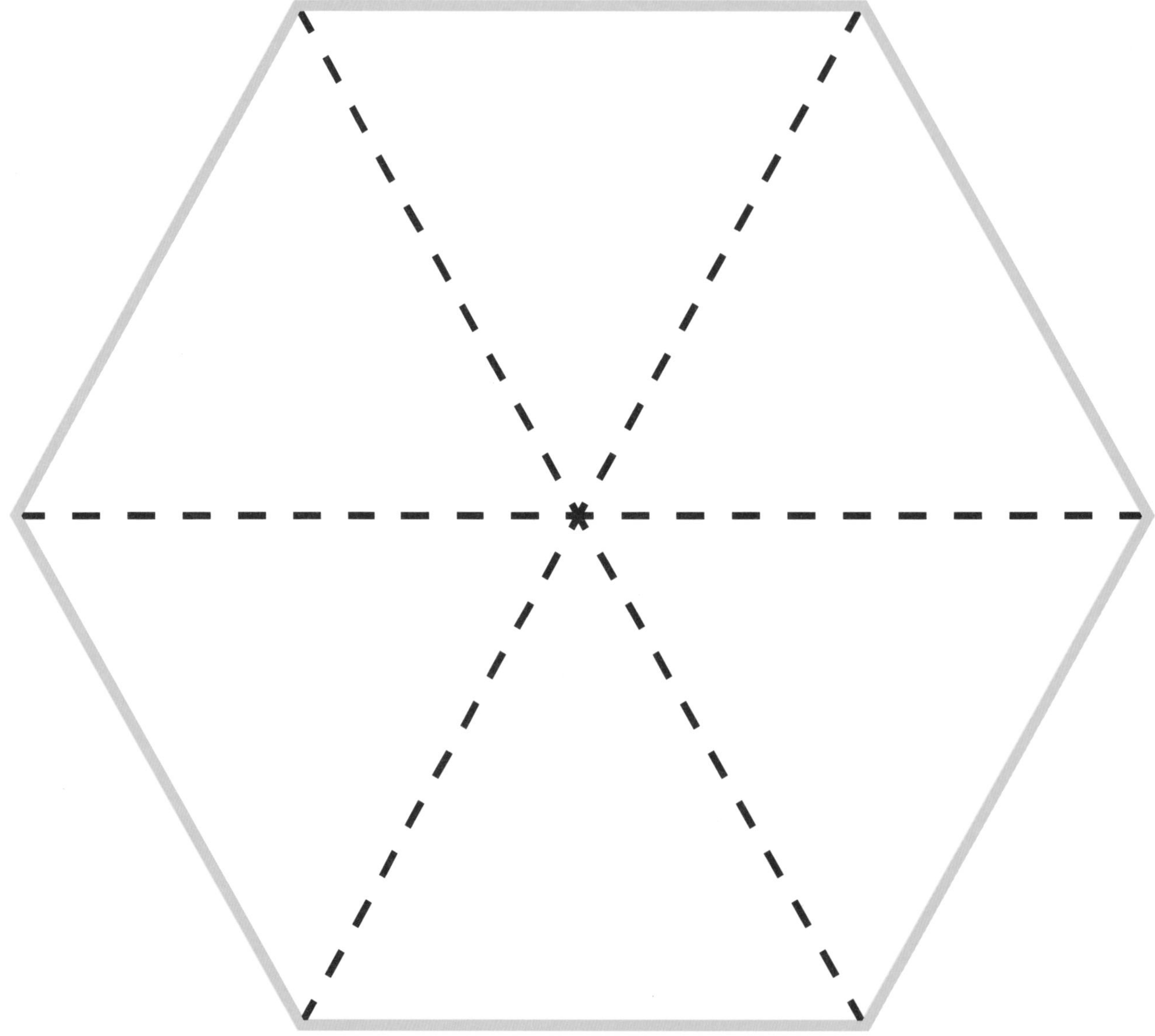

2. How many triangles are formed? ☐

3. **Color** two triangles yellow to form a diamond shape.

4. **Color** two triangles green to form a diamond shape.

Date: ____________

Color the small circles red.
Color the big square blue.
Color the largest triangle green.
Color the small stars yellow.
Color the rectangles orange.

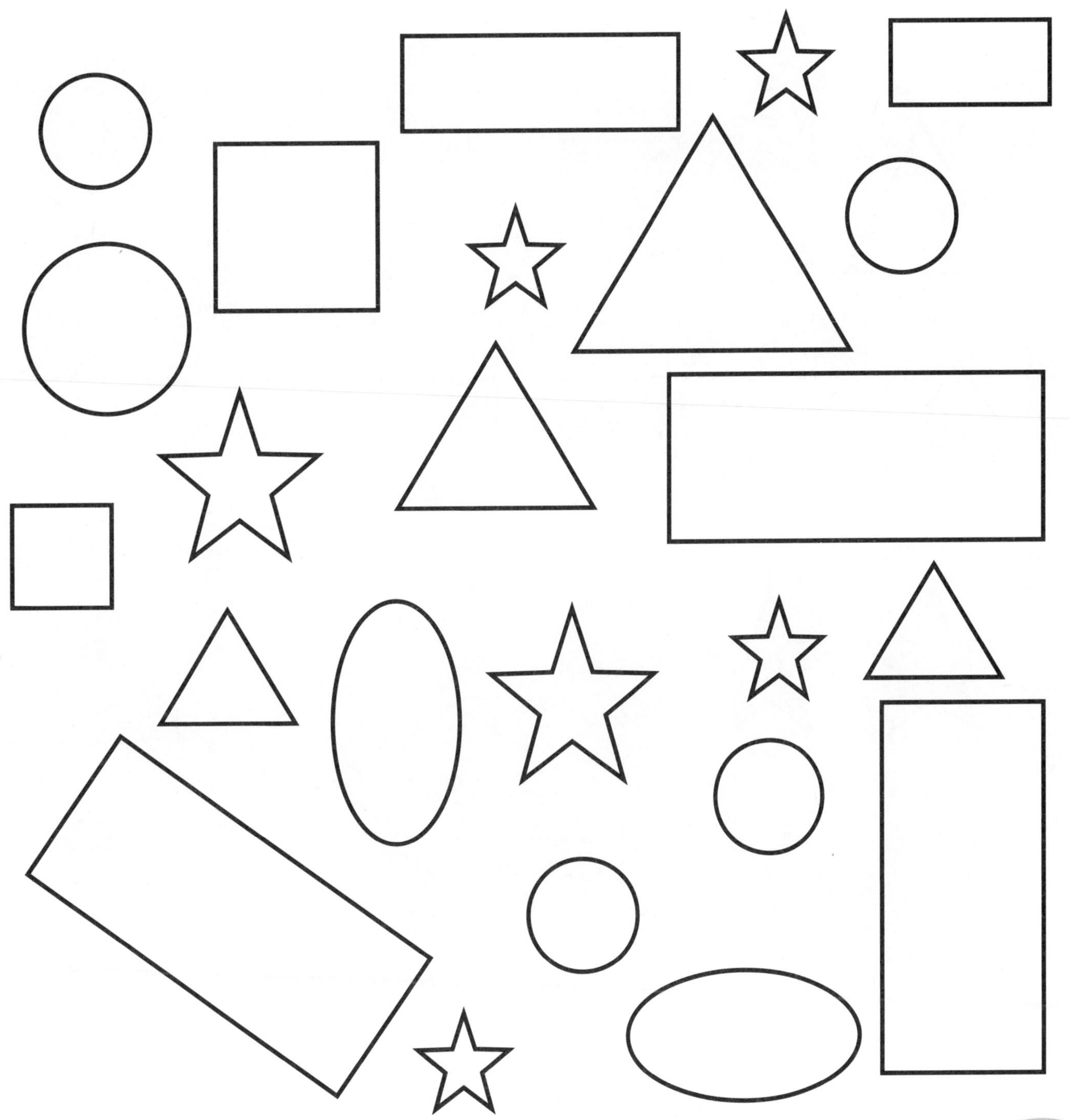

Date: ___________

Draw a line to the shape that comes next.

1. 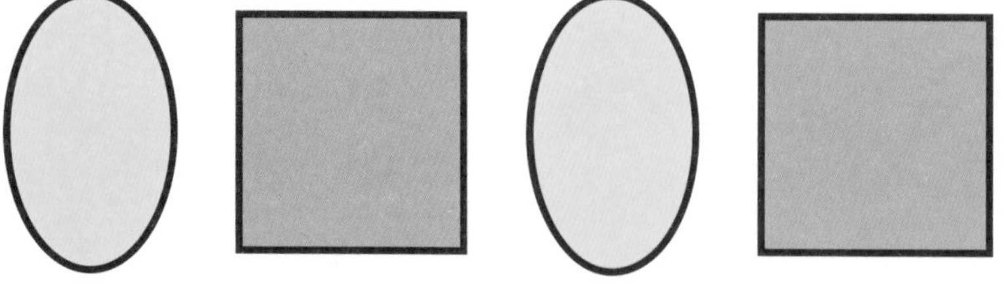

2. 

3. 

4.

5. 

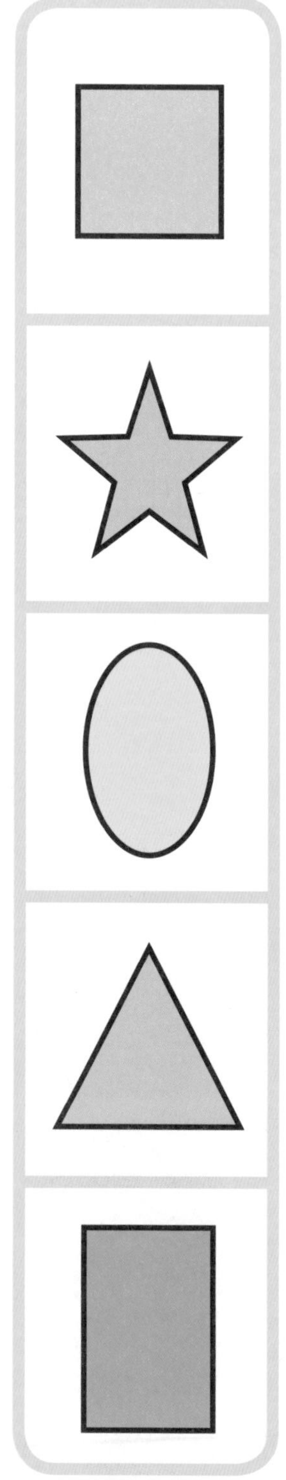

Date: ____________

Draw a line to the shape that comes next.

1. 

2. 

3. 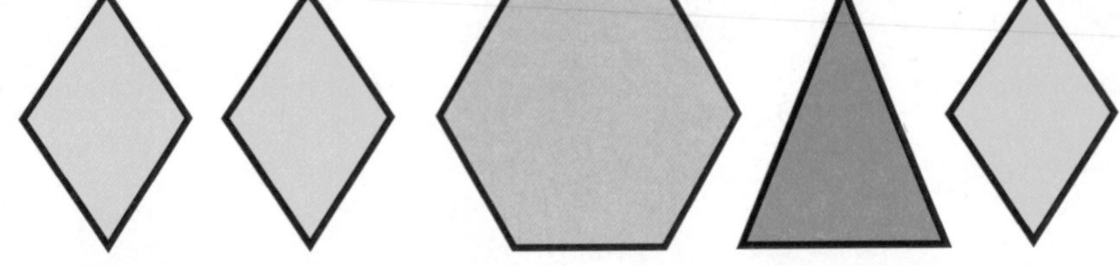

4. 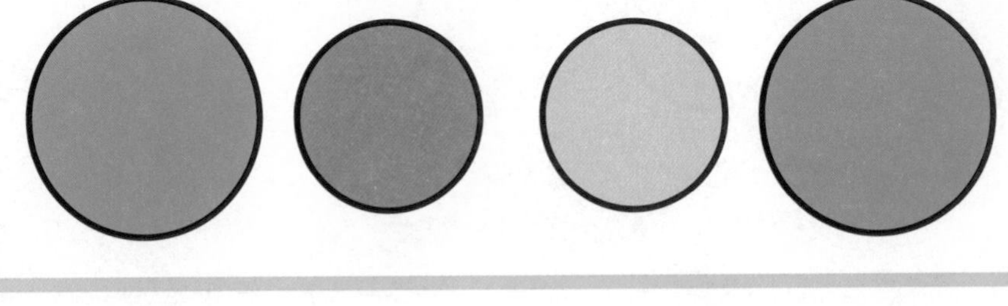

5. 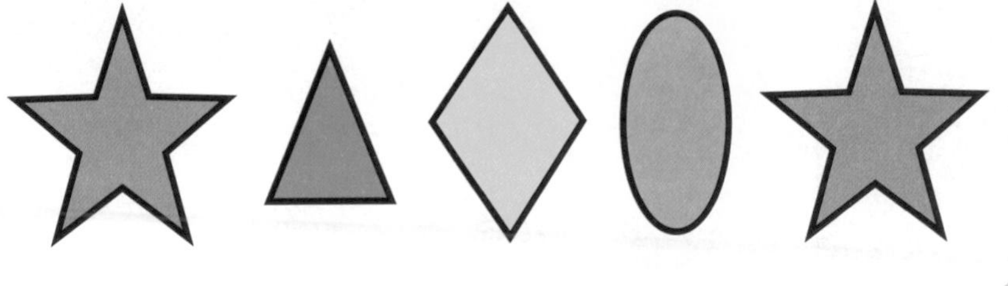

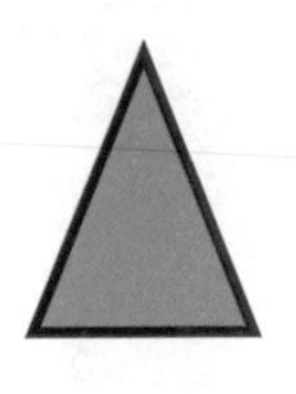

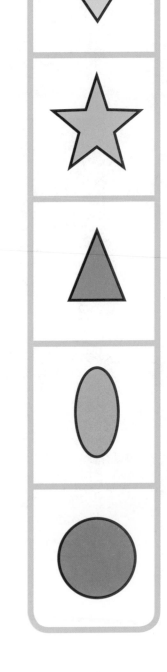

Date: ____________

Draw what comes next in the box at the end of each row.

1. 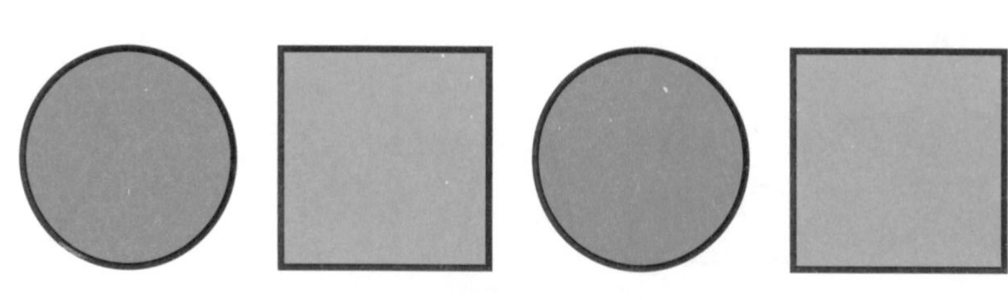

2. 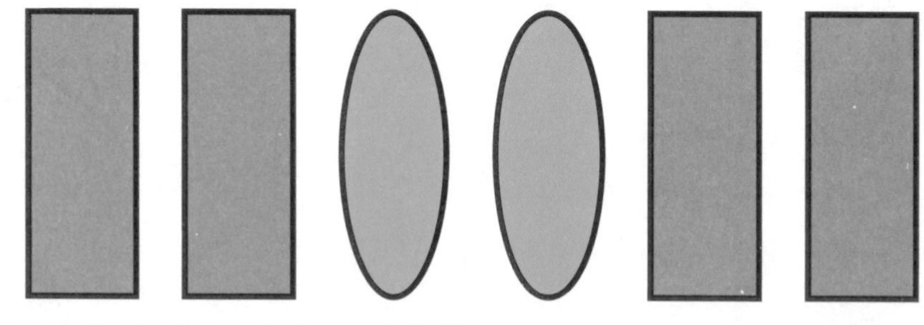

3. 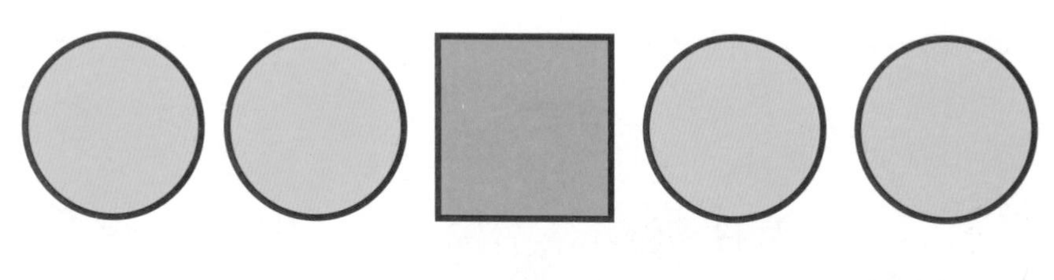

4. 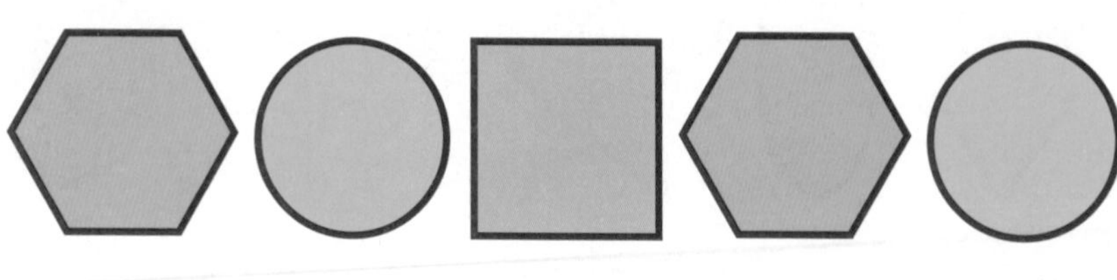

Date: ________________

Draw what comes next in the box at the end of each row.

1.

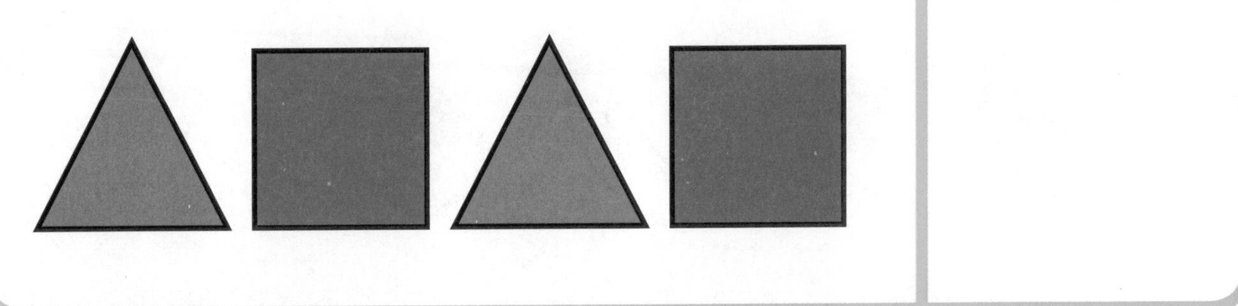

2.

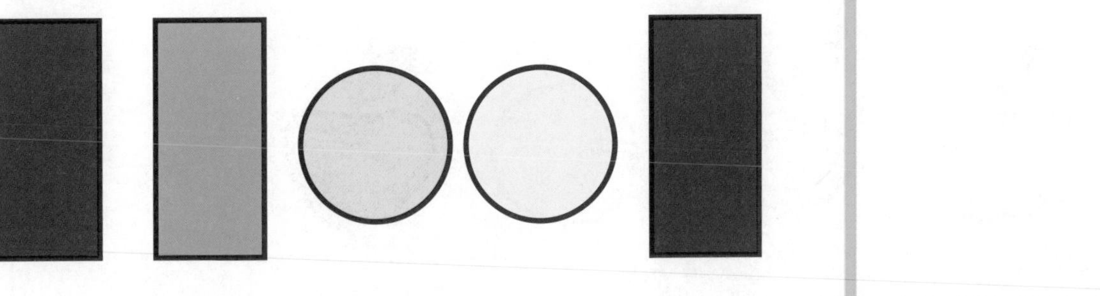

3.

4.

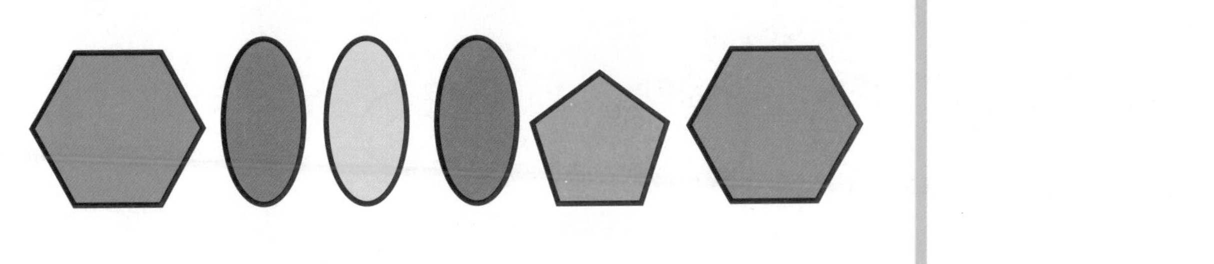

Date: ____________

Draw what comes next in the box at the end of each row.

1.    

2.   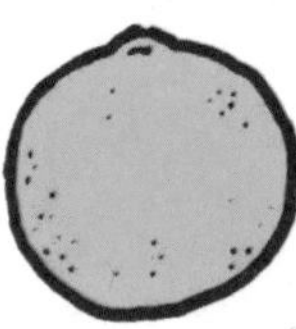 

3. 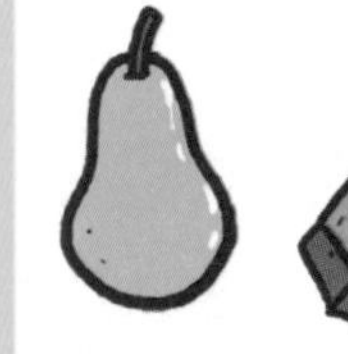    

4.    

Date: ____________

Draw the missing fruit to complete the pattern.

1. 

2. 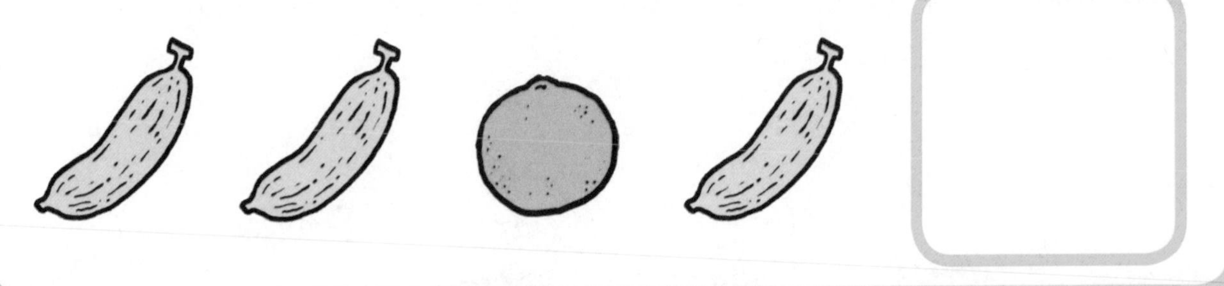

3. 

4. 

Date: ____________

Look at the pictures. Write the number of the correct vehicle to complete the pattern.

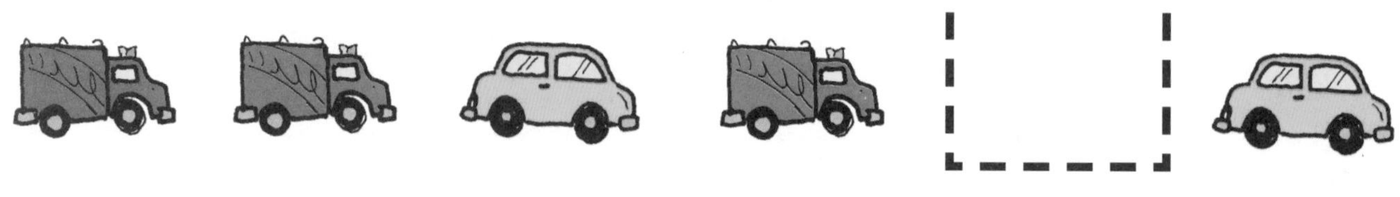

Date: ____________

Color the last vehicle in each row to complete the pattern.

1.     

2. 

3.     

4.     

Date: ____________

Look at the pictures. Write the number of the correct insect to complete the pattern.

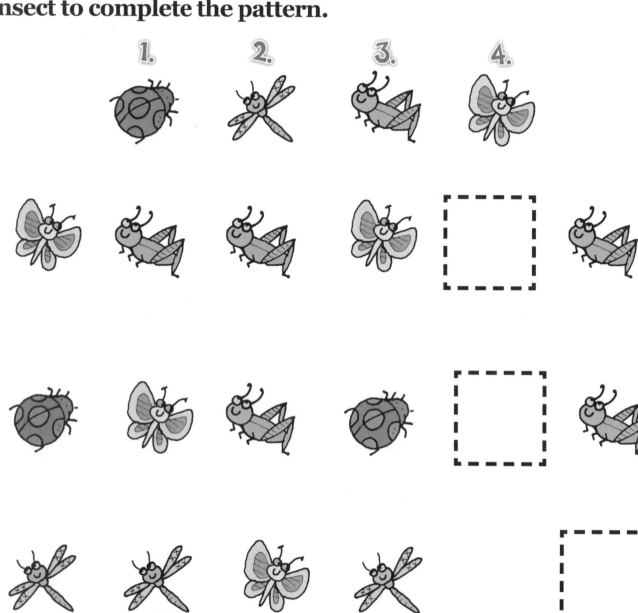

1. 2. 3. 4.

Date: ____________

Color the last insect in each row to complete the pattern.

1. 

2. 

3. 

4. 

Date: ____________

Draw lines to match the flowers that complete the patterns.

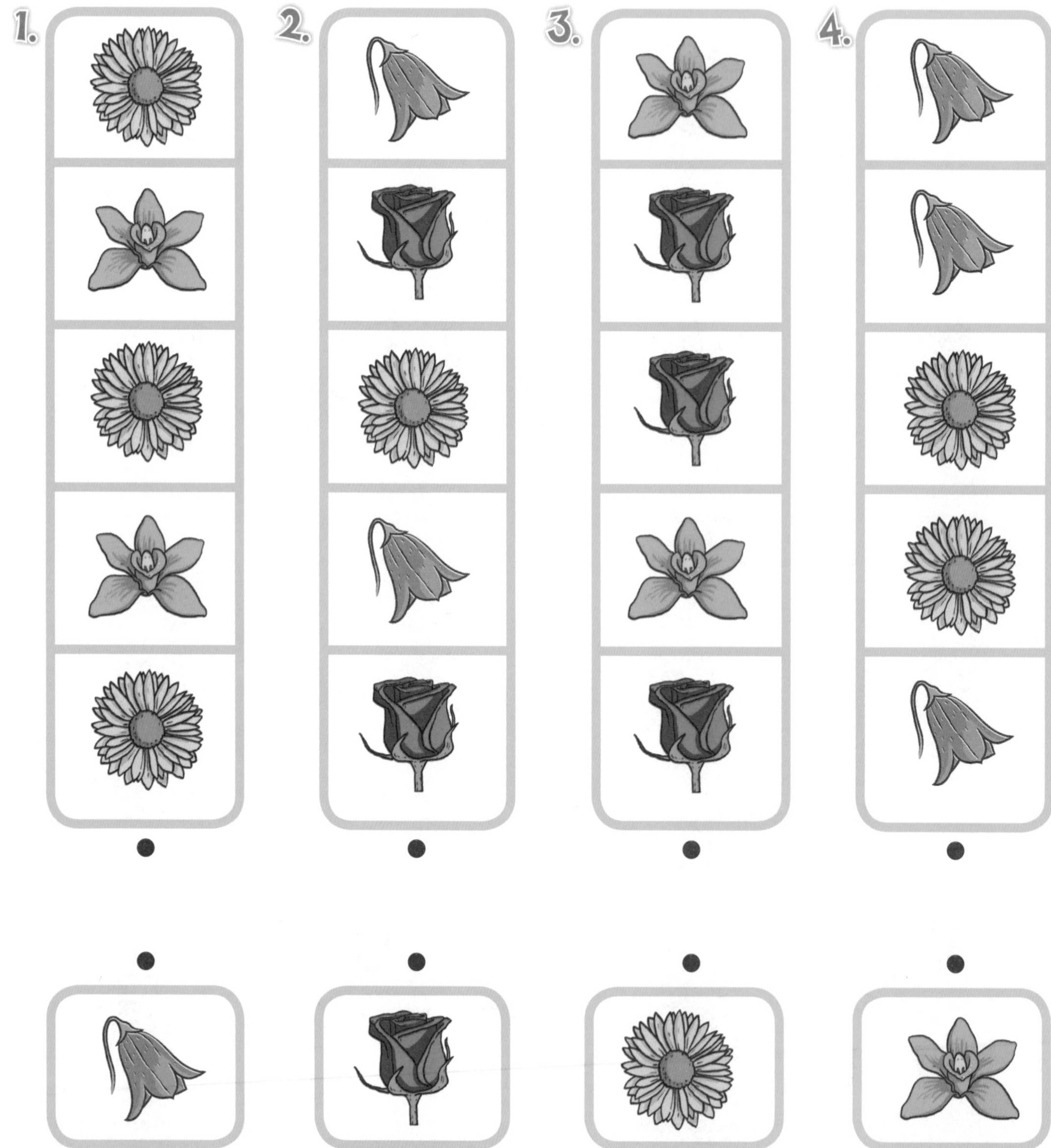

Date: ____________

Color the flower at the end of each row that completes the pattern.

1. 

2. 

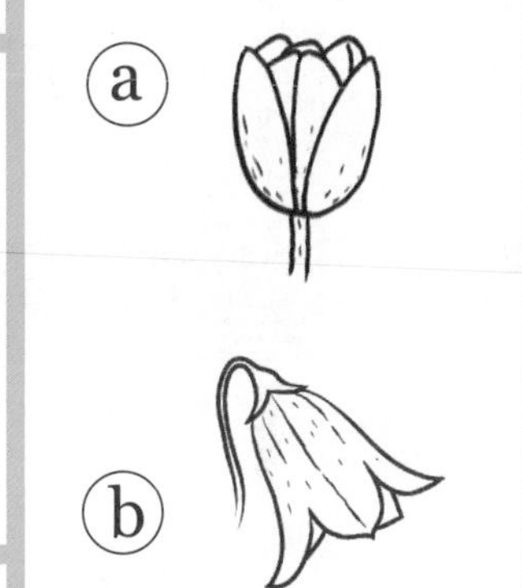

3. 

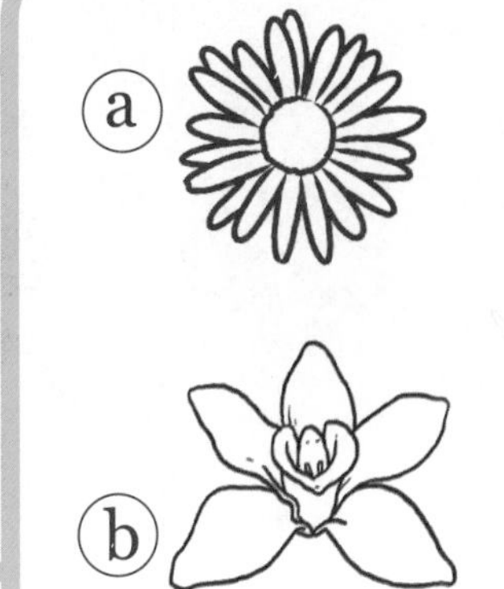

Date: ____________

Color the leaf at the end of each row that completes the pattern.

1\. 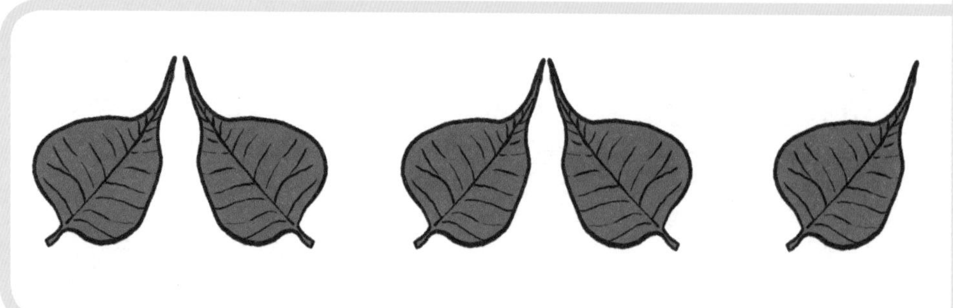

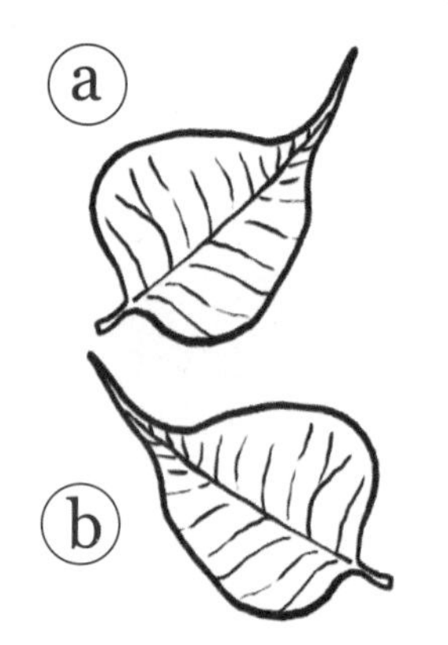

2\. 

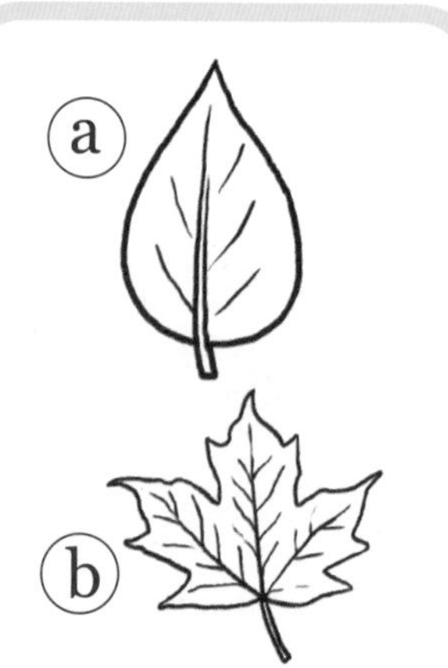

3\. 

a 

b 

Date: ____________

Draw lines to match the correct leaf in each row to complete the pattern.

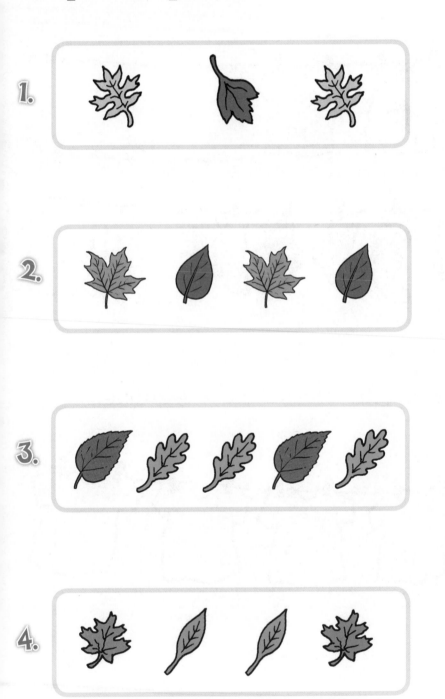

1.

2.

3.

4.

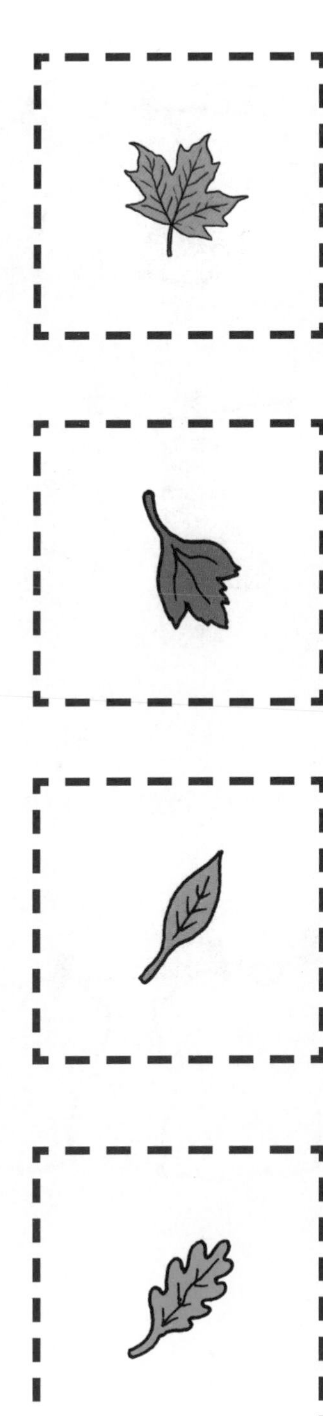

Date: ____________

Draw the correct object to complete each pattern.

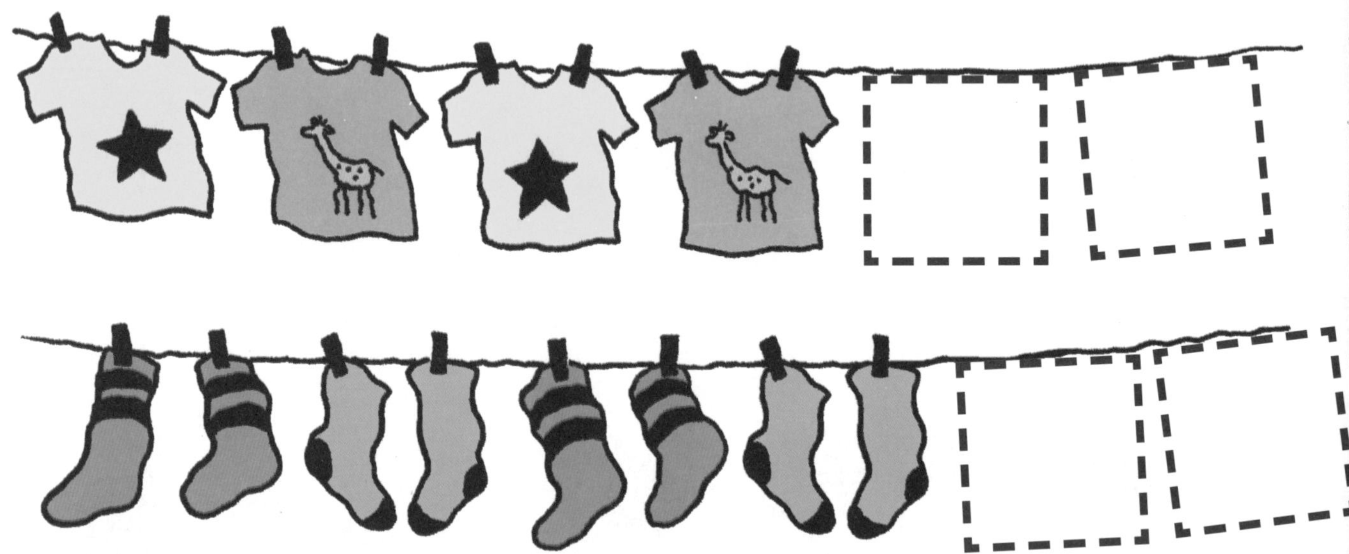

Draw and color your own patterns on these T-shirts.

Date: ____________

Continue labeling each pattern.

1.    

A B A B 

2.    

A A B A 

3. 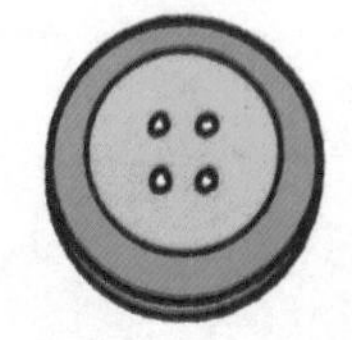   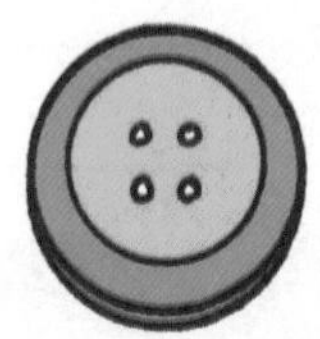 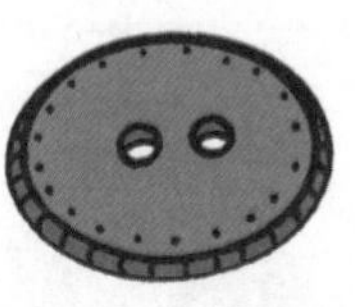

A B C A 

Look at each pattern. What kind of pattern is it? Circle the answer.

4. 

AAB AB

5.     

ABC ABB

Date: ____________

These shapes are making a pattern on the frame of a picture. Draw and color the missing shapes.

Date: ____________

These shapes make a pattern on the frame of a mirror. Draw and color the missing shapes.

Date: ____________

Look at the pattern. Color the other squares to continue the pattern.

Date: __________

Look at the pattern. Draw and color the shapes to continue the pattern.

Date: ____________

Look at the pattern. Circle the correct pair of squares that completes the pattern.

(a)

(b)

(c)

Date: ____________

Look at the pattern. Circle the correct pair of squares that completes the pattern.

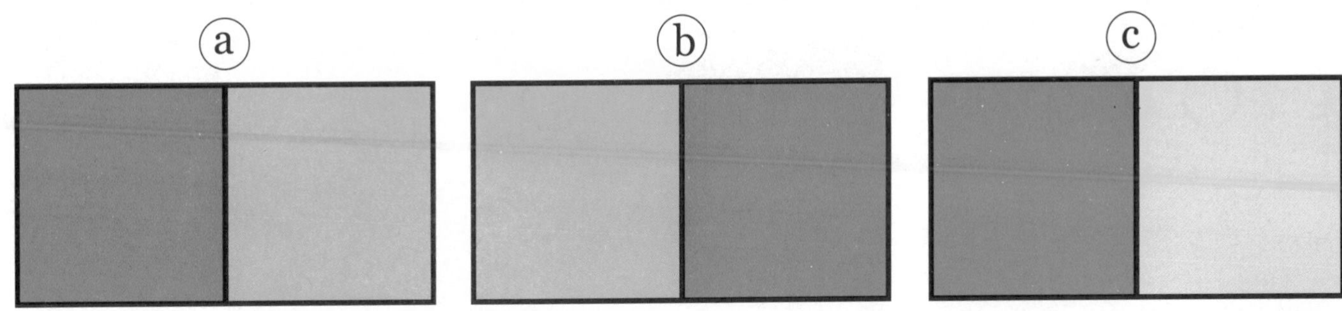

Color the bubble next to the correct answer.

1. How many sides does a square have?

○ **A** 1

○ **B** 2

○ **C** 3

○ **D** 4

2. How many sides does a hexagon have?

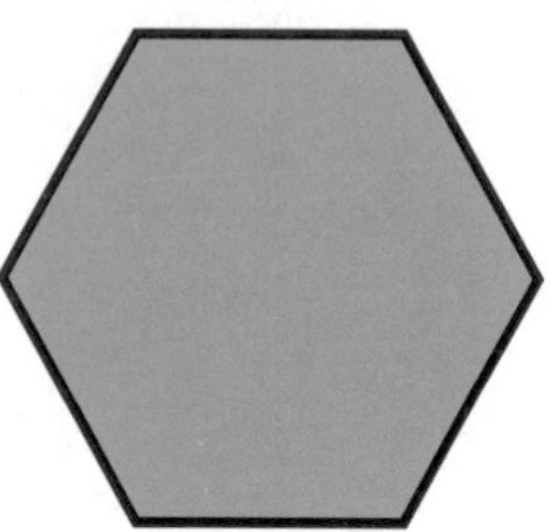

○ **A** 6

○ **B** 5

○ **C** 4

○ **D** 3

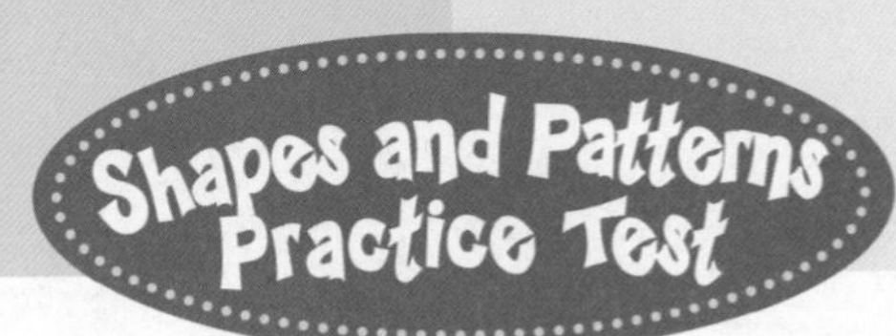
Shapes and Patterns
Practice Test

Color the bubble next to the correct answer.

3. Which shape comes next in the pattern?

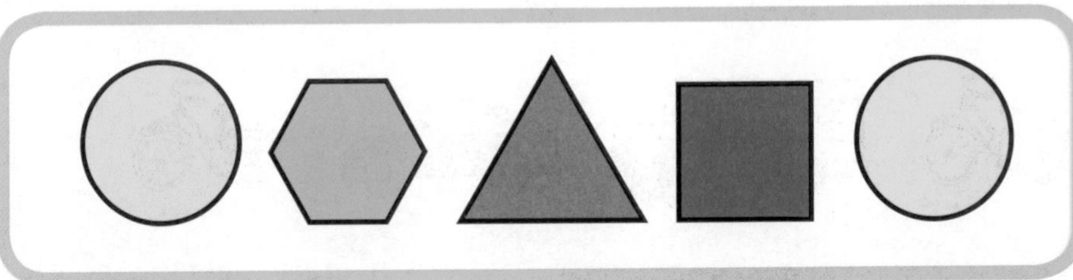

- ◯ **A** circle
- ◯ **B** hexagon
- ◯ **C** triangle
- ◯ **D** square

4. Which shape comes next in the pattern?

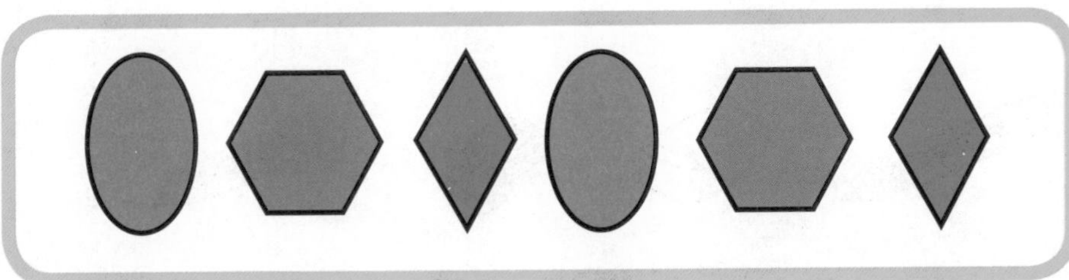

- ◯ **A** oval
- ◯ **B** hexagon
- ◯ **C** diamond
- ◯ **D** circle

Color the bubble next to the correct answer.

5. Which object comes next in the pattern?

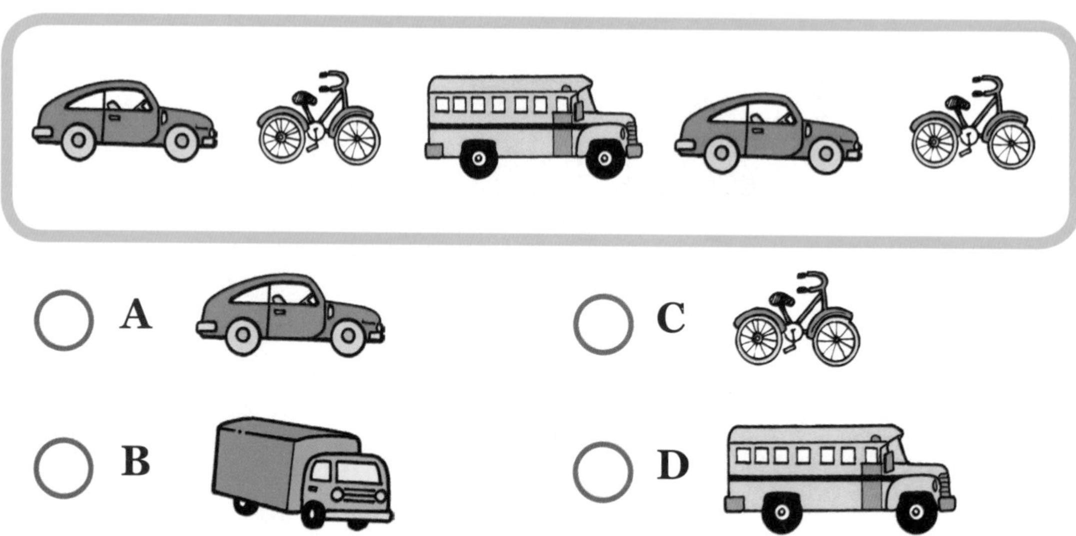

6. Which object comes next in the pattern?

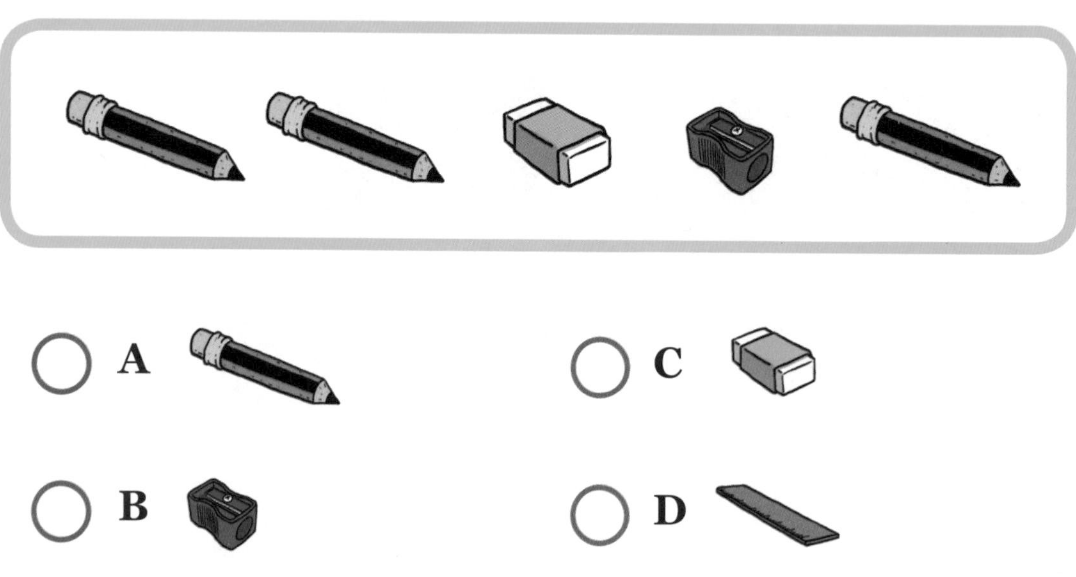

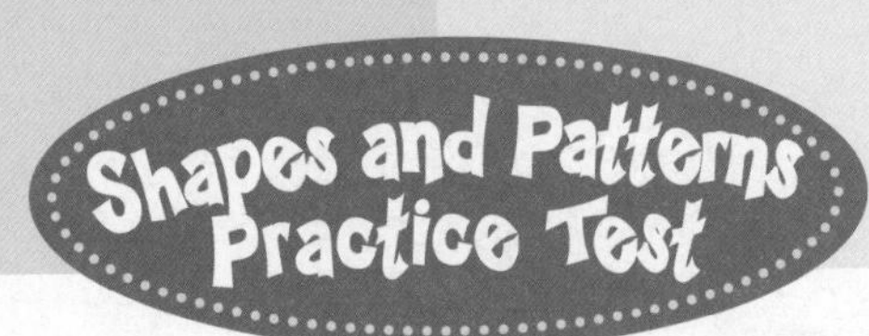

Color the bubble next to the correct answer.

7. Which shapes complete the pattern?

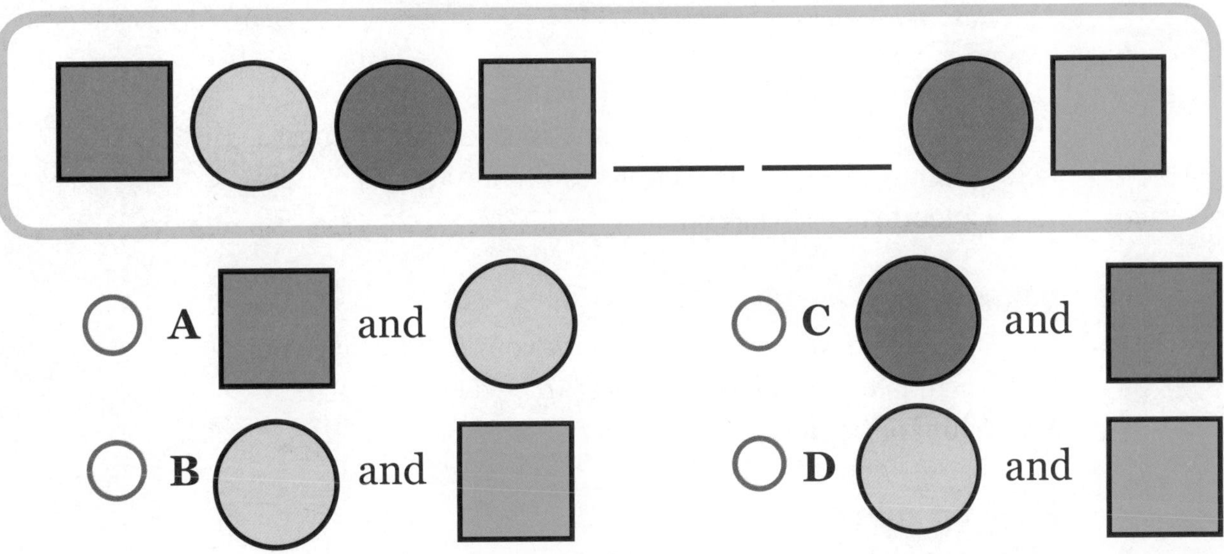

8. Which shapes complete the pattern?

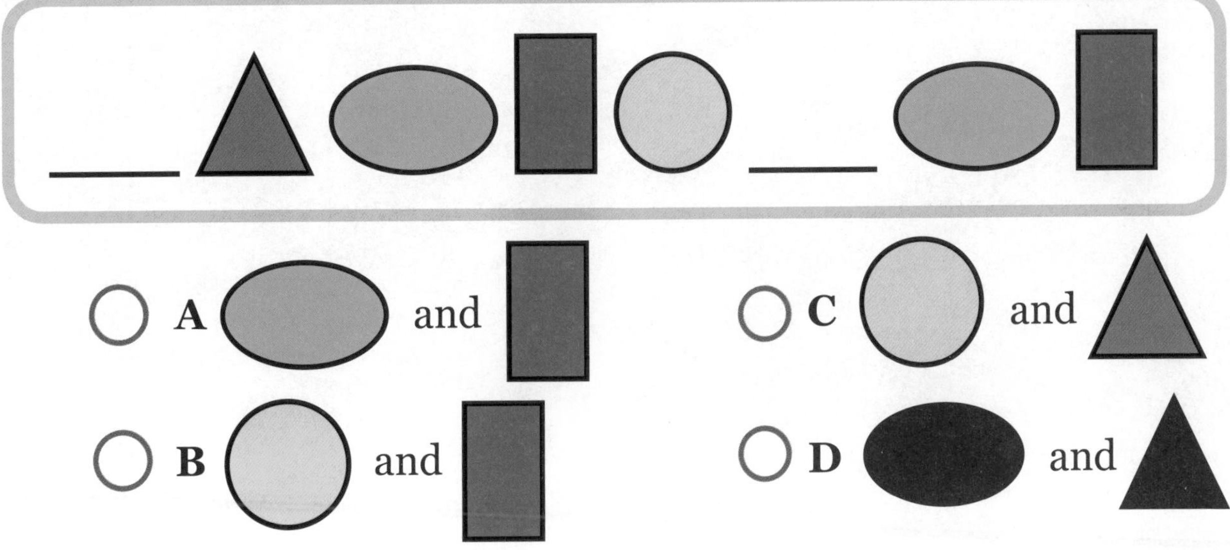

Problem Solving

Have you heard the old saying, “A picture is worth a thousand words”? Pictures can sometimes explain things better than words. In this section, your child will learn how to use pictures to solve problems.

What to do

Read the directions on each page with your child. Have your child complete the activities. Together, review the work. Praise him or her for being a “super sleuth”.

Keep on going!

With your child, put together puzzles or play games that require your child to find a way out of a maze.

Date: ______________

Look at the picture. Write the number.

How many?

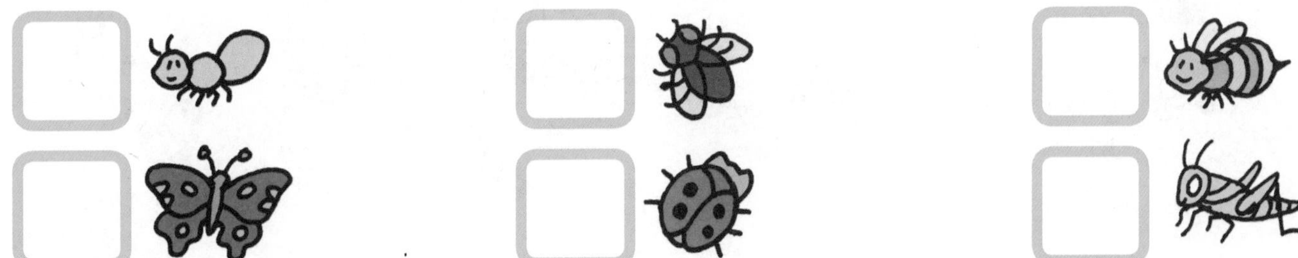

How many in all?

Date: ____________

Circle how many you see in the picture.

1.		1	5
2.		4	2
3.		8	5
4.		6	3
5.		7	10
6.		2	8
7.		9	7
8.		10	7
9.		3	1

Circle how many you see in all.

10.		+		=	8	9	10
11.		+		=	3	8	9
12.		+		=	6	2	4

Date: ________________

Look at the picture. Write the number.

How many?

How many in all?

Date: __________

Help the baby ducks find the mother duck.

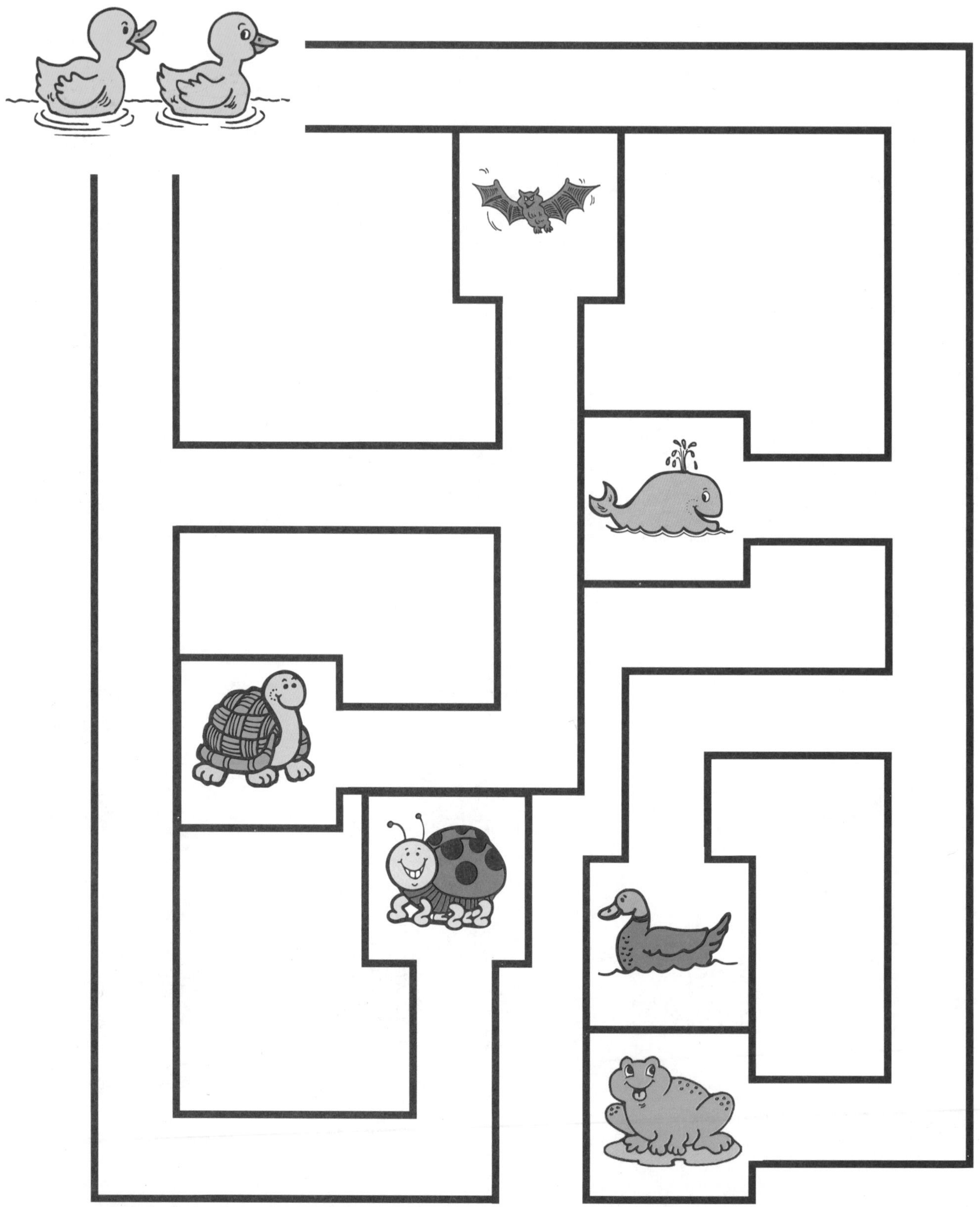

Date: ____________

Help the bee find its way to the hive.

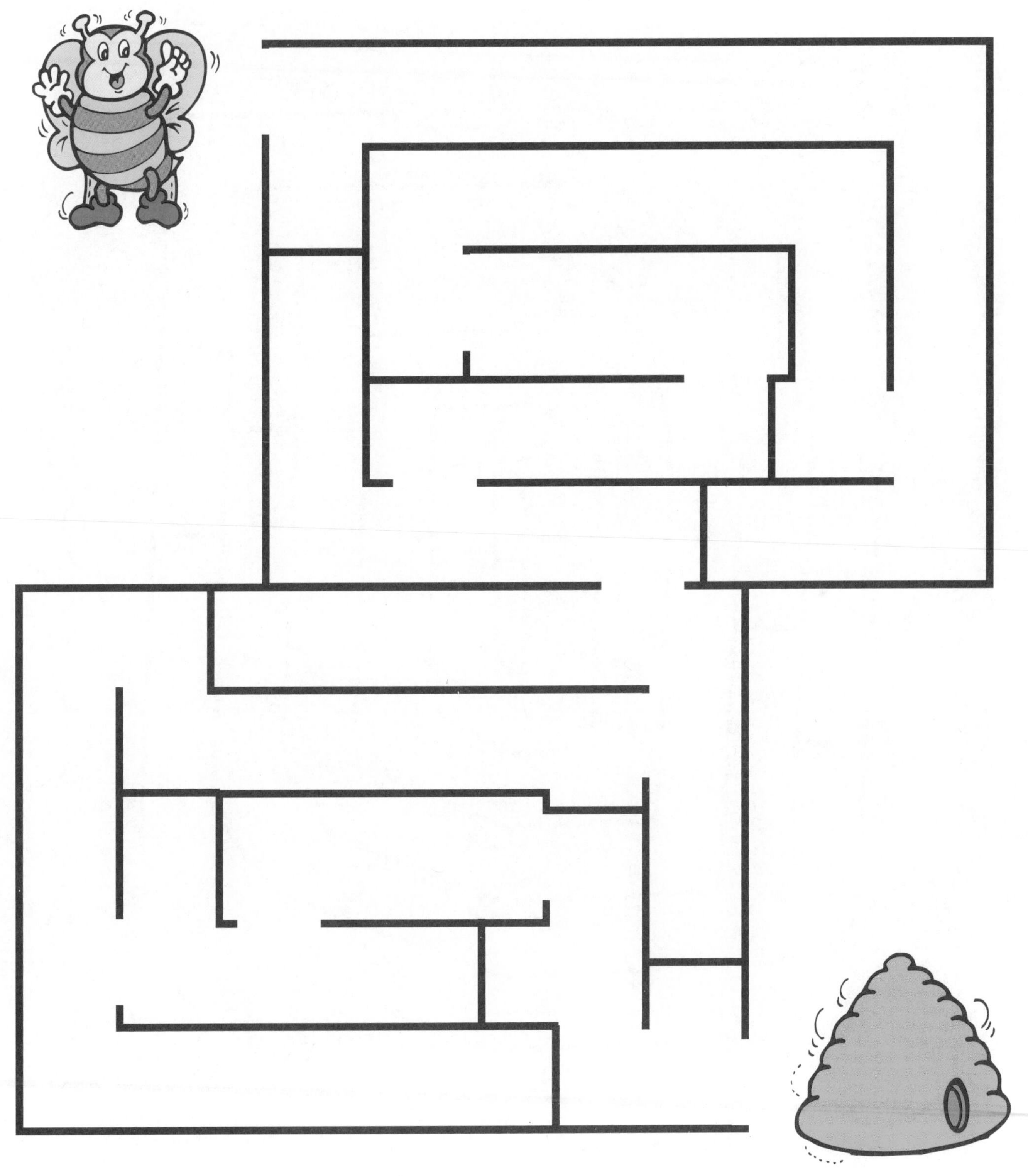

Date: ____________

Help the sunshine reach the flowers.

Date: ____________

Help the bat finds its way to the cave.

Date: ____________

Help the musician find the trumpet.
Follow the red and blue pattern.

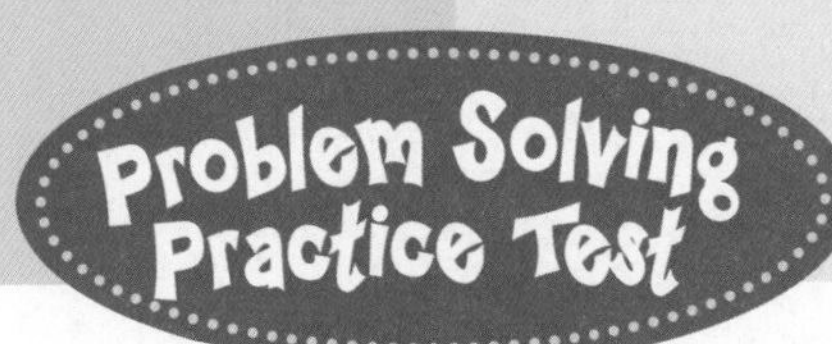

Color the bubble next to the correct answer.

Example

Which does **not** belong?

1	P	8	6

○ **A** 1 ○ **B** P ○ **C** 8 ○ **D** 6

1. Which does **not** belong?

C	2	Y	X

○ **A** C ○ **C** Y

○ **B** 2 ○ **D** X

2. Which does **not** belong?

W	B	L	9

○ **A** W ○ **C** L

○ **B** B ○ **D** 9

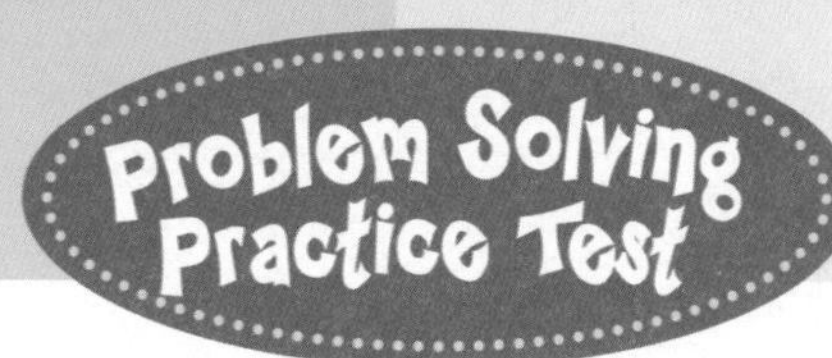

Color the bubble next to the correct answer.

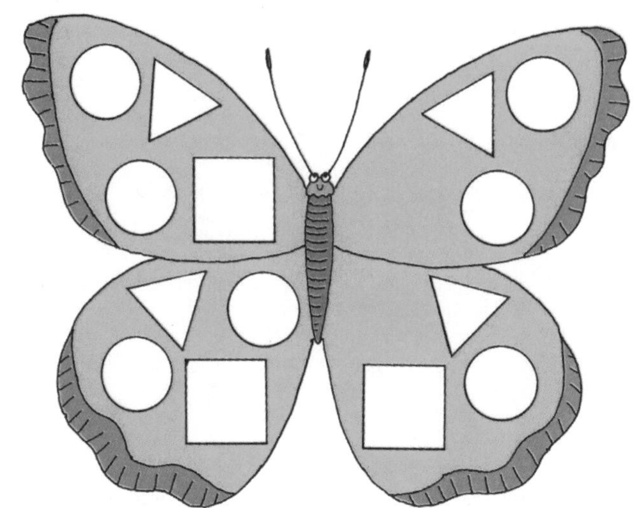

3. How many triangles are on the butterfly?

○ **A** 1 ○ **C** 3

○ **B** 2 ○ **D** 4

4. How many circles are on the butterfly?

○ **A** 3 ○ **C** 7

○ **B** 5 ○ **D** 9

5. How many squares are on the butterfly?

○ **A** 6 ○ **C** 8

○ **B** 3 ○ **D** 1

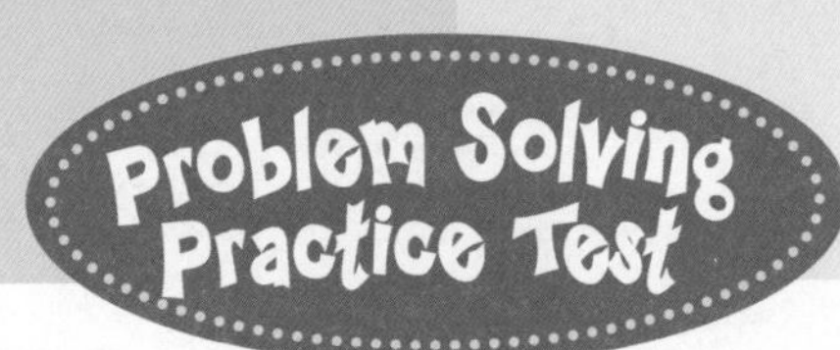

Color the bubble next to the correct answer.

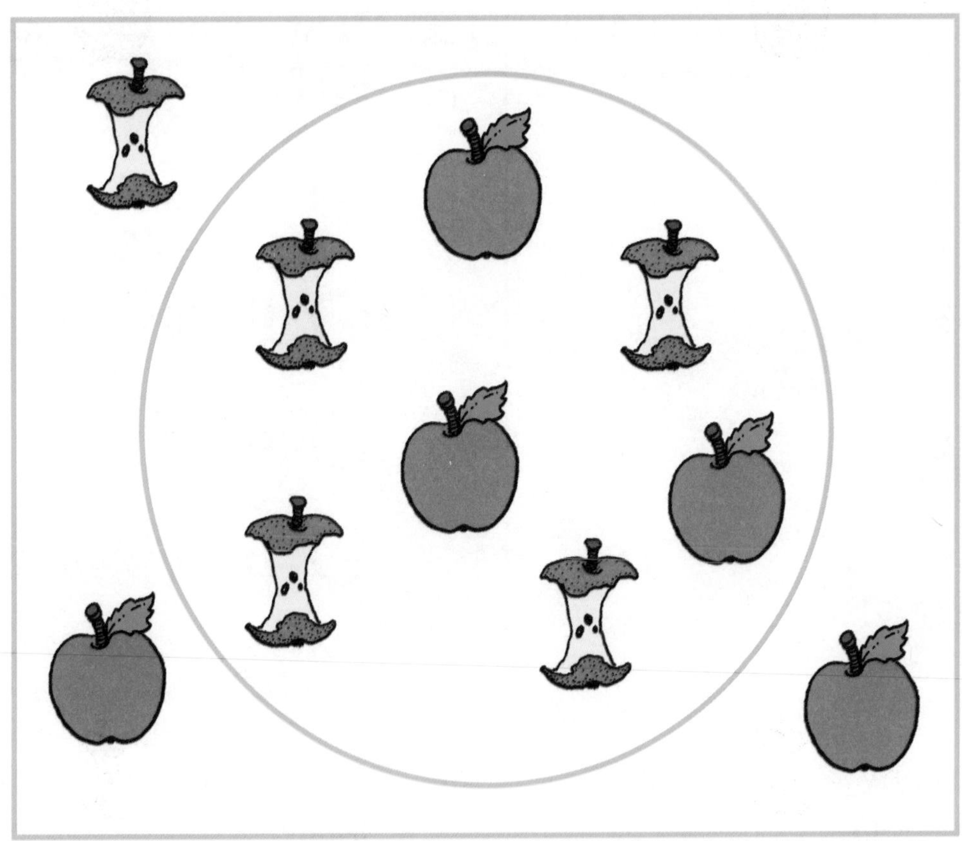

6. How many are in the circle?

- ○ **A** 3
- ○ **B** 4
- ○ **C** 6
- ○ **D** 7

7. How many  are in the circle?

- ○ **A** 3
- ○ **B** 4
- ○ **C** 6
- ○ **D** 7

Problem Solving Practice Test

Color the bubble next to the correct answer.

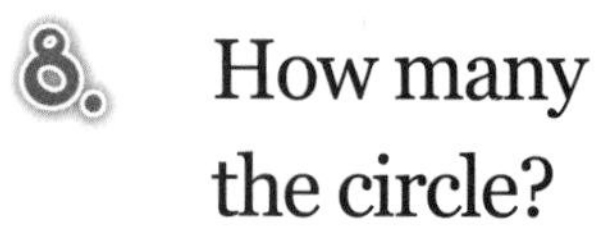

8. How many   are **not** in the circle?

- ○ **A** 1
- ○ **B** 2
- ○ **C** 4
- ○ **D** 4

9. How many  are **not** in the circle?

- ○ **A** 1
- ○ **B** 2
- ○ **C** 3
- ○ **D** 4

10. How many  are there in all?

- ○ **A** 3
- ○ **B** 5
- ○ **C** 7
- ○ **D** 9

11. How many  are there in all?

- ○ **A** 4
- ○ **B** 5
- ○ **C** 8
- ○ **D** 9

Answer Key

Page 9-24, 29-44, 49-66
Review letter formation, spelling, drawing and coloring on each page.

Page 25
1. F 2. G 3. H

Page 26
1. D 2. G 3. E

Page 27
1. g 2. f 3. h

Page 28
1. f 2. h 3. c

Page 45
1. N 2. M 3. P

Page 46
1. N 2. M 3. K

Page 47
1. o 2. n 3. p

Page 48
1. m 2. o 3. k

Page 67
1. V 2. X 3. Z

Page 68
1. X 2. U 3. U

Page 69
1. w 2. v 3. y

Page 70
1. w 2. u 3. v

Page 71

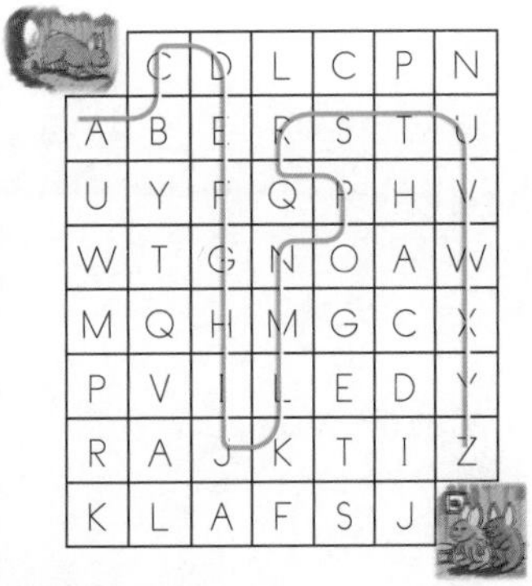
C D L C P N
A B E R S T U
U Y F Q P H V
W T G N O A W
M Q H M G C X
P V I L E D Y
R A J K T I Z
K L A F S J

Page 72

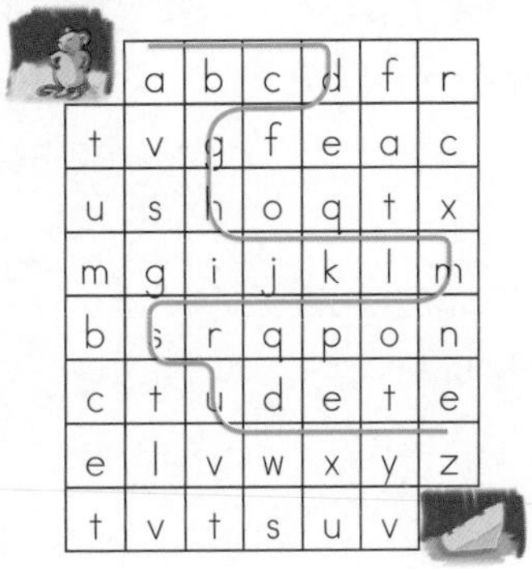
a b c d f r
t v g f e a c
u s h o q t x
m g i j k l m
b s r q p o n
c t u d e t e
e l v w x y z
t v t s u v

Page 73-79
1. I J 2. H I 3. W X
4. M N 5. c d 6. t u
7. l m 8. q r 9. balloon
10. quilt 11. rice 12. water
13. yacht 14. horse

Page 81
21 consonants; Color: F, M, B, J, X, L

Page 82
Circle: bird, ball, belt, boat, banana, basket, bell, books, boots, bat
Extra: bee

Page 83
Color: domino, dog, duck, dinosaur, deer, dice, door
Extra: dentist

Page 84
Circle: fox, five, fish, fork, fan, feather, four
Extra: firefighter

Page 85
Circle: lamp, lace, leaf, ladder, ladybug, lake, lamb, leg, lightning, lemon, letter, lettuce, lips, lizard, lobster, log
Extra: love

Page 86
Circle: motorcycle, milk, mop, mirror, mouse, mitten, monkey, moon, money
Extra: mother

Page 87
Color: nose, nine, needle, nail, nuts, necklace, net
Extra: newspaper

Page 88
Write p on: popcorn, pineapple, porcupine, penguin, police officer, pin, puppet, pencil, paper
Extra: pizza

Page 89
Circle: rest, run, ride, rock, rake, roll, read, rope, rip, row, race, rush
Extra: rocket

Page 90
Circle: saw, six, sun, school bus, sink, soap, starfish, seal
Extra: sandwich

Page 91
Color: tiger, tortoise, teapot, toast, telephone, television, table, tape
Extra: tent

Page 92
Willy, worm, wanted, watermelon, window, wagon, wiggled, wall, wow, was, wonderful
Extra: wind

Page 93
k sound: couch, cow, corn, coin, coat, cake, cobra, cat, coconut, comb
s sound: centipede, cinnamon roll, cereal, ceiling, celery, circles

Page 94
g sound: gate, girl, gift, guitar, gum, goose, gorilla
j sound: gingerbread man, giant, gerbil, general, gymnast

Page 95
Color: horn, house, helicopter, hammer, hand, heart, horse, hose, hat, hanger

Page 96
vase, vegetables, violin, vest, vacuum

Page 97
Circle: kitten, kiss, key, kick, kangaroo, kite, king

Page 98
1. y 2. q 3. w
4. h 5. v 6. r

Page 99
1. lamb, l 2. camel, c 3. deer, d
4. fish, f 5. bat, b

Page 100
bear – r, dog – g, cat – t, racoon – n, deer – r, camel – l, lamb – b, lion – n,
Extra: octopus

Page 101
n, l, r
n, m, k
d, x, g
r, l, f
Extra: dream

Page 102
1. rug, flag, g 2. spoon, sun, n 3. chair, star, r
4. broom, gum, m 5. hat, foot, t 6. ball, bell, l

Page 103
Orange: dress, mouse
Purple: ball, bell, shell
Green: map, rope, lamp

Page 104
1. six 2. sun 3. flag 4. bread
5. bib

Page 105
1, pot, pumpkin 2. nest, nine
3. duck, dog 4. fox, farmer
5. bike, cake 6. bus, dress
7. hat, goat 8. ball, bell

Page 106
1. cub 2. wig 3. pail
4. fox 5. leg

Page 107
Review that directions have been followed.

Page 108
1. rat 2. hat 3. tack
4. mask 5. fan 6. lamp
7. cap 8. Dad 9. trap
10. hand 11. clap 12. black

Page 109
1. an 2. and 3. as
4. had 5. at 6. can
7. lamp 8. fast

Page 110
Color: leg, net, belt, desk, neck, ten, sled, nest
Extra: yes

Page 111
en: ten, end; et: get, let
7. red 8. yes 9. get
10. let 11. ten 12. end

Page 112
Color: chick, igloo inn, fish, bib, chin, ship, pin, six

Page 113
i: if, is; h: him, his
7. big 8. him 9. if
10. sit 11. is, his

Page 114
Green: mop, hot, hop, log, sock, dog, frog, clock

Page 115
op: hop, top; ot: got, not
7. top 8. fox 9. hop
10. on

Page 116
Circle: rug, drum, gum, tub, but, rut, dust, bug, sub, club, mug, mud, cub, cup, slug, dug, hug, sun, plug, jug, nut, must, duck, truck

Page 117
two-letter: up; three-letter: but, run mud, bug
7. mud 8. jump 9. but 10. run 11. bug
12. up

Page 118
hat, cat, bat, mat
Extra: sat, fat, vat, pat, etc.

Page 119
dad, mad, sad, glad

Page 120
man, fan, pan, can

Page 121
1. pan 2. cat
3. mad 4. van

Page 122
ten, men, hen, pen

Page 123
red, bed, sled

Page 124
jet, pet, net, wet, vet

Page 125
wing, sing, ring, string

Page 126
Answers vary. E.g.
C, D, B, A, E

Page 127
Answers vary. E.g.
A, C, E, B, D

Page 128
mop, hop, stop, top

Page 129
Answers vary. E.g.
B, A, C, E, F, D

Page 130
run, bun, sun

Page 131

1. book	2. rake	3. log
4. fire	5. bell	6. ring

Page 132
1. gate, late, skate
2. fail, pail, tail
3. save, wave, brave
4. gain, stain, train

Page 133
ay: day, play, stay
ai: rain, tail, wait

7. wait	8. day	9. rain
10. tail	11. stay	12. play

Page 134
Brown: wheel, feet, meat, teeth, peach, queen, sheep, key
Extra: eraser

Page 135
ee: tree, need, see, feet

7. see	8. tree
9. we	10. feet
11. me	12. need

Page 136
hide, side, tide, wide, glide, pride
nice, rice, price, slice, spice, twice
dine, line, mine, vine, shine, spine
lime, crime, chime, grime, prime, slime
light, might, sight, tight, flight, bright
hike, like, pike, spike, trike, strike

Page 137
i_e: like, kite; y: by, my, fly

7. like	8. kite	9. by
10. I	11. my	12. fly

Page 138
goat, goal, soap, toast, roast, toad, foam, road, coat
Extra: toad

Page 139
o_e: home, bone, note, rope

7. note	8. rope	9. home
10. bone	11. go, so	

Page 140
1. fruit, rude, duke
2. cube, flute, clue
3. rule, June, true
Extra: blue

Page 141

1. rude	2. flute	3. chute
4. dune	5. huge	6. June
7. cute		

Page 142
Review that directions have been followed.

Page 143
Review that words and pictures are matched correctly.
Extra: blood

Page 144

1. bread	2. brain	3. bracelet	4. bride
5. bricks	6. bridge	7. broom	8. brush

Extra: bruise

Page 145
Orange: clap, clock, claws, climb, clothes, clouds, clover, clam
Extra: closet

Page 146
5, 1, 4, 6, 2, 3

Page 147
Color: drain, drive, dragonfly, dress, drop, drum, drill, drink, dryer

Page 148-151

1. C	2. A	3. Y
4. U	5. B	6. D
7. C	8. B	9. A
10. B		

Reading Skills

Page 153
1. 3, 2, 1
2. 2, 1, 3

Page 154
3, 1, 2
1 - First, 2 - Next, 3 - Last

Page 155
3, 1, 2
1 - First, 2 - Next, 3 - Last

Page 156
Nest with baby birds.

Page 157
Girl on ladder.

Page 158
Bread and peanut butter.

Page 159
Review that directions have been followed.

Page 160-162
Review that directions have been followed.

Page 163-166

1. C	2. B	3. C	4. C
5. C	6. A	7. D	8. B

Page 168-169
Review that numbers have been colored and instructions have been followed.

Page 170
2, 4, 8, 10
Review that the dots are joined in the right order.

Page 171
1. three, five, six
2. six, eight
3. eight, ten

Page 172-201
Review that numbers and words are formed and directions have been followed.

Page 202

1. 9	2. 12	3. 10	4. 15

Page 203

1. one	2. seven	3. fourteen	4. fifteen
5. ten	6. twelve	7. thirteen	8. nine
9. four	10. seven		

Page 204
1, 4, 6

Page 205
3, 4

Page 206
2, 3

Page 207
1, 2, 3, 5

Page 208
1, 5

Page 209
2, 3, 6

Page 210
2, 4

Page 211
Review that directions have been followed. 18

Page 212
3

Page 213

1. 18	2. 20	3. 20	4. 19
5. 20	6. 18		

Color: 2, 3, 5

Page 214-217
Review that directions have been followed.

Page 218
Top: 13, 17
Bottom: 14, 16
The numbers in the top row are odd and the numbers in the bottom row are even.

Page 219
two, three, four, five, six, seven, eight, nine, ten, eleven, twelve, thirteen, fourteen, fifteen, sixteen, seventeen, eighteen, nineteen, twenty

Page 220
Review that directions have been followed.

Page 221

1. 13	2. 20	3. 19	4. 13
5. 11	6. 15		

Page 222

1. 16	2. 17	3. 14	4. 12
5. 15	6. 18		

Page 223
Color stars and planets.
20 stars, 1 moon, 14 comets, 12 rockets, 20 planets, 8 globes, 1 sun

Page 224-229
Review that directions have been followed.

Page 230

1. a	2. b	3. a	4. b

Page 231
Review that directions have been followed.

Page 232

1. 19	2. 12	3. 19	4. 14
5. 20	6. 15		

Green: broccoli
Red: beetroots

Page 233-238

1. C	2. C	3. B	4. D
5. D	6. C	7. B	8. A
9. D	10. C	11. C	12. B
13. A	14. D		

Shapes and Patterns

Page 240-247
Review that directions have been followed.

Page 248
Triangle: sign, flag, stamp
Circle: clock, coin

Page 249
square: picture frame, stamp
Diamond: kite, clock

Page 250-256
Review that directions have been followed.

Page 257
1. square
2. triangle
3. hexagon
4. circle
5. star

Page 258

1. circle
2. oval
3. star
4. triangle
5. hexagon
6. rectangle

Page 259

1. rectangle
2. triangle
3. circle
4. pentagon
5. hexagon

Page 260-271

Review that directions have been followed.

Page 272

1. oval
2. rectangle
3. square
4. star
5. triangle

Page 273

1. star
2. oval
3. diamond
4. circle
5. triangle

Page 274

1. circle
2. oval
3. square
4. square

Page 275

1. red triangle
2. green rectangle
3. orange diamond
4. green oval

Page 276

1. banana
2. apple
3. watermelon slice
4. lemon

Page 277

1. cherries
2. banana
3. watemelon slice
4. kiwi fruit

Page 278-281

Review that directions have been followed.

Page 282

1. pink orchid
2. yellow daisy
3. red rose
4. bluebell

Page 283

1. a
2. b
3. b

Page 284

1. b
2. a
3. a

Page 285-286

Review that directions have been followed.

Page 287

1. A, B
2. A, B
3. B, C
4. AB
5. ABC

Page 288-291

Review that directions have been followed.

Page 292

c

Page 293

b

Page 294-297

1. D
2. A
3. B
4. A
5. D
6.A
7. A
8. C

Problem Solving

Page 299

3 ants, 5 flies, 4 bees, 2 butterflies,
1 ladybug, 2 grasshoppers

1. 7
2. 6
3. 6
4. 4

Page 300

1. 1	2. 4	3. 5
4. 3	5. 10	6. 2
7. 9	8. 7	9. 3
10. 10	11. 8	12. 6

Page 301

3 planes, 4 trucks, 5 vans, 5 cars, 2 helicopters, 1 bicycle

1. 8	2. 7	3. 6
4. 7		

Page 302-306

Review that directions have been followed.

Page 307-310

1. B	2. D	3. D
4. C	5. B	6. A
7. B	8. B	9. A
10.B	11.B	

SCHOLASTIC

Learning Express

Congratulations!

Paste a photo or draw a picture of yourself.

I, ____________________

am a Scholastic Superstar!

I have completed Reading and Math Jumbo Workbook K.

Presented on ____________________

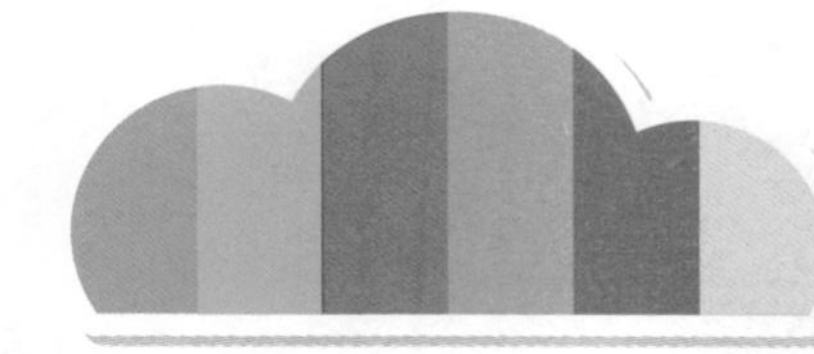

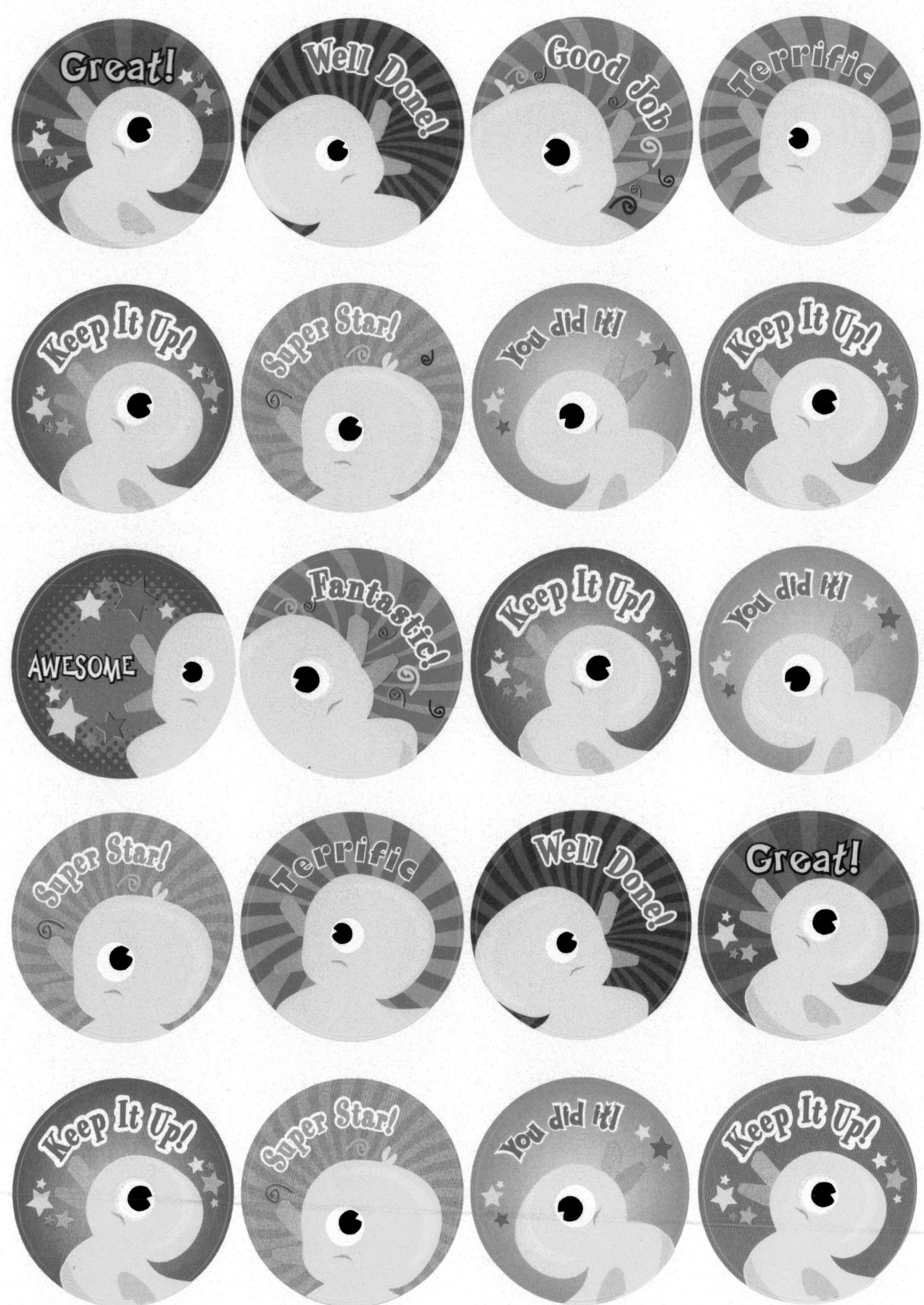

STK011015X PO# 445566